THE EARLY
BATTLES OF
EIGHTH ARMY

The Early Battles of Eighth Army

'CRUSADER' to the Alamein Line 1941–1942

by

ADRIAN STEWART

LEO COOPER

First published in Great Britain in 2002 by
Leo Cooper
an imprint of
Pen & Sword Books Ltd
47 Church Street
Barnsley
South Yorkshire
S70 2AS

ISBN 0 85052 851 8

Typeset in 10/12.5pt Plantin by
Phoenix Typesetting, Ilkley, West Yorkshire

Printed by
CPI UK

To my daughter Judith.
Much overdue!

CONTENTS

LIST OF ILLUSTRATIONS

(*My grateful thanks to the Taylor Library for their assistance in providing these illustrations.* A.S.)

LIST OF MAPS

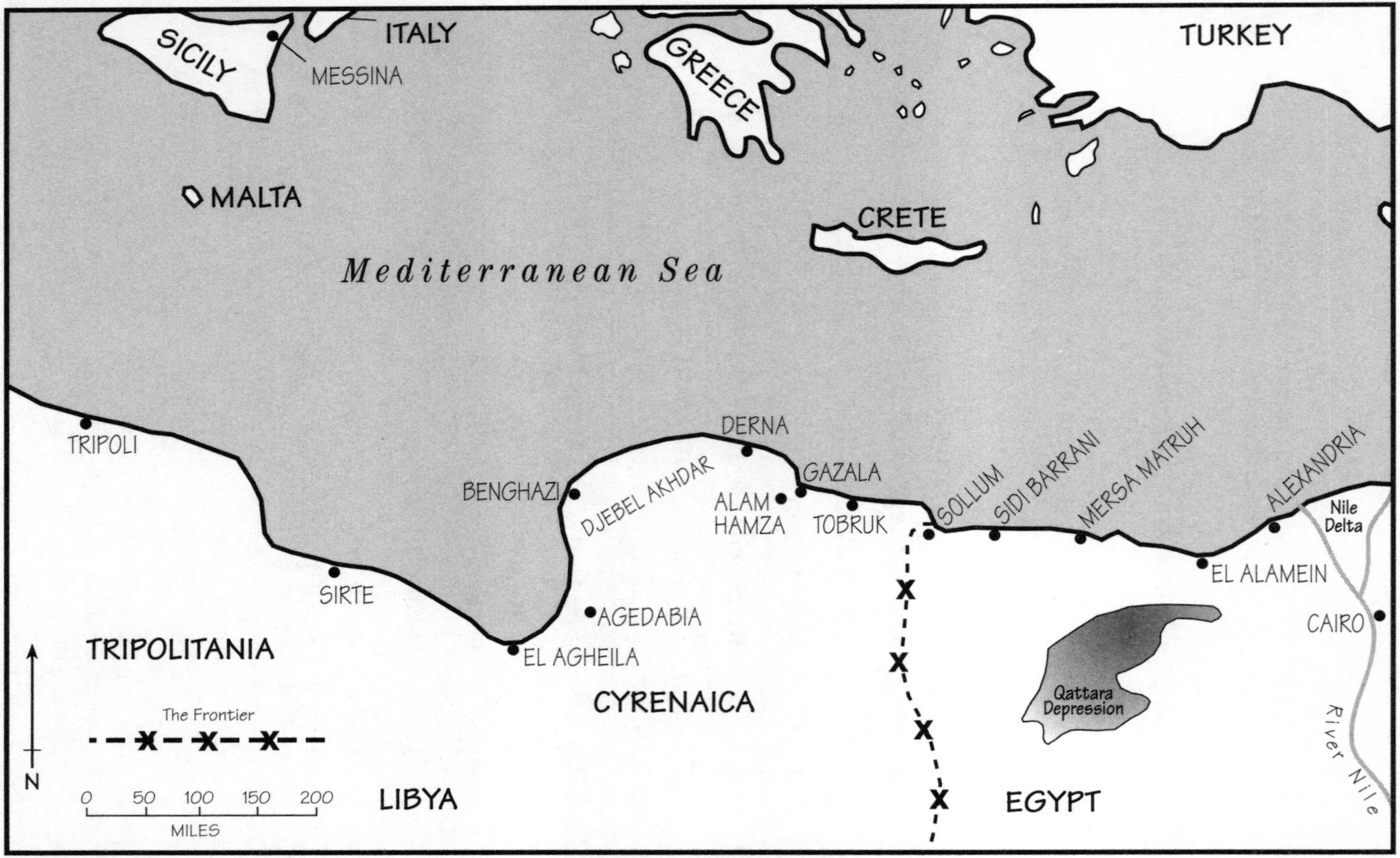

Map I. The Battleground

1

A DAY IN THE DESERT

It was, perhaps, the most bizarre sight yet to have appeared in the Western Desert.

By 5 August, 1942, the soldiers of Britain's Eighth Army and the airmen of the Desert Air Force had become rather unconventional in the matter of uniform. Even when properly dressed, the men in the ranks sported a wide variety of headgear: the berets of the Royal Tank Regiment, the turbans of some of the Indian troops, the slouch-hats of the Australians, the romantic-looking 'kepis' of the Fighting French. Apart from these, however, they frequently wore nothing else above the waist during the day, while in the hours of darkness, which were often bitterly cold, they usually added civilian-style pullovers to their official attire.

The attitude of their officers was, if anything, still more casual. Wing Commander John Darwen, who delighted an armoured-car patrol by emerging from a crash-landed Hurricane wearing riding-boots, riding-breeches, and a hunting-pink coat, was perhaps considered a shade eccentric, but few officers were seen in any recognized article of military clothing except their caps. Flexible suede 'desert boots' with rubber soles, corduroy trousers, shaggy sheepskin coats, brightly coloured silk scarves – all emphasized the independent spirit of the 'old desert hands'.

Yet even in the Western Desert, the appearance of Winston Churchill, clad in a black siren suit, crowned by a white pith helmet, which reminded those who had served in India of railway guards, and brandishing a white sunshade, was regarded as somewhat amusing. This sense of amusement was not of course shared by the higher ranks of the Eighth Army who were well aware that the Prime Minister's visit was by no means purely formal. Nor was there anything whatever amusing about Churchill's companion, alert, intense, severe, unsmiling – General Sir Alan Brooke, Chief of the

Imperial General Staff, professional head of the British Army, whose responsibility it was, in Churchill's words, 'to appraise the quality of our generals.'

Churchill and Brooke had every reason for discontent. Eighth Army had received continual reinforcements of men and equipment, carried by vessels making a passage of some 14,000 miles round the Cape of Good Hope at a time when a shortage of shipping was crippling all Allied plans, and at the cost of ruinous consequences in the Far East – and the results hitherto had been woeful. Far from being driven out of North Africa as Churchill had envisaged, Eighth Army's enemies, the German-Italian forces under the tactical command of General (later Field Marshal) Erwin Rommel, had invaded Egypt and were now holding their ground only some 70 miles from the main British base of Alexandria. It was not that Eighth Army had never enjoyed success; what was really disheartening was that its successes had brought no lasting benefits and seemed always to be followed by still more humiliating failures.

By August, 1942, a decisive victory by Eighth Army had become a necessity for many reasons. Much stress would later be laid on the political importance to Churchill of such a victory. In fact, despite some grumbling, Churchill's own position was probably secure enough, at least for the time being, since only the previous month he had defeated a Motion of Censure in the House of Commons by 475 votes to 25. What did concern him was the effect that Eighth Army's failures might have on Britain's two great wartime allies.

Relations between Britain and Soviet Russia were inevitably tense. It was difficult to forget that the Russians had not joined the fight against Nazi Germany until 22 June, 1941, and then only because they had been attacked. Prior to that date, they had supplied the Germans with valuable strategic raw materials, watched with callous indifference the Nazi occupation of Western Europe and taken the opportunity to seize half Poland and the Baltic States and to invade Finland – an action that had resulted in Russia's expulsion from the League of Nations.

After leaving the Middle East, Churchill and Brooke would fly to Moscow where the Soviet dictator, Josef Stalin, would heap abuse on them, demanding to know when Britain would start fighting and assuring them that this would not prove too bad once they had tried it. The leaders of a country that had fought Germany since September, 1939, and her ally Italy since June, 1940, at heavy cost and for much of the time alone, listened to such sneers with justified resentment, but also with a deep anxiety. They feared that if the Russians were not encouraged by a belief that Britain could oppose Germany effectively, they might either collapse or seek a separate peace at the expense of their western territories – as indeed, so some Russian historians have suggested, had already been attempted in October, 1941.

By contrast, the relationship between Britain and the United States was based on mutual trust and respect. However, it was complicated by the fact that both countries, unlike Russia, faced another dangerous foe in the Far East. Churchill and his Service Chiefs had so far persuaded the Americans that their primary strategic objective should be the defeat of Germany but many of President Franklin Roosevelt's advisers were eager to divert their country's main efforts to the struggle with Japan. The longer decisive success continued to elude the Eighth Army, which was the only British or American force engaged in active combat with the German Army in the field, the louder the objections to the 'Germany first' policy would become.

In addition, Churchill and Brooke felt a strong moral obligation towards the Americans. Both had recently been in Washington when Roosevelt and his Chief of Army Staff, General George Marshall, had ordered the shipment to Eighth Army of 300 Sherman tanks, superior to any Allied tank then in the Middle East. Neither ever forgot the generosity of this gesture and each was determined that when the Shermans arrived in the Desert, they would be put to the best possible use.

That Churchill was therefore right to desire a victory for political reasons is surely undeniable. Yet even had none of the above factors applied, Eighth Army would still have had to gain success for purely military considerations. In the first place, the Western Allies had planned a joint invasion of Vichy French North Africa, which was given the inspiring code-name of TORCH by the Prime Minister, for the end of October, 1942. It was correctly felt that the reception of the landing forces would depend very much on whether the Eighth Army had previously achieved an unquestioned triumph.

The most crucial reason of all for an Eighth Army victory, however, related to the most important focal point in the Desert War – which, paradoxically, lay outside the Desert. While Allied shipping had to travel the weary miles round the Cape of Good Hope, Axis supplies needed to cross only some 350 miles of sea from the port of Messina in northern Sicily to Tripoli, the main base in Italy's North African colony of Libya.

Fortunately for the Allied cause, sixty miles south of Sicily was the island-fortress of Malta, from which surface-warships, submarines and aircraft could decimate the Axis convoys. Rommel, who had the best possible reasons to know, would later point out that: 'With Malta in our hands, the British would have had little chance of exercising any further control over convoy traffic in the central Mediterranean . . . It has the lives of many thousands of German and Italian soldiers on its conscience.'[1] The Italian Official History sadly remarks: 'Malta was the rock upon which our hopes in the Mediterranean foundered.'

By mid-1942, Malta's situation was desperate. The island was still sending its aircraft and submarines to attack enemy shipping, but its own fall was imminent unless it could receive the supplies of food and fuel that it required. The scanty rations issued to troops and civilians alike had had to be cut to the absolute minimum and unpleasant skin diseases caused by malnutrition had begun to appear. Fuel was still more scarce. Malta's Governor, Viscount Gort, who set a sterling example to his people throughout their ordeal, sharing their hardships and, living and eating very simply, toured his capital, Valetta, on a bicycle, rather than use precious petrol.

Malta's troubles had become acute since the Eighth Army had been driven from Cyrenaica, the eastern province of Libya. This had given the Luftwaffe airfields from which British ships bound for the island could be attacked, while at the same time it had deprived the Desert Air Force of bases from which they could be protected. It was not for nothing that the seas between Cyrenaica and Crete had become known as 'Bomb Alley'. A series of misfortunes had culminated in June with the total repulse by enemy aircraft of a large convoy making towards Malta from Alexandria.

If it was clear that no ships could get to Malta from the east, it was hoped that convoys from Gibraltar, for which aircraft-carriers could provide fighter-cover for at least part of the way, might have a better chance of success. In June, two merchantmen had reached Malta from the west, thereby providing a breathing-space. In August, a much larger convoy, code-named 'PEDESTAL', set out for the island. While Churchill and Brooke were in Moscow, four of its freighters, loaded with a mixture of flour, ammunition and aviation fuel in cans, and the American-built tanker *Ohio*, won through to preserve Malta for the Allied cause. However, the loss of nine more merchantmen and several warships, including the aircraft-carrier *Eagle*, warned that this costly success was unlikely to be repeated. Yet if Malta was to survive, it had to receive further supplies by the end of November.

There was only one way in which the delivery of those supplies could be guaranteed. The ships carrying them would have to enjoy strong fighter protection. For this to be possible, Eighth Army would have to recapture the Cyrenaican aerodromes, especially the airfield complex at Martuba, just south of the town of Derna in the north-east of the Cyrenaican 'bulge'. This would necessitate an advance of some 480 miles through enemy-occupied territory. It was a matter of grave reflection that in July, 1942, Eighth Army, though blessed with an immense superiority in troops and equipment, had made five attempts to drive back the Axis forces, all of which had failed miserably.

Indeed not only would Eighth Army have to win a decisive offensive victory, it would first have to win one when fighting on the defensive. It was known that Rommel was preparing for a further advance at the end of August. Neither fresh troops nor the new Shermans would have reached

Eighth Army by that date, whereas throughout the month Rommel was receiving strong reinforcements of men, aircraft, anti-tank guns and tanks, among the last-named some Mark IV Specials, superior even to the Shermans. Rommel's original thrust into Egypt had been halted only by much greater numbers and then more as a result of the enemy's exhaustion than any other factor. There was thus a good deal of understandable pessimism as to Eighth Army's ability to meet a new assault coming at a time when, as Captain B.H. Liddell Hart points out in his *History of the Second World War*, 'the strength of the two sides' would be 'nearer to an even balance than it was either before or later.'

Already the Royal Navy had withdrawn most of its units, including all its remaining capital ships, through the Suez Canal to the Indian Ocean. Should Rommel's final thrust succeed, the loss of Egypt would not only virtually ensure the starvation of Malta into surrender, it would also prevent those warships from returning to the Mediterranean, save by passing all the way round the Cape of Good Hope. The Mediterranean would thus become an Axis lake, enabling the Axis dictators, Adolf Hitler and Benito Mussolini, to pour into Alexandria, then, of course, an Axis and not a British base, as many men and supplies as they considered necessary for the conquest of the remainder of the Middle East, in particular the oil-fields of Iraq. Even set-backs in Russia might well not have checked the flow, for the Axis leaders could easily have chosen to 'reinforce success', especially as they would then be able to strike at Russia's own oil-supplies in the Caucasus from the south.

With these tremendous issues at stake, it can be imagined that when Churchill and Brooke left Heliopolis Airport, outside Cairo, early on 5 August 1942, for their day in the Desert, they must have been consumed by anxiety and tension – particularly, perhaps, Brooke. He had hoped for some time that he could visit Eighth Army 'to see what was wrong. But for this I wanted to be alone.' Instead, the day before his departure, he had learned that Churchill intended to join him, with the result that Brooke would have to grapple not only with the problems of the Middle East but with the impulsive intuition of a Prime Minister who was intent, in his own words, on 'sensing the atmosphere'.[2]

Churchill and Brooke first flew to Burg el Arab on the Mediterranean coast where the so-called desert 'sand' – it was really gritty dust – changed from its normal brownish-yellow to grey and the beaches were a pure, dazzling white. At the Headquarters of the Desert Air Force they were greeted by its leader, the New Zealander Air Vice-Marshal Arthur Coningham, his superior, the Air Officer Commanding-in-Chief, Middle East, Air Chief Marshal Sir Arthur Tedder, and General Sir Claude Auchinleck, who was not only the Commander-in-Chief of the Middle East Land Forces but had also assumed personal leadership of Eighth Army. The whole party then drove up to the Eighth Army's defensive positions which were collectively, if rather misleadingly, known as the Alamein Line.

At the northern end of the defences, Churchill and Brooke met Major General Leslie Morshead, the small, quiet but immensely determined ex-shipping executive who commanded 9th Australian Division and the tall, talkative but obstinate Major General Dan Pienaar, who had won an immediate DSO in the field earlier in the war and was now the leader of 1st South African Division. They then moved south to where the rock base that underlay the shallow 'sand' emerged to form the ugly Ruweisat Ridge, near to which Auchinleck had established his Headquarters. Here the distinguished visitors were entertained to breakfast in, according to Churchill, 'a wire-netted cube, full of flies and important military personages'. Here also Churchill questioned Auchinleck about his plans for dealing with Rommel's anticipated attack and for the subsequent advance of Eighth Army and was not reassured by Auchinleck's replies.

The Prime Minister was much more impressed by Lieutenant General William 'Strafer' Gott who was among the officers gathered at Eighth Army Headquarters. He talked privately to Gott, 'looked into his clear blue eyes and questioned him about himself.' Churchill then returned to Burg el Arab where he heard the Air Force's assessment of the situation before flying back to Cairo. Brooke, meanwhile, continued his tour of the Alamein defences. He too subsequently had a private and utterly frank conversation with Gott. He returned to Cairo via Burg el Arab late that evening.

The views that Churchill and Brooke heard during 5 August were, says General Sir William Jackson in *The North African Campaign 1940–43*, 'many and varied and did not flatter the senior commanders.' As might have been expected, the officers of the Desert Air Force and of those Army units which came from the Dominions, as the self-governing parts of the British Commonwealth were then known, were particularly forthright in their comments.

As a result of their experiences, Churchill and Brooke quickly reached two conclusions. The first, declares the British Official History,[3] was that 'a drastic and immediate change should be made to impart a new and vigorous impulse to the Army and to restore confidence in the High Command.' The second was that past misfortunes had in no way resulted from any lack of calibre in the men in the ranks. As Churchill signalled to London that evening: 'Troops were very cheerful and all seem confident and proud of themselves, but bewildered at having been baulked of victory on repeated occasions.'

Churchill was later to sum up Eighth Army at this time as being 'brave but baffled'. It was a very expressive description, for the men of Eighth Army, in spite of their bravery, had certainly been 'baffled' repeatedly in the sense of being 'thwarted' in their attempts to defeat their enemies. As a result, they had also become 'baffled' in that word's other meaning of 'confused'; they could not understand why their efforts had brought such inadequate rewards.

Churchill and Brooke seem to have judged the basic reasons why Eighth Army had been 'baffled' in both senses with remarkable accuracy. Of course there was more information available to them than to many later commentators, while, faced with the prospect of losing the greatest, most important war in human history, they were naturally not much concerned about the effects that their decisions might have on any luckless individual.

By contrast, accounts of Eighth Army's early battles which appeared in the first fifteen years or so after the war's end often seemed less concerned with the details of the conflict than with inflating or protecting individual reputations, whether Allied or Axis. In any case, for a long time it was simply not possible for the full story to be told. Many important military figures were barred from comment because they were still serving officers; the mass of records – summaries, orders, reports, signals – which together made up the War Diaries of General Headquarters, Middle East and of the Headquarters of Eighth Army and its subordinate Corps were not available for publication; and the ability to intercept enemy signals – the celebrated 'Ultra' Intelligence – was still a closely guarded secret. By the time that all this information had been revealed, a number of myths were already so deeply ingrained that they are still repeated in the face of all the evidence to the contrary.

This is the more regrettable because when the myths are stripped away, the picture that emerges both confirms and illuminates the conclusions reached by Churchill and Brooke. Moreover if it demonstrates why the men of Eighth Army had been baffled, it serves to remind us that they had also been very brave and they had gone on being brave for a very long time.

Among those who had accompanied Churchill to the Middle East was Colonel Ian Jacob, later Director-General of the BBC but then Military Assistant Secretary to the War Cabinet. Jacob did not join the Prime Minister on his visit to Eighth Army because Auchinleck was rightly reluctant to receive a large party of visitors which might be spotted and attacked from the air. Instead Jacob spent the day obtaining opinions from officers of his own or similar rank, as a result of which, interestingly enough, he reached conclusions very similar to those of Churchill and Brooke. On the following day, 6 August, he made this entry in his diary:[4]

> As the result of my own conversations with the various people of my own standing whom I met in the Middle East, I gathered a number of interesting impressions. . . . The Army in the Middle

East is in a rather bewildered state. They have just lost a big battle, which they felt they ought to have won. They are disturbed by various happenings in the Desert, and nearly everyone you talk to has a different explanation of why there was a failure. There are certain things, however, on which all agree. . . .

Notes

1   *The Rommel Papers*, edited by Captain B.H. Liddell Hart. All quotations from Rommel come from this source.
2   All quotations from Churchill are from his massive history of *The Second World War Volume IV: The Hinge of Fate*. Those from Brooke (unless otherwise stated) will be found in Sir Arthur Bryant's *The Turn of the Tide 1939–1943* which is based on Brooke's wartime diaries.
3   *The Mediterranean and Middle East* Volume III (September 1941 to September 1942) *British Fortunes Reach their Lowest Ebb* by Major General I.S.O. Playfair with Captain F.C. Flynn RN, Brigadier C.J.C. Molony and Group Captain T.P. Gleave.
4   This and the subsequent quotations from Colonel Jacob's Diary are recorded in *From Churchill's Secret Circle to the BBC: The Biography of Lieutenant General Sir Ian Jacob* by General Sir Charles Richardson.

2

'CRUSADER'

Our misfortunes in the Western Desert are not universally attributed to inferior equipment. In fact one officer of the Royal Armoured Corps, of considerable experience, went so far as to say that equipment had nothing to do with the outcome of the battle.

Colonel Jacob's Diary.
6 August, 1942.

As Alan Moorehead, the Australian War Correspondent, reports in his book *The Desert War*:

> All the orders were given, the guns placed, the tanks grouped and ready, and the empty beds standing row on row in the field hospitals. It seemed a calculated cruelty. The inevitability of the battle was the hardest thing to accept.

The battle in question was Operation CRUSADER. It began on 18 November, 1941, and was the first to be fought by the Eighth Army, which had officially only come into existence at midnight on 26 September. Of course such dates are somewhat artificial. The massive expansion of the British and Commonwealth forces in Egypt, which inevitably resulted in the creation of Eighth Army, had begun in July, while the situation which faced its soldiers had been created by previous actions in a struggle that had started as long ago as midnight on 10 June, 1940, when Italy had entered the Second World War.

Thereafter the fighting would ebb and flow right up to the time of Churchill's and Brooke's visit. It was the Italians who advanced first. The RAF Official History[1] picturesquely describes how:

From 13 September the enemy lorries were crossing the frontier and winding down the huge escarpment that frowns above the emerald-and-white beauty of Sollum. Constantly harassed by our ground and air forces [the former under the command of a certain Brigadier Gott] they pressed on through a nothing called Buq Buq, and in the evening of 16 September arrived at the small collection of houses and huts unduly dignified by the name of Sidi Barrani.

Though the main British defences at Mersa Matruh were still some sixty miles further east, the invaders now halted, to begin building a chain of forts stretching away to the south-west. These were stocked with every available luxury but were neither properly protected nor mutually supporting.

The fact was that Mussolini's armed forces had neither been trained nor equipped to fight a modern war. Their artillery was demoralizingly in-effective; their tanks were described by their pitying foes as 'useless death traps' or 'mobile coffins'; and their CR 42 biplane fighters, though superior to the RAF's biplane Gladiators, were no match for the more modern Hurricanes.

Consequently, when the British Western Desert Force, under the over-all leadership of General Sir Archibald Wavell, Commander-in-Chief, Middle East and the tactical control of Lieutenant General Sir Richard O'Connor, began an offensive of its own on 9 December, this succeeded beyond the most optimistic hopes. Though the strength of the British and Common-wealth soldiers never exceeded two divisions, their professional skills and their determination were so much greater than those of their enemies, that by 8 February, 1941, they had over-run the whole of Cyrenaica and had reached the frontier post of El Agheila on its western boundary. In the process they had annihilated an Italian army of nine divisions and captured 130,000 men, 1,300 guns and 400 tanks, all at a cost of only 500 killed, 1,373 wounded and 55 missing.

At El Agheila the coastal plain was hemmed in by deep sand, formidable 'wadis' (dry watercourses) and salt marshes which approached very close to the sea, but such had been the scale of the British triumph that O'Connor was confident that he could easily press on through this 'bottle-neck' to Tripoli. Unfortunately, Churchill had other ideas. With Wavell's approval, he preferred instead to dispatch large military and air forces to Greece, a country already at war with Italy but now threatened by a German invasion as well. His decision would lead to disastrous British defeats, in Greece, in Crete – and in Cyrenaica.

Far more formidable enemies were now about to reach North Africa. On 6 February, Adolf Hitler had issued instructions to General Erwin Rommel, whom he had personally selected to lead the troops he was sending to aid his faltering ally. Before a week had passed, Rommel was in Tripoli. On 31 March, the Axis forces in their turn embarked on an audacious offensive against Wavell's now weakened command.

By 8 April, the situation had been almost completely reversed. Most of Cyrenaica was back in Axis hands, O'Connor was a prisoner of war and Rommel was talking of carrying his advance to the Suez Canal. Fortunately, Wavell had been able to retain the little port of Tobruk, thus depriving his opponent of a vital harbour, while its garrison could pose a constant threat to Rommel's line of communications. German light forces, bypassing Tobruk, did continue their advance to the Egyptian frontier but near Sollum they were brought to an abrupt halt by a new mobile force, Gott's 7th Support Group from 7th Armoured Division, which also had 22nd Guards Brigade under command.

Next it was the British who went onto the offensive but this time with very different results. Attacks on 15 May and 15 June both ended in failure in the face of the highly effective German anti-tank guns. Thereupon, on 21 June, the day before the German invasion of Russia, Churchill, believing Wavell had been exhausted by the weight of his responsibilities, replaced him by Auchinleck, previously the C-in-C, India.

The reorganization which was to turn the Western Desert Force into the Eighth Army began at the same time.[2] Reinforcements poured into Egypt: 600 tanks, 800 guns, Indian infantrymen from Syria, South Africans from Abyssinia, where they had played a major part in another rout of the Italians, New Zealanders back from their ordeals in Greece and Crete. Whereas Wavell's last offensive had been mounted with just one under-strength armoured division and two infantry brigades, by November, 1941, Eighth Army's leader, Lieutenant General Sir Alan Cunningham, controlled two full Corps plus the garrison of Tobruk. Of these formations, the last-named, commanded by Major General Scobie, was the smallest, consisting of the 70th (British) Division, the 1st Polish Brigade and the 32nd Army Tank Brigade.

The principal infantry formation was XIII Corps under Lieutenant General Godwin-Austen. This contained the three brigades of the 2nd New Zealand Division, led by Major General Bernard Freyberg VC, and the three brigades of Major General Frank Messervy's 4th Indian Division which, in reality, was British-Indian, since it was the usual practice for the men of one battalion in each Indian Army brigade to be British while those of the other two were Indians or Gurkhas. The 1st Army Tank Brigade provided support.

The main armoured formation was to be found in Lieutenant General Willoughby Norrie's XXX Corps. This was the British 7th Armoured

Division with its famous badge of the jerboa, the desert rat. Commanded by Gott, now a major general, it consisted of the 4th, 7th and 22nd Armoured Brigades plus the infantry and artillery of 7th Support Group, now under Brigadier Campbell. Also part of XXX Corps was Major General Brink's 1st South African Division, though this contained only two South African brigades, its third formation being Brigadier Marriott's 22nd Guards Brigade. Three more South African brigades, forming the 2nd South African Division under Major General de Villiers, remained in army reserve.

At the start of CRUSADER, Eighth Army possessed 710 tanks, not counting light tanks carrying only machine-guns. Moreover, there were a further 500 in reserve as reinforcements if necessary. XIII Corps and the Tobruk garrison between them had some 200 of the heavy 'I' (for 'Infantry') tanks – Matildas or the later, faster Valentines – while 7th Armoured had mainly Crusaders or the new American Stuarts, which had been re-christened 'Honeys' by their delighted crews.

On the opposing side was ranged an Axis army nominally commanded by the Italian General Ettore Bastico but taking its operational orders from Rommel. His infantry consisted of the five Italian divisions of Lieutenant General Navarini's XXI Corps together with one German division recently formed out of a number of independent units, including ex-members of the French Foreign Legion. Commanded by Major General Max Sümmermann, this bore the hideous title of *Zur Besonderen Verfügung* [For Special Services] *Afrika*, but in defiance of chronology, it will henceforth be called by the name it would receive on 15 December and thereafter make famous: 90th Light.

Rommel's armoured formations were the German Afrika Korps under Lieutenant General Ludwig Crüwell and the Italian XX Corps under Lieutenant General Gastone Gambara. The former contained Major General Walther Neumann-Silkow's 15th Panzer Division – 8th Panzer Regiment[3] and 115th Motorized Infantry Regiment – and Major General Johann von Ravenstein's 21st Panzer Division – 5th Panzer Regiment and 104th Motorized Infantry Regiment. The Italian Corps was made up from the Ariete (Armoured) and Trieste (Motorized) Divisions.

These armoured units were considerably weaker than those of their opponents. Gambara had only 146 obsolete tanks. Crüwell had almost 250 but some seventy of these were Mark IIs, armed only with machine-guns, while of his 174 gun-armed tanks, thirty-five were Mark IVs, which fired high-explosive shells from a short-barrelled 75mm gun, devastating when used against infantry but unsuitable for action against hostile armour. Crüwell had no reserves on hand and little chance of receiving any. Moreover, as will be examined later, the majority of the Allied tanks were slightly superior to those of the Germans and all were vastly superior to those of the Italians. Rommel did, however, have one great advantage. He possessed ninety-six 50mm long-barrelled anti-tank guns, more effective than the British 2-pounders or indeed the short-barrelled 50mms carried on his own Mark III tanks. In addition he had thirty-five of the even more deadly 88mm anti-aircraft guns, which in their desert role of tank-destroyers had already earned a reputation as formidable as it was well-deserved.

Eighth Army's supporting air arm, which on 9 October had officially become known as the Western Desert Air Force, though in practice the word 'Western' was rarely used, also out-numbered its opponents. Coningham had under his command one Free French and five British squadrons equipped with Blenheim bombers, two Southern African squadrons flying Marylands, 24 Squadron SAAF with the latest Bostons, and the equivalent of no less than nineteen fighter squadrons: thirteen British, three South African, two Australian and one Southern Rhodesian. These flew half-squadrons of Beaufighters and Fleet Air Arm Martlets, five full squadrons of Tomahawks and thirteen squadrons of Hurricanes, one of which – 80 Squadron RAF – was equipped with 'Hurribombers' carrying four 40lb bombs under each wing; the first of a long line of fighter-bomber units to serve in the Desert.

In all, Coningham controlled some 500 serviceable aircraft. He could also call on large reserves, including Wellington bombers, back in the area of the Nile Delta. By contrast, Major General Frölich, the *Fliegerführer Afrika*, could only muster some 300 serviceable machines, of which only one third were German – though it was admittedly easier for the Axis powers to send reinforcements of aircraft to North Africa than it was for them to provide ground troops. Frölich's position moreover was made vastly more difficult by the heaviest rainstorm of the year which occurred on the evening prior to the opening of CRUSADER. This flooded the Axis airfields but largely missed those of the Desert Air Force.

In addition, the Axis ground and air forces alike were desperately short of supplies, especially petrol. The main reason for this was that their convoys across the Mediterranean were under constant attack from aircraft, submarines and surface vessels operating from Malta. In September, 28 per cent of all cargoes sent to Rommel failed to reach him. In October, the proportion lost was 21 per cent. In November, it rose to a staggering 63 per cent. Nor did Malta's aircraft attack only shipping. On the night of 21–22 October for instance, a raid on the oil storage depot at Naples set off fires which the bomber crews described as the biggest they had ever seen.

Finally, the soldiers of Eighth Army were ready in every respect for the coming encounter. Their confidence had been lifted by the great increase in their strength and it seemed at the time that their preparations had been very thorough, for Auchinleck had rightly resisted pressure from Churchill to commence his assault prematurely. Whereas apart from the Italian Savona Division which, stiffened by German detachments, was holding the Egypt-Cyrenaica frontier posts, Rommel's troops were quite unprepared to resist an Allied attack. Instead they were taking up positions for an assault of their own on Tobruk, planned for 21 November. In fact, Rommel, who had been at a conference in Rome, only flew back to North Africa – via Athens – just before the battle began. He had received several warnings of Eighth Army's offensive from the Italians, not to mention his own Intelligence staff, but these he had rejected with scorn. Even after CRUSADER had begun, he would not at first concede that it was any more than a reconnaissance in force.

There was thus an apparently justifiable belief that Eighth Army, as Churchill proclaimed in a stirring signal to Auchinleck, would 'add a page to history which will rank with Blenheim and with Waterloo.' The only person who appears to have entertained doubts was the then Chief of the Imperial General Staff, General Sir John Dill. He was greatly concerned because the ground and air forces sent to North Africa had been provided at the expense of the Far East, pointing out that: 'It has been an accepted principle in our strategy that in the last resort the security of Singapore comes before that of Egypt. Yet the defences of Singapore are still considerably below standard.' Moreover despite the personal friendship of the two men, Dill felt that 'Auchinleck, for all his great qualities and his outstanding record on the Frontier, was not the coming man of the war as the Prime Minister thought.'

Nor indeed was it fair to expect that he would be, for his previous commands in India and briefly in Norway had provided Auchinleck with few precedents to assist him in his current task – and that task was made no easier by his selection of the man to lead Eighth Army. Both Churchill and the Chiefs of Staff had urged the claims of Lieutenant General Sir Henry Maitland Wilson. This officer was then in charge of the Allied troops in Syria but previously as Commander, British Troops in Egypt it was his 'organizational ability and knack of inspiring realism in training' which, according to General Jackson, had 'provided the standard of professionalism needed' to achieve the destruction of the Italians. The advice was not accepted.

Instead, as mentioned earlier, Auchinleck had entrusted the task to Lieutenant General Sir Alan Cunningham, telling Dill somewhat curtly that: 'I am convinced that I am right, and have now no further doubts in the matter.' Yet the choice was a peculiar one. Cunningham had proved extremely successful against the Italians in East Africa but he had never fought Germans before and he was utterly inexperienced in armoured warfare. Moreover, when he took up his post in September he was confronted with a couple of potential plans for CRUSADER which, as the

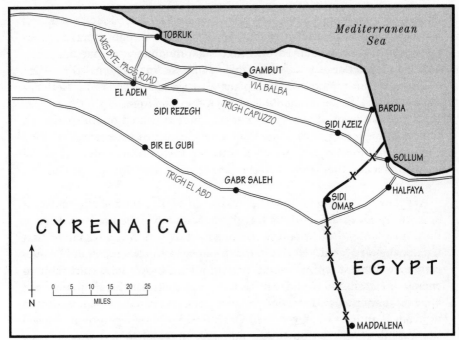

Map IIA: The 'CRUSADER' Battlefield.

Map IIB: Sidi Rezegh.

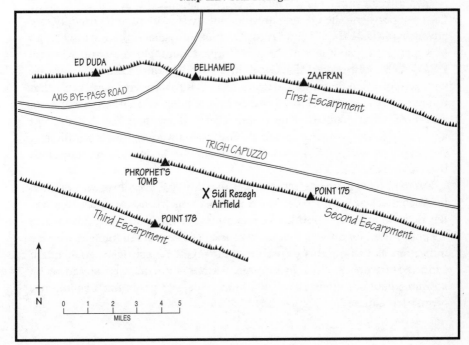

Official History makes clear, had been prepared by Auchinleck's staff and had received Auchinleck's personal approval after he had 'weighed every conceivable course open to Rommel.' Cunningham was naturally disinclined to question the express wishes of his Commander-in-Chief.

This was unfortunate, for both plans were singularly bad ones. Both envisaged that XIII Corps should pin down the Axis frontier positions while XXX Corps advanced westward. For this there appeared on the map to be three possible routes, the coastal Via Balbia and two rough tracks, the Trigh Capuzzo and the Trigh el Abd, but since the first two were blocked by the enemy defences, the Trigh el Abd might have seemed the only practicable choice.

Auchinleck's planners, however, came up with a further alternative, a huge sweep far to the south by way of the oases along the northern edge of the impassable Great Sand Sea. Luckily this was the alternative that Cunningham rejected, rightly believing that such an advance would be over extremely difficult terrain, would present a long supply line, vulnerable to enemy air attack, and would split his two corps so widely that they could not hope to be mutually supporting. Nonetheless a ghost of the plan remained to haunt Eighth Army, for a small Oasis Force was sent to mount a diversion on this route. Although this did cause Rommel some uneasiness, its only real effect on the battle was to deprive Eighth Army of the troops – 29th Indian Brigade and some South African armoured cars – of which it was composed.

Auchinleck's other plan, which Cunningham accepted, called for XXX Corps to out-flank the German frontier defences south of Sidi Omar, before advancing astride the Trigh el Abd. Even in this version there was likely to be a dangerous gap between the two Corps. Cunningham attempted to fill it by detaching Brigadier Alec Gatehouse's 4th Armoured Brigade, together with supporting infantry and artillery from 7th Armoured Division, so that it could either protect Godwin-Austen's left flank or assist Norrie's main armoured thrust as proved necessary. It was a compromise that did not appeal to Norrie who felt that Gatehouse's tasks were mutually conflicting, but his protests were over-ruled by Cunningham who in turn was supported by Auchinleck.

Yet the plan's major defect was that the aim of XXX Corps was defined by Auchinleck as being 'to destroy the enemy tank forces', after which it was felt that the relief of Tobruk, the reconquest of Cyrenaica, the advance to Tripoli, would follow as a matter of course. Unhappily Auchinleck gave no indication as to how this desirable result might be achieved. As Captain Liddell Hart points out, 'an armoured force is not in itself suited to be an immediate objective. For it is a fluid force, not easily fixed as infantry formations can be.'

The task of XXX Corps was made still more difficult by the particular problems of operating in a desert. It was never easy to pinpoint any position accurately, the more so since distances tended to be extremely deceptive. Dust-storms or heat hazes not only made matters worse but often rendered it impossible to tell friend from foe except at close range, including, indeed especially, from the air; that each side used captured vehicles added to the problem. Radio communications, poor to begin with, were often interrupted by electric storms or enemy interference. Few available maps were either detailed or reliable.

In such circumstances, it was appallingly difficult to gain an accurate picture of the situation, to tell where friendly forces, let alone enemy ones, were located. It was highly probable therefore that if it attempted to track down the enemy armour, XXX Corps would become confused, dispersed and vulnerable to counter-attack.

Thus, as Liddell Hart observes, the only way to ensure an effective encounter with Rommel's tanks was to force them 'to cover or retrieve some point of key importance.' To Norrie's credit, he realized this, urging an immediate advance of the whole of XXX Corps on the airfield at Sidi Rezegh. This would threaten not only to relieve Tobruk but to sever the Axis bypass road round the Tobruk salient which was the supply route to Rommel's frontier garrisons. Again Cunningham rejected his subordinate's advice, deciding instead, once more with Auchinleck's approval, that the British armour should proceed to a place called Gabr Saleh, though this had no practical importance, being merely a convenient landmark in an otherwise featureless part of the desert. Here it would pause to await the enemy's reaction, thereby in effect handing all initiative to Rommel.

Surprisingly, perhaps, matters did not go badly at first. The storm that had struck the Axis airfields enabled the Desert Air Force to destroy numerous enemy aircraft on the ground on 18 November, as indeed happened on the next two days as well. The Beaufighters, a flight of 272 Squadron, improved the occasion by shooting down seven Junkers Ju 52 transports. Opposition was minimal. The Hurricanes of 33 Squadron, having strafed Italian aerodromes, were met only by three Fiat CR 42 biplane fighters. These they promptly destroyed, two falling to the guns of Pilot Officer Wade, a young Texan who had joined the RAF as a volunteer in December 1940. He would rise to the rank of Wing Commander with twenty-five enemy machines to his credit before being killed in an air-accident in January 1944.

On the ground Eighth Army also met little resistance, for Rommel still refused to accept that his opponents had launched a major offensive. The only enemy encountered were the armoured cars of the German 3rd and 33rd Reconnaissance Units, detached from 21st and 15th Panzer Divisions respectively; these naturally fell back before the Allied advance. By evening XXX Corps had reached Gabr Saleh but Rommel's armour had still not been sighted. Next morning therefore 7th Armoured Division split up in search of its elusive objective. 7th Armoured Brigade headed for Sidi Rezegh, 22nd Armoured on its left flank made for Bir el Gubi, while 4th Armoured remained at Gabr Saleh apart from its 3rd Battalion of the Royal Tank Regiment[4] which set off north-eastward after the German light forces.

The exploits of the British armoured formations during the Desert War have rarely received proper appreciation, mainly because they have been distorted by a number of myths. The first of these concerns the tanks' performance. As late as January 1944, Auchinleck could write to Brooke claiming that there was at this time 'not a great deal in the way of armour' with which to deal with Rommel – a surprising complaint from a commander whose numerical advantage in tanks was immense – and in any case he had only 'inferior armament and equipment'. Even in his official Despatch long after the close of hostilities, Auchinleck could state, not as an opinion but as a fact, that British tanks were inferior to those of the Germans.

Certainly the British tanks in the Desert had their faults. The Matildas and Valentines, particularly the former, lacked speed; the Crusaders lacked mechanical reliability; the Stuarts lacked range. Yet in their really important qualities – gun power and armour – all were, if anything, superior to their German rivals.

At the time of CRUSADER, Rommel's Mark IIIs and Mark IVs carried a short-barrelled low-velocity 50mm gun or a short-barrelled low-velocity 75mm gun respectively. Both of these had less penetrative power than the 2-pounders used in all the British tanks or the equivalent 37mm of the Stuarts.

All German tanks originally had 30mm armour over the entire hull and the turret. This was considerably less than the Matildas with 78mm of armour on the hull and 75mm on the turret or the Valentines with 60mm of armour on the hull and 65mm on the turret; both were virtually immune from enemy tank-guns save at very short range. The side plates of the crusaders (28mm) and the Stuarts (25mm) were slightly less strong than those of their opponents but their front hull plates (33mm and 44mm) and their turret armour (49mm and 38mm) were thicker. For this reason the Germans had begun to modify their tanks by adding a further plate to the front of the hull. This doubled the thickness of armour, which was thus superior to that of the Crusaders or Stuarts – though not to that of the British heavy tanks – but did not prevent their turrets from remaining as vulnerable as before. In any case though some conversions took place during the winter of 1941–42, the fury of battle ensured that the majority of the German tanks had still not been improved by the time CRUSADER ended.[5]

Thus, throughout the battle, the British tanks had not only a big advantage in quantity but a definite advantage in quality as well. Their mishaps arose not from inadequate equipment but from mistaken tactics. The criticism usually made is that the British armour was dispersed far too widely, as indeed happened on 19 November. It should be recalled, however, that it was not easy to achieve concentration in the conditions of a desert war. In fact on numerous occasions during CRUSADER and later battles, the Afrika Korps was far more widely dispersed than the armoured formations of Eighth Army. On 19 November for instance, only 21st Panzer, and then only its 5th Panzer Regiment, under Lieutenant Colonel Stephan, came into action, its opponents being the remaining two units of Gatehouse's 4th Armoured Brigade, 8th Hussars and 5th Royal Tanks.

Another criticism directed against Eighth Army's tank commanders is that they were staid and conservative in comparison with the Afrika Korps led by the dashing Rommel. Yet ironically the real mistake the British made was that of being too brave, too daring. They scorned standing on the defensive. They persisted in regarding the tank not as a mobile protected gun but as a steel-plated horse. While the Germans preferred to use their tanks against weaker targets such as supply echelons or unprotected infantry, the British delighted in making charges at the enemy armour – although in the tanks of that period it was extremely difficult to fire the gun accurately whilst on the move.

On 19 November, Gatehouse's Stuarts made just such a charge against Battle Group Stephan. In so doing they encountered their most deadly enemies, the anti-tank guns. These were much the Germans' most effective weapons and were always used in combination with their tanks, in defence forming a screen in front of their armour, in attack pushing out boldly ahead of it. Though Gatehouse claimed many successes, the Germans really lost only three tanks, one of which was a Mark II armed only with machine-guns. 4th Armoured Brigade lost twenty-three Stuarts, though twelve of these were repaired later.

Elsewhere on the same day, Brigadier Scott-Cockburn's 22nd Armoured Brigade charged the Italian positions at Bir el Gubi, defended by the Ariete Armoured Division. This attack had more success, destroying thirty-four Italian tanks, damaging fifteen, and knocking out twelve guns. Nevertheless the Italians held their ground, destroying twenty-five of Scott-Cockburn's Crusaders. Qualitatively of course this was far more serious than the loss of the obsolete Italian armoured vehicles. These were slower than any of the British types except Matildas, mechanically unreliable, poorly armoured – 30mm on the hull, 40mm on the turret – and mounting a low-velocity 47mm gun which was inferior to any on the Allied side. That Ariete was often able to hold off superior numbers of British tanks during CRUSADER is conclusive evidence that the misfortunes of the British armour were caused by faulty tactics rather than inadequate equipment.

Brigadier Davy's 7th Armoured Brigade was the most successful on 19 November. At about 1630 in the afternoon, it overran the Sidi Rezegh airfield, destroying nineteen enemy aeroplanes on the ground. Next day Campbell's 7th Support Group joined Davy, while Brigadier Armstrong's 5th South African Brigade also prepared to move to his aid and Brigadier Dan Pienaar's 1st South African Brigade to mask Bir el Gubi. Meanwhile XIII Corps had begun to wheel round the Axis frontier defences at Sidi Omar and in the evening orders were sent to Scobie to commence a break-out from Tobruk on the following day.

Throughout 20 November indeed, Eighth Army consolidated its advantages, helped considerably by the fact that Rommel's armour was still widely separated. Battle Group Stephan withdrew in the morning to rejoin the rest of 21st Panzer, before moving off in pursuit of 3rd Royal Tanks, the numbers of which had been much exaggerated. Since 3rd Royal Tanks had rejoined Gatehouse early that same day, this action proved a wild-goose chase which ended with 21st Panzer running out of fuel. While it was replenishing, 15th Panzer attacked Gatehouse on its own at about 1630, its main assault ironically enough falling on 3rd Royal Tanks. Gatehouse lost twenty-six more Stuarts but it seems reasonable to suppose that the failure of the two Panzer Divisions to join forces saved him from far greater destruction.

It appeared that the fighting at Gabr Saleh would be resumed next morning with even greater intensity. During the night, 22nd Armoured had arrived to assist Gatehouse, while Crüwell had at last concentrated his Afrika Korps by bringing up 21st Panzer. By then, however, the whole aspect of the battle had changed. At 2100, a BBC news bulletin announcing that Eighth Army had 'started a general offensive in the Western Desert, with the aim of destroying the German-Italian forces in Africa' had at last alerted Rommel to the seriousness of the situation. He at once ordered Crüwell to 'follow the enemy tanks which have advanced towards Tobruk. Objective the airfield of Sidi Rezegh.'

The airfield lay on a little plateau about three miles wide running roughly south-east to north-west between two of the three escarpments or rocky cliffs to be found in this area. These have been given various names in different British accounts, but since the fighting at Sidi Rezegh was to be complicated enough in all conscience, it may be permissible to simplify this aspect of it at least by following the German example of calling them the First, Second and Third Escarpments reading from the sea. South of the airfield was the Third Escarpment, the highest part of which was Point 178. The Second Escarpment formed the northern boundary of the plateau, its most prominent features being a natural one, Point 175 which, because of the angle at which the escarpment ran, was almost due east of the airfield and, to the north-west, a man-made one, the white marble tomb of the prophet after whom Sidi Rezegh is named.

North of the Second Escarpment lay the Trigh Capuzzo, the middle one of the three routes running westward from the frontier. Beyond this was the First Escarpment which the Axis bypass road crossed between the high points of Belhamed, north of the prophet's tomb, and Ed Duda to its north-west. North-west again of the latter lay Tobruk, the garrison of which had been such a thorn in Rommel's side and was even now making preparations to torment him still further.

During the next three days, beginning with 21 November, the battlefield in general and this area in particular saw a series of combats of a ferocity unprecedented in the Desert. These were fought not only by the rival armies but also by their supporting airmen as they strove to protect their own ground troops and savage those of the enemy. The Axis pilots clearly had the better of these encounters, but their casualties were too heavy to be endured by a weaker force which had already suffered crippling losses earlier – on the 20th, for instance, the Beaufighters of 272 Squadron had destroyed fourteen Junkers Ju 87 Stuka dive-bombers on the ground plus four more in the air. The ultimate result of these clashes therefore was the slow but sure attainment of aerial supremacy by the Desert Air Force.

At 0845 on 21 November, Cunningham ordered XIII Corps, which by now had out-flanked the frontier defences, to engage. 4th Indian Division accordingly attacked the Axis strongpoints from the rear, making a series of gains, though at high cost, over the next three days. Meanwhile 2nd New Zealand Division moved northward, continued its advance during the pitch-black night of 21–22 November, and cut both the Via Balbia and the Trigh Capuzzo west of Bardia early next morning. Thereafter, leaving his 5th Brigade at Sidi Azeiz to watch the enemy forces holding Bardia, Freyberg directed his 4th and 6th Brigades westward towards Sidi Rezegh.

Even earlier on 21 November, at 0800, Scobie's 70th (British) Division, supported by Brigadier Willison's 32nd Army Tank Brigade – 1st, 4th and 7th Battalions of the Royal Tank Regiment – began an assault which ulti-mately broke through the enemy positions surrounding Tobruk. Heavy casualties were suffered. The 2nd Battalion, The Black Watch lost three-quarters of its strength. Some sixty tanks were knocked out, though half of them were later repaired. Yet a salient 4,000 yards deep was secured and over 1,000 prisoners were taken, half of them Germans from 90th Light.

Though failure elsewhere prevented any chance of Scobie's men advancing further for the time being, during that day and those following they consolidated their salient with stubborn fortitude. On the 21st, Sergeant Allan Appleby, in temporary command of a troop of tanks won a

Distinguished Conduct Medal, to earn which a soldier must display not only great courage but also outstanding initiative. Sergeant Appleby certainly showed both. His three tanks were trapped in a minefield, two of them being immobilized. Throughout the day, Appleby fought off enemy attacks, repairing his damaged tanks in the intervals between engagements. By evening, with both casualties repaired, the troop retired to Tobruk. On the way, Appleby found another crippled tank which he also towed to safety.

Two days later, 32nd Army Tank Brigade in general and 4th Royal Tanks in particular won an even higher decoration when Captain Philip Gardner left his tank under intense fire to help a wounded officer lying near a disabled armoured car. Lifting him into this vehicle, Gardner fixed a tow-rope to it then, returning to his tank, he attempted to pull it to safety. The rope snapped, so Gardner again ran over and this time carried the casualty to the tank, remaining outside it holding on to him while it withdrew. Sad to relate, the injured officer died shortly afterwards, but Gardner, though wounded in arm and leg, survived – to receive a Victoria Cross.

It was not the earliest nor the only VC to be won during CRUSADER. At 0830 on 21 November, 1st Battalion, King's Royal Rifle Corps from Campbell's 7th Support Group, reinforced by a company of 2nd Battalion, The Rifle Brigade and backed by forty-two guns, attacked the Second Escarpment at Sidi Rezegh. During that attack, Rifleman John Beeley earned the Eighth Army's first VC – alas, a posthumous one – by taking an enemy post single-handed. A two-mile section of the escarpment was taken, as were 800 German and Italian prisoners, twice the number of the attackers. 6th Royal Tanks from 7th Armoured Brigade then drove on over the escarpment making for Ed Duda, only to meet the iron resistance of four 88mms ordered up by Rommel in person. These, as so often, halted the British armour with very heavy losses.

Sidi Rezegh then came under attack from German tanks. As previously mentioned, Crüwell's Afrika Korps had been ordered to retire from Gabr Saleh to the airfield, and the pursuit by 4th and 22nd Armoured Brigades had not been as effective as might have been hoped, partly because they believed the Germans to be in full retreat, partly because the move was protected by an efficient screen of anti-tank guns. Even so, the enemy suffered losses and did not manage to break away until the British armour had run out of fuel.

Nonetheless, Crüwell's evasion of his pursuers had grim consequences for the Eighth Army units at Sidi Rezegh. Brigadier Davy, threatened from the south-east by two panzer divisions, moved his remaining armoured regiments, 7th Hussars and 2nd Royal Tanks, to meet them, but the odds were too great. As Davy reports,[6] 'the enemy tanks were accompanied and in some cases preceded by anti-tank guns which were not at first recognized as hostile as they were mingled with British trucks and lorries' – as ill-luck would have it, Crüwell's advance had taken him into the supply echelons of 7th Support Group. It was these guns that did the main damage. Some held off an attempt by 2nd Royal Tanks to attack 15th Panzer's flank, while others, accompanying 21st Panzer, devastated the luckless 7th Hussars who lost their Commanding Officer, Lieutenant Colonel Byass, and all but ten of their armoured vehicles.

While the anti-tank guns, which Davy notes were 'very boldly handled', engaged the British armour, some of 21st Panzer's tanks, as was usual, sought softer options. They attacked a company of 2nd Rifle Brigade which, backed by the guns of 60th Field Regiment and 3rd Regiment Royal Horse Artillery, had been stationed near the eastern end of the Third Escarpment to protect the right-rear of the British positions. In the first clash four of the attacking tanks were set ablaze by 3rd RHA's mobile 2-pounder anti-tank guns – transported on lorries known as 'portees' – under 2nd Lieutenant George Ward Gunn. Two 2-pounders were also destroyed, however, leaving only two still in action.

The Germans retired – but only temporarily. They soon returned in full force, the high-explosive shells of their Mark IVs causing havoc among the British infantry positions. Another 2-pounder was lost. All the crew of the remaining gun were killed or wounded and its driver, understandably enough, was withdrawing from the fray when Major Bernard Pinney, commanding a battery of 3rd RHA, called on Ward Gunn to stop him. This Ward Gunn did and, joined by Pinney, brought the gun back into action. Hits set the portee on fire but Pinney fought the blaze while Ward Gunn continued the battle, destroying two more enemy tanks, damaging others, until he was killed instantly by a bullet through the forehead. Pinney then went on firing until further hits made the gun inoperable, after which he drove it away. Both officers were recommended for the VC. Since this decoration is rightly given sparingly, it was awarded only to Ward Gunn, possibly because he had given his life in the action whereas Pinney had survived. Tragically, that was only until next day, for he was killed by a stray shell in a comparatively quiet area.

Meanwhile, 15th Panzer had turned its attention to 2nd Royal Tanks, its accompanying 88mms again inflicting terrible casualties. The belated approach of 4th and 22nd Armoured Brigades finally ended the fighting. Crüwell retired to the north-east, 15th Panzer making for Gambut, 21st Panzer for Belhammed.

Neither side showed much activity on the morning of the 22nd but the afternoon saw the conflict swing very much in favour of the Germans. At about 1500, 5th South African Brigade assaulted Point 178 on the Third Escarpment from the south, but was repulsed with loss by units of 90th

Light. At about the same time, an attack was launched by 21st Panzer alone – for once more the enemy armour had not been concentrated – against the airfield. Its infantry regiment the 104th engaged the British-held part of the Second Escarpment from the north, while the gap between the Second and Third Escarpments was invaded from the west by 5th Panzer Regiment, urged on personally by Rommel. The infantry assault was dispersed by artillery fire but 5th Panzer Regiment broke onto the airfield.

Here the pattern of the previous day was repeated. The German anti-tank guns finished off what was left of 7th Armoured Brigade and then decimated 22nd Armoured Brigade as it tried to counter-attack. Next the German tanks assaulted the Second Escarpment from the rear, forcing the surrender of most of its defenders, 1st Battalion The King's Royal Rifle Corps.

Again, Eighth Army's courage illuminated what would otherwise have been a dismal day. Sergeant Stanley Burrage, his tank destroyed and his crew killed, set up a first-aid post in the middle of the battlefield, where he tended the injured amidst the thickest fighting, an action recognized by the award of the DCM. Brigadier 'Jock' Campbell – his real names were John Charles – who had already shown heroic leadership on the previous day, proved inspirational on the 22nd, driving about in his open staff car, banging on the sides of tanks to attract attention and lead them against the enemy, leaping out to help serve his guns and constantly shouting encouragement to anyone he felt needed it. He won a VC.

It was all in vain. By 1545 the Germans held the airfield. 4th Armoured Brigade moved up to oppose them but, coming under fire from anti-tank guns, retired to reorganize with the exception of a troop of 3rd Royal Tanks which the indomitable Campbell personally led into the attack. Under cover of this, the remains of his battered 7th Support Group fell back south of the Third Escarpment to a position east of the 5th South African Brigade. As a crowning misfortune, 15th Panzer, at last appearing on the scene at about 1700, ran into the Headquarters of 4th Armoured Brigade which was then accompanied by a detachment of the 8th Hussars. Gatehouse was away at a conference but his second-in-command was captured as were sixteen other officers and 150 men. Some thirty-five tanks were destroyed or taken. The German officer who achieved this coup, Major Fenski, was killed in action next day. By nightfall 7th Armoured Division had only 144 tanks fit for action. The Afrika Korps had 173.

Although a fair number of the latter were Mark IIs and such a comparison also takes no account of the heavy 'I' tanks with XIII Corps or of Eighth Army's reserves, his recent successes had understandably led Crüwell to believe that he could break British resistance with one last great effort on 23 November. This as it happened was the Sunday before Advent or in the Lutheran calendar *Totensonntag* – the Sunday of the Dead.

Crüwell's plan was simple. Von Ravenstien was ordered to send 21st Panzer's 104th Infantry Regiment to reinforce units of 90th Light on the Third Escarpment, while his 5th Panzer Regiment joined Neumann-Silkow's 15th Panzer Division which had both 8th Panzer Regiment and 115th Infantry Regiment already under command. Crüwell intended all these forces to turn south towards Bir el Gubi, link up with the Ariete Division and then swing northwards to crush the remains of XXX Corps against the escarpment. On the way, Crüwell encountered the supply vehicles of 7th Support Group and 5th South African Brigade. Every Allied tank or gun within range offered desperate resistance, urged on by Campbell who for all practical purposes now won his VC a second time, on this occasion sitting on top of an Armoured Command Vehicle, waving red and blue scarves as signals for 'Stop' and 'Go', his whole attitude summed up by one unforgettable signal to a troop of guns: 'Expect no orders. Stick to me. I shall advance soon!'[7]

Though Neumann-Silkow wished to finish off his present opponents, Crüwell persisted in his southward drive. This next encountered Pienaar's 1st South African Brigade which was moving north to join the forces at Sidi Rezegh, having left 22nd Guards Brigade to hold its former position at Bir el Gubi. The South Africans turned their artillery fire onto the enemy but, having no tanks of their own, were forced to halt; nor did they resume their advance that day. These encounters had cost Crüwell eleven more tanks. He had 162 under his command when he joined Ariete at about 1235.

At 1500 Crüwell's two Panzer Regiments, accompanied by artillery and the 115th Regiment in lorries, lined up to make what General Jackson calls a 'charge en masse' against 5th South African Brigade. Ariete made little impact on the left of the line, allowing the remnants of 22nd Armoured Brigade to deliver attacks on the Germans' left flank – but nothing could stop Crüwell's onslaught. By nightfall the South Africans' defence had finally disintegrated. Brigadier Armstrong was captured along with some 2,000 of his men, though many others got away to join Pienaar, while Major Cyril Cochran took a group of about 200 north-eastward to reach the advancing New Zealanders with whom they fought for the remainder of the battle, Cochran earning a DSO in the process.

At first glance this seemed an Allied disaster. In fact it was the Afrika Korps that had suffered the real injuries. Crüwell had forfeited his hard-won superiority in armour by the loss of seventy-two tanks. In 8th Panzer Regiment both the battalion commanders and five of the six company commanders had been killed or wounded. Colonel Zintel had died at the head of his 115th Regiment while casualties among his infantrymen had been horrifyingly high. 'Crüwell', says Ronald Lewin in *The Life and Death of the Afrika Korps*, had 'cut the heart out' of his command.

Notes

1   *'Royal Air Force 1939–1945' Volume I: The Fight at Odds* by Denis Richards.
2   In retrospect it is amusing to note that many of the old hands regretted the change, feeling that a unique formation had become 'just another army'.
3   A German panzer regiment was roughly equivalent to a British armoured brigade.
4   At full strength a battalion of the Royal Tank Regiment was the equivalent of a normal armoured (cavalry or yeomanry) regiment.
5   Full details of the Allied and Axis tanks can be found in the Official History which has provided the main source for the facts set out here or hereafter.
6   In his own regimental history of the 7th Hussars, *The Seventh and Three Enemies*.
7   Campbell was promoted to major general after the battle. He was killed on 5 March, 1942, when his staff car overturned on a road recently repaired with wet clay that had not had time to harden.

3

PYRRHIC VICTORY

The well-tried principle that the best results from artillery are obtained by its centralized control was forgotten.

Colonel Jacob's Diary.
6 August, 1942.

By one of those ironies which were so pronounced a feature of the Desert War, it was in fact the Commander of Eighth Army who now 'lost heart'. During 23 November, greatly exaggerated reports of the British tank losses had been reaching Cunningham who, it should not be forgotten, was quite without experience in armoured warfare. As accounts of the destruction of 5th South African Brigade also came in, Cunningham's anxieties increased. He began to give serious consideration to abandoning the struggle so as to fall back to the frontier.

Fortunately, Cunningham's Brigadier General Staff, Brigadier 'Sandy' Galloway, strongly disagreed. His firm stand was supported by both of Cunningham's Corps Commanders. At a conference with Cunningham and Galloway held at about mid-day, Godwin-Austen – though learning for the first time of the casualties suffered by XXX Corps – stated categorically that he was 'horrified' by any suggestion of a retreat. Norrie, even more commendably, also remained undaunted. Consulted by wireless, he declared that he was 'perfectly able to deal with the situation for the rest of the day in the event of a counter-attack.' Cunningham listened to their advice to the extent of making no decision before asking Auchinleck to join him at his Headquarters at Maddalena to discuss the whole question. Galloway, more alarmed by his commander's fears than by the situation, also rang Cairo to make certain that the C-in-C, Middle East did just that.

Auchinleck, accompanied by Tedder, reached Eighth Army's head-quarters that evening. Here he was urged to continue the battle by the resolute Galloway, who in General Jackson's words, 'refused to reflect the depression of his commander – a difficult thing to do under such circum-stances. The two British Corps Commanders were consulted and were equally adamant that the offensive should go on.' Their arguments were the more readily acceptable because earlier that same day Auchinleck had learned through 'Ultra' interceptions that his enemy was 'fully stretched and desperate', short of supplies, especially petrol, and with no hope of receiving any reinforcements in the immediate future – in sharp contrast to the reserves available to Eighth Army.[1] In addition, Auchinleck had just received a signal from Churchill – also kept well informed by 'Ultra' – which gave him a timely reminder that 'a prolongation of battle must wear down enemy with his limited resources.'

Thus encouraged, Auchinleck rightly forbade any withdrawal and by his decision ensured that the battle would not be lost by default. It still had to be won, however. On 24 November Auchinleck issued a formal instruction to Cunningham but, as is pointed out by Field Marshal Lord Carver[2] in his *Dilemmas of the Desert War*: 'It was full of stirring phrases such as "relent-lessly using all resources down to the last tank", and "to the limit of endurance", "determined effort", "utmost boldness", "worth immense risks which will be taken"; but contained no more of practical value than the simple directives of the previous evening.' In turn, apart from suggestions about the use of the Long Range Desert Group and the Oasis Force, neither of which could hope to have any real effect, those directives had amounted to a simple command to 'recapture the Sidi Rezegh-Duda ridge at the earliest possible moment and join hands with Tobruk garrison'; they gave no indication as to how this was to be achieved.

Indeed the only tactical change which was initiated at this time was an increased use of 'Jock Columns'. Named after the irrepressible Brigadier Campbell, who had first employed them, these were small, highly mobile groups of motorized infantry and field guns. They appealed to those officers and men who liked individual, independent action and also to Auchinleck, who had had experience of similar formations during his service in India. Throughout the last phases of CRUSADER, his correspondence refers to them repeatedly in terms of high praise: they were 'excellent', 'invaluable', 'just what we want', 'doing awfully well', and he gloats over the fact that 'more and more' were being organized.

Unfortunately, that meant that more and more British formations were being weakened. For the 'Jock Columns', as their founder openly stated, had many weaknesses. They could raid, harass and confuse but they could not capture strong enemy positions or repel strong enemy attacks. Moreover their use began that tendency to split up British units which would long continue with increasingly harmful effects. In particular it would result in a dispersal of the British artillery which was recognized, even by the enemy, as the most efficient element in Eighth Army. Ironically, on 22 October, Auchinleck had received a long memorandum from Churchill which began:

> Renown awaits the commander who first in this war restores
> artillery to its prime importance on the battlefield, from which it
> has been ousted by heavily armoured tanks.

Auchinleck had filed it away, annotating it: 'Keep as history.'

As Auchinleck's official Despatch confirms, Cunningham accepted the decision to fight on 'loyally' and issued 'orders to give effect to it'. Nonetheless the C-in-C, Middle East had been much disquieted by the Eighth Army Commander's pessimism. After his return to Cairo on 25 November therefore, he held further consultations with Tedder, Coningham, his own Chief of Staff, Major General Arthur Smith and the Minister of State, Middle East, Oliver Lyttelton, as a result of which he determined to relieve Cunningham of his command. It must have been a bitter moment for Auchinleck since it was he who had insisted on appointing Cunningham in the face of much advice to the contrary and he who had assured Dill that Cunningham would 'bring a fresh brain to problems which I feel are getting a bit stale and fishlike.' It cannot have been very pleasant for Cunningham either, particularly as, to save everyone's 'face', Auchinleck ordered him to 'agree to being placed on the sick list and to go into hospital for a period' which, as Auchinleck appreciated, Cunningham disliked intensely. Moreover, on his return to Britain, Cunningham found that, despite his previous successes in East Africa, it had been decided that he would not be given another operational command. Though he would loyally fill a number of important posts, including Commandant of the Staff College, GOC Northern Ireland and High Commissioner in Palestine, he would always remain bitter at having thus been 'put on the shelf'.

To replace Cunningham, Auchinleck appointed his own Deputy Chief of the General Staff, Major General Neil Ritchie. This was another strange choice, for Ritchie lacked experience of high command in battle as well as of desert operations in general; he was also placed in a most invidious position in that he was junior to both his Corps Commanders. He was understandably reluctant to accept the post, arguing that it would be better for Auchinleck to assume direct command, at least until a new officer could be sent out from England. Churchill urged a similar course of action, but Auchinleck was deaf to all advice. What makes his decision the more surprising in retrospect is that in the future he would, in the words of the Official History, spend 'days at a time' at Ritchie's Headquarters, during which 'all important operational matters' would be discussed between them. Starting on 1 December for instance, Auchinleck stayed for ten days at Eighth Army Headquarters giving 'advice' which, as even the Official History remarks, could scarcely have been distinguishable from 'orders'.

Luckily all this drama made little practical difference at the time. While it was taking place, CRUSADER was being won by the officers and men of Eighth Army – with the unintentional assistance of the enemy commander. At 1040 on 24 November, Rommel had begun a reckless, if daring, advance eastward along the Trigh el Abd at the head of 5th Panzer Regiment, followed at intervals by the rest of 21st Panzer Division, 15th Panzer Division and finally Ariete. His intention was to crush the 2nd New Zealand and 4th Indian Divisions against his frontier positions, an achievement which he blithely assured his Chief Operations Officer, Lieutenant Colonel Siegfried Westphal, who was left in charge of his headquarters at El Adem, would take only twenty-four hours; thirty-six at the most.

Since the New Zealanders were already moving away from the frontier; while 4th Indian Division had occupied part of the original Axis defences, Rommel really had no prospect of achieving his aim. He did scatter the XXX Corps supply echelons which lay in his path and he all but captured the luckless Cunningham, who had been visiting Norrie's Headquarters, unaware of his impending dismissal. Cunningham escaped only by dashing to a waiting Blenheim which took off under fire.

As Auchinleck would state in his Despatch, however, Rommel's thrust 'inflicted little material damage and the moral effect was almost negligible.' The scattered transport units 'soon reassembled and reorganized themselves' and the XXX Corps supply and maintenance services were hardly affected. The Desert Air Force evacuated Landing Grounds 123 and 124 successfully, while the Germans passed just clear of Landing Grounds 122 and 128, on the former of which 175 aircraft were packed wing-tip to wing-tip. Furthermore, Rommel inexplicably failed to attack two massive British supply dumps lying south of the Trigh el Abd, although Major General Freiherr von Mellenthin, then a lieutenant colonel and Rommel's Chief Intelligence Officer, states in his *Panzer Battles* that their location was known 'from captured documents'.

In the event, it was the Axis columns which suffered heavy loss. The artillery of 7th Support Group engaged them from the north and the artillery of 1st South African Brigade from the south. Coningham's Hurricanes and Tomahawks joined in, though not his bombers, due to fear of errors in identification. It is almost amusing to read accounts of Rommel's ability to concentrate his armour while that of Eighth Army was dispersed and then to turn to the situation on the evening of 24 November which saw Ariete stopped in its tracks and the remaining seventy-six tanks of the Afrika Corps (twenty of them Mark IIs) scattered over miles of desert, with Rommel, Crüwell and their Chiefs of Staff cut off from their troops in enemy-held territory, escaping disaster only because their Armoured Command Vehicle was a captured British one.

Next day the Axis casualties increased. Coningham's Blenheims and Marylands now joined the fighters in their assaults, and the 'Hurribombers' of 80 Squadron proved particularly deadly against Rommel's supporting motorized infantry or supply lorries, as well as causing gruesome casualties among tank crews who were decapitated when they opened their hatches to see what was happening or blown to pieces when caught by surprise outside their vehicles.

For its part the German armour inflicted little damage. 15th Panzer did not even reach the frontier area until the morning of the 25th. Thereafter its only achievement was the destruction of a British field workshop after a gallant defence by sixteen disabled Matildas of 42nd Royal Tanks. 21st Panzer was even less successful. Lieutenant Colonel Stephan, still commanding 5th Panzer Regiment, was killed by strafing fighters on the 25th, after which his unit lost eight tanks in an attack on the 1st Field Regiment. The British had five guns knocked out temporarily but they were back in action next day. As a culmination to these misfortunes, 5th Panzer Regiment, under Rommel's personal direction, lost seven more tanks making an attack across a minefield against the dug-in artillery of 25th Field Regiment. On 26 November both Panzer Divisions retired independently to Bardia for fuel and ammunition.

Nor did 'the antics of the Afrika Korps in the area of the frontier', as Field Marshal Carver rather unkindly calls them, have any effect on the Eighth Army units in the Sidi Rezegh area. They, it appears, were blissfully unaware of the actions of both Rommel and Auchinleck alike. When Ritchie arrived at his headquarters in the late afternoon of 26 November, he found, to quote Carver again, that:

> . . . the situation had been largely restored, not by any direct contribution of Auchinleck's, but by the toughness of the New Zealanders and the determination of Freyberg, egged on by Godwin-Austen, to push westward towards Tobruk.

Their spirit may be summed up in Freyberg's words to Brigadier Barrowclough's 6th New Zealand Brigade: 'You will receive no further orders but you will start fighting.'

The New Zealanders' first major success had come at dawn on 23 November when 6th Brigade over-ran the Afrika Korps Headquarters. Crüwell was away, preparing for *Totensonntag*, but 200 prisoners were captured including all Crüwell's cypher staff, as were numerous vehicles, among them all the Afrika Korps' wireless trucks. During the day, Barrowclough's men continued their westward drive, as did 4th New Zealand Brigade under Brigadier Inglis and the Matildas and Valentines of the supporting 1st Army Tank Brigade under Brigadier Watkins.

At about 1130, 6th Brigade's leading battalion, the 25th, assaulted the Second Escarpment. Enemy anti-tank guns destroyed twelve of the sixteen Valentines engaged, but the infantry captured Point 175, only to be driven off it again in the afternoon. The New Zealanders suffered 450 casualties in these encounters, 120 of them fatal, mostly in 25th Battalion, whose CO, Lieutenant Colonel McNaught, was wounded three times. Next morning, 6th Brigade renewed the attack and captured Point 175 once more, as it did the Sidi Rezegh airfield on the 25th. Meanwhile 4th Brigade had captured Gambut on the Via Balbia on the afternoon of the 23rd, and although unfortunately it did not move north of the road, which would have brought it to the main enemy supply dumps, it then advanced to Zaafran on the First Escarpment east of Belhamed and north of Point 175, seizing this on the morning of the 25th.

That night, Eighth Army mounted three attacks. Scobie's Tobruk garrison pushed forward to within three miles of Belhamed, Captain James Jackman of the 1st Royal Northumberland Fusiliers earning a posthumous Victoria Cross for his cool leadership under fire in the process. 4th New Zealand Brigade, fighting its way westward, captured Belhamed in the early hours of the 26th. 6th New Zealand Brigade thrust north-westward towards the Prophet's Tomb – but was thrown back by the men of the 9th Bersaglieri Regiment, whose courage was an honour to the Italian Army.

At dawn on the 26th, Inglis attempted to lead 4th New Zealand Brigade to Ed Duda but his advance too was checked, this time by enemy 88mms which destroyed seven Matildas. While the attention of the enemy on the First Escarpment was directed eastward, however, at 1210 they were engaged from the north-west. In the face of heavy artillery fire and a mis-directed British bombing attack, the Tobruk garrison finally captured Ed Duda, to come within two miles of the positions secured by Inglis.

Once more darkness brought no respite. Throughout the night, Barrowclough's men persisted in their attacks on that part of the Second Escarpment remaining in enemy hands. They met with savage resistance, the anti-tank guns firing into the New Zealand infantry at point-blank range with results too ghastly to be described. Nonetheless early in the morning of the 27th, the Prophet's Tomb was captured and the whole of the Second Escarpment at last came into Eighth Army's hands.

Meanwhile a further attempt to link up with Scobie was made by the 4th New Zealand Brigade, supported by the Matildas of Lieutenant Colonel Yeo's 44th Battalion of the Royal Tank Regiment. An attack by an armoured formation at night had previously not been considered possible, since it was believed that the tanks could not be controlled effectively and would not even be able to keep in touch with each other. Fortunately, Brigadier Watkins, commanding 1st Army Tank Brigade of which 44th Royal Tanks formed part, had felt for some time that it was perfectly feasible for tanks to fight after dark, provided their crews were adequately trained, and moreover that doing so would reduce the heavy losses that were being inflicted on the British armour by the 88mms. He had therefore set in train a programme of night exercises and dummy attacks for which Yeo's men were now to provide a dramatic justification.

By 0100 on the 27th, the New Zealanders and the Matildas had broken through to Ed Duda without the loss of a tank and at the cost of one infantry casualty. The siege of Tobruk had been raised, though for Yeo the joy of the achievement was tragically marred by the news that his son, a captain in 1st Royal Tanks with the Tobruk garrison, had been killed in action less than two hours earlier.

By now the hapless Westphal at El Adem was sending desperate signals for the Afrika Korps to return to the Sidi Rezegh-Tobruk area, his pleas being repeated by Crüwell. On 27 November Rommel reluctantly agreed to abandon his 'antics' in the frontier zone. As his forces moved westward, 15th Panzer attacked the headquarters of the 5th New Zealand Brigade at Sidi Azeiz, taking over 700 prisoners including Brigadier Hargest, though only after a defence for which the Brigade Commander later received Rommel's congratulations – well deserved but probably of little consolation in the circumstances.

By this time, 7th Armoured Brigade had been withdrawn from the battle to refit but further tanks had arrived from Eighth Army's reserves to bring Gott's numbers to forty-five in 22nd Armoured Brigade and seventy-seven in 4th Armoured Brigade. As 15th Panzer moved westward along the Trigh Capuzzo in the early afternoon of the 27th – 21st Panzer was using the Via Balbia – it fell into an ambush set by 22nd Armoured which also earned the Germans' admiration. 4th Armoured then attacked from the flank and though held off by anti-tank guns, caused havoc among the enemy's transport echelons. These were only saved from total destruction by the approach of night.

Unfortunately, the 7th Support Group was no longer with Gott, having been split up into 'Jock Columns' in order to harass the various Axis formations scattered throughout the battle area. This resulted in there being no infantry or artillery units on hand to block the Trigh Capuzzo after dark. The British tanks did not block it either because, in accordance with current tactical thinking, both armoured brigades withdrew southward to spend the night in a protective leaguer. 15th Panzer promptly continued its westward journey during the hours of darkness. On the 28th, both Panzer Divisions rejoined the Axis forces near the old Sidi Rezegh battlefield.

The situation which Rommel and Crüwell now faced was not encouraging. The Afrika Korps had passed to the north of the main body of XXX Corps. This now consisted only of the remaining units of 7th Armoured Division plus 1st South African Brigade – 22nd Guards Brigade had also been dispersed in 'Jock Columns' – and lay south-east of the Third Escarpment. That escarpment was still in Axis hands as was the area north of the First Escarpment. The First Escarpment proper, however, was held by Eighth Army from Ed Duda, secured by the Tobruk garrison, eastward to the 4th New Zealand Brigade's positions at Belhamed and Zaafran. So was the Second Escarpment which was in the hands of 6th New Zealand Brigade.

The German commanders remained undaunted. They planned a major assault in the Sidi Rezegh area on 29 November, though it is worth noting that yet again they did not concentrate their armour for this purpose. 21st Panzer was due to advance into the gap between the First and Second Escarpments but early that morning its commander, von Ravenstein, returning from a conference with Crüwell, was taken prisoner when he drove into a well camouflaged New Zealand position. His place was taken by Major General Böttcher, originally in charge of Rommel's heavy artillery but more recently commanding the troops on the Third Escarpment. Perhaps as a result of his inexperience, 21st Panzer attempted little and achieved less over the next three days.

Neumann-Silkow's 15th Panzer moved first to the north of the Third Escarpment, then to the west of the Second Escarpment, and finally attacked Ed Duda on the First Escarpment at 1300. The fight raged all afternoon but the Tobruk garrison held firm until after dark when a skilful counter-attack by their Matildas flung back their assailants with heavy losses.

Only the Italian armour proved successful. Ariete Division, entrusted with the task of protecting the German rear, advanced slowly northward towards Sidi Rezegh. The British tanks which Gott had concentrated under Gatehouse's command attempted to pursue but were halted by Ariete's anti-tank guns. In consequence, Gatehouse was unable to reach the Second Escarpment, with the result that Pienaar's 1st South African Brigade, which was intended to join 6th New Zealand Brigade on the escarpment, was also reluctant to proceed too far north unsupported, for fear of suffering the fate of its sister-brigade on *Totensonntag*.

Unhappily, the New Zealanders were hourly expecting the South Africans' arrival. At 1515, Lieutenant Bayley's armoured car did reach the escarpment, convincing everyone that Pienaar's main body was not far behind. When, in the late afternoon, a strong force appeared making for Point 175 from the south-east with no attempt at concealment, it was believed to be the South Africans. In fact this was Ariete, approaching casually because, by an unlucky mischance, the Italians thought the position had already fallen to their allies. By the time the New Zealanders had discovered the mistake it was too late. By nightfall Point 175 had been lost, together with 200 prisoners. Next day Norrie, in an armoured car, personally led an attempt by 1st South African Brigade to regain it, but the attack did not go in until after dark and was repulsed with some ease.

By then, in any case, the situation had changed once more in favour of the enemy. All morning on 30 November, German artillery had pounded 6th New Zealand Brigade's remaining positions on the Second Escarpment. A force of Stukas with strong fighter escort attempted to join in the attack but was routed by the Tomahawks of 112 Squadron RAF and 3 Squadron RAAF which together claimed fifteen enemy aircraft destroyed and another fifteen damaged for the loss of four Tomahawks but no pilots. At about 1600, 15th Panzer Division, recalled from Ed Duda, backed by German infantry from the Third Escarpment under Lieutenant Colonel Mickl, and supported by a westward advance from point 175 by Ariete, fell on the New Zealanders. By 1730, the whole of the Second Escarpment was back in Axis hands and a further 600 prisoners had been taken, the surviving defenders retiring to join their 4th Brigade at Belhamed.

Early on 1 December, Neumann-Silkow continued his advance, driving the New Zealanders from Belhamed also. Godwin-Austen's Headquarters Staff, as well as most of Freyberg's transport vehicles, took refuge in Tobruk, the defenders of which were now once more cut off from the main body of Eighth Army. At this point Gatehouse's tanks finally arrived on the scene but, after covering a New Zealand retreat to Zaafran, the British armour returned to its former position south-east of Sidi Rezegh. Freyberg's artillery, however, was able to hold off a further thrust by 15th Panzer, while 21st Panzer, which could have blocked his line of retreat, obligingly chose instead to move westward out of the way. The New Zealanders fell back towards the frontier in good order.

It seemed as though Rommel had achieved another success. In reality he had brought his army to the brink of ruin. Like 5th South African Brigade earlier, the New Zealanders had not been overcome easily. Rommel had suffered further savage losses and his men were now mentally and physically exhausted. Even those New Zealanders who had been taken prisoner would report later that their captors were 'practically sleepwalkers' who showed no sign of any elation.

Eighth Army had also endured much but it had the priceless advantage of fresh reserves to throw into the fight. More tanks moved up to bring the number with 7th Armoured Division to a total of 136, while Messervy's 4th Indian Division, plus the remainder of 5th New Zealand Brigade, also headed for the Sidi Rezegh area, being replaced on the frontier by 2nd South African Division.

Still Rommel stubbornly refused to accept the inevitable. On 2 December he ordered motorized infantry columns eastward along the Via Balbia and the Trigh Capuzzo to help his frontier garrisons. Next day, they were attacked by the Desert Air Force, then ambushed, the former by 5th New Zealand Brigade, the latter by 4th Indian Division. Both retired with ruinous losses. On the 4th, 21st Panzer attacked Ed Duda, still held by the Tobruk forces, but was repulsed. Meanwhile, 15th Panzer and Ariete made another attempt to get through to the frontier. Ritchie, who now had Auchinleck at his headquarters to give him 'advice', suggested that Norrie should move to meet this threat, but the XXX Corps Commander who had planned an advance of his own towards El Adem protested against conforming 'to every movement of Rommel's' – what a later Eighth Army Commander would have called 'dancing to Rommel's tune'. He would receive definite orders to deal with this incursion on 5 December, but by that time the enemy were already retiring of their own accord.

Rommel had at last concluded, with some reluctance, that he could not help his frontier garrisons, isolate Tobruk and still oppose Norrie. He therefore began to withdraw all his fighting forces and as much transport as possible from the areas north of the Via Balbia and around Sidi Rezegh. Covered by Ariete, these withdrew to a line running from west of Ed Duda via El Adem to the neighbourhood of Bir el Gubi. By 6 December this movement had been completed and Eighth Army had re-established contact, permanently this time, with Scobie in Tobruk.

Attention meanwhile had already turned to Bir el Gubi, near which XXX Corps had concentrated. It had been joined by 11th Indian Brigade from Messervy's Division which on both 4 and 5 December attempted to storm Bir el Gubi but was thwarted by a battalion of the Young Fascists, aided as usual by anti-tank guns. Despite their lack of success, these attacks convinced Rommel that a major British offensive was developing from this area, as indeed Norrie had originally intended. This, Rommel felt, he must check at all costs. On 5 December a Stuka raid on Norrie's positions was intercepted by the Tomahawks of 112 and 250 Squadrons which claimed eighteen of the dive-bombers or their escorting fighters for the loss of five of their own machines and two pilots. On the same day, however, the Afrika Korps, which had at last been re-united, fell on the unhappy 11th Indian Brigade, dispersing it.

Next day, the Panzer divisions, further reinforced by Ariete, attacked the British armour. Their advance met heavy resistance on the ground and from the air. Neumann-Silkow was killed when a shell hit his command tank, nothing whatever was achieved and, by the end of the day, the Afrika Korps had only forty tanks left.

On 7 December Rommel learned that, mainly as a result of the activities of the British forces in Malta, he could expect no replacements of men, ammunition or equipment for at least a fortnight. With considerable moral courage therefore, he finally acknowledged defeat. He detached 90th Light to Agedabia to guard against the risk of a British thrust south of the Djebel Akhdar, the 3,000-feet-high Green Mountain in the Cyrenaican 'Bulge' between Benghazi and Derna. The bulk of his forces he ordered back to a new line running south of Gazala which had been fortified by the Italians earlier in the year.

These moves, as Rommel recognized, entailed the irrevocable loss of his troops in the frontier positions. Their reduction was entrusted to 2nd South African Division but, despite heavy bombing raids, the defenders remained resolute and an attack on Bardia by the 3rd South African Brigade beginning on 16 December, failed with heavy losses.

Accordingly there was a pause until 1 January 1942, when the assault was undertaken by 8th and 44th Royal Tanks from 1st Army Tank Brigade, which, it will be recalled, had become highly proficient in night operations and which had 3rd and 4th South African Brigades under tactical command for the operation. After preliminary moves in the daylight hours, the armour duly launched a major attack after dark, under cover of a powerful artillery bombardment. Once again this proved successful and at dawn on the following day the garrison surrendered. 6th South African Brigade overran the Axis defences in the Sollum area on 12 January and the last outpost, Halfaya, guarding a pass up the giant escarpment, surrendered on the 17th. In all 13,800 Axis soldiers became prisoners of war and at Bardia 1,177 Allied soldiers, who had been captured earlier in the battle, were liberated.

The pursuit of the main Axis army was far less successful. Curiously enough no adverse comments are ever made about the conduct of this, although a similar pursuit by Eighth Army almost a year later has been subjected to much bitter criticism. Yet in November, 1942, Eighth Army took just nineteen days to reach El Agheila from El Alamein, a distance of some 840 miles by the coast road. To reach El Agheila after CRUSADER, Eighth Army had to advance only some 470 miles by the coast road, but this took it thirty days.

Admittedly, at the time of CRUSADER the Axis forces had suffered a far less shattering defeat than would be the case at El Alamein, but even so it is difficult to escape the impression that the advance after the earlier battle was far less competent. Auchinleck and Ritchie entrusted it to Godwin-Austen's XIII Corps, to which Gatehouse's tanks were transferred, rather than to

Norrie's XXX Corps which was experienced in and had been specially trained and equipped for just such mobile operations. Furthermore this decision resulted in an inevitable delay to allow the necessary re-organization to take place. Norrie again protested but again without success.

In consequence, the initial Axis retirement was hindered only by the Desert Air Force. On 8 December the 'Hurribombers' of 80 Squadron left almost a mile of the coastal road covered with blazing transports. They also beat off an attack by enemy fighters, destroying at least two without loss. Next day, during another raid on German vehicles, No 80's CO, Squadron Leader Michael Stephens, was engaged by an Italian Macchi MC 202 fighter. Wounded, with his aircraft in flames, Stephens remained at the controls long enough to shoot down his attacker. He then baled out, beating out his burning clothes during his descent. He recovered, to be awarded a DSO.

Of course not all air-actions were successes. On 10 December six unescorted Bostons of 24 Squadron SAAF, attacked by a dozen enemy fighters, were all shot down except one which crash-landed on its return to base. The South Africans at least preserved their sense of humour. Henceforth they referred to this affair as the 'Boston Tea Party'.

By 11 December, 90th Light was well on its way to Agedabia, though it had lost its commander, Sümmermann, killed by strafing fighters on the 10th; while Rommel's main strength was established in the Gazala Line. It was not troubled by Eighth Army until the 13th, when the 5th Brigade of 4th Indian Division advanced directly on a key escarpment at Alam Hamza and its 7th Brigade swung round to outflank the escarpment to the south. The latter, counter-attacked by Crüwell's panzers, was only saved from disaster by the gunners of 25th Field Regiment which destroyed twelve enemy tanks at a cost of seven officers and fifty-eight men. The attacks of 5th Brigade were also beaten back except for that of the 1st Battalion, The Buffs (Royal East Kent Regiment)[3] which captured Point 204 in the south-west of the escarpment.

On the 15th, the offensive was resumed all along the line but without success. It was hoped that this would divert attention from a wide sweep around the whole enemy position by 4th Armoured Brigade, but sadly this had no effect at all, for the ground over which 4th Armoured had to travel proved far too difficult for rapid progress. As a result, The Buffs, isolated on Point 204, bore the brunt of a full-scale counter-attack by 15th Panzer which, though not without considerable casualties, overran their position at about 1530, killing, wounding or capturing almost a thousand men.

Under cover of this success, Rommel began a further retirement on the night of 16–17 December, this time intended to take him all the way back to El Agheila. Eighth Army set out after him but since the British lines of communication were now becoming dangerously long, there were considerable delays as supplies, especially of petrol, were brought forward. Rommel, by contrast, was finally receiving reinforcements. Though two merchant vessels had been sunk on 13 December, taking forty-five tanks to the bottom with them, a third, the *Ankara* with twenty-two tanks on board, reached Benghazi safely on the 19th,[4] while a fourth, the *Monginevro*, arrived at Tripoli on the same day with a further twenty-three tanks which were also in Crüwell's hands soon afterwards.

Thus strengthened, the Germans turned on their pursuers. By 27 December the retreat had halted at Agedabia. The position was attacked by 22nd Guards Brigade but unsuccessfully. At the same time 22nd Armoured Brigade attempted an outflanking manoeuvre through the open desert but Crüwell, now with sixty tanks – though sixteen of these were Mark IIs – attacked it in turn from the flank, destroying thirty-seven British tanks for the loss of only seven of his own. Two days later, he renewed the action, destroying another twenty-three British tanks but again losing only seven German ones. The Axis troops then resumed their retreat to El Agheila which they reached on 6 January, 1942, without further molestation.

Eighth Army had won its victory, but not, alas, one to rank with Blenheim or Waterloo. It bore a much closer resemblance to that Battle of Heraclea in 280 BC, which had led to the celebrated comment of King Pyrrhus of Epirus – another such victory would ruin his cause. In the first place on that same 7 December when Eighth Army's superior resources finally triumphed over Rommel, Japan had entered the war, whereupon, as Dill had warned, the consequences of providing those resources at the expense of the Far East became hideously apparent. Hong Kong, where the armed forces consisted of just six battalions on the ground and five obsolete machines in the air, was lost on 25 December. In Malaya, defended mainly by inexperienced Indian troops, many of whom had never seen a tank before, protected until almost the end of the campaign only by slow, unmanoeuvrable American Buffalo fighters, one defeat followed another. They culminated on 15 February, 1942, when the fall of Singapore brought with it the surrender of some 85,000 men, about 70,000 of whom were fighting soldiers. Many had only recently arrived from Britain, sent out in haste, and could do little more than swell the numbers of those taken prisoner.

Disaster in Malaya was swiftly followed by disaster in Burma. Its capital, Rangoon, fell on 8 March. On 1 May, Mandalay was abandoned. Twelve days later, the remaining British forces were driven out of Burma altogether. British prestige in the Far East would never recover from these experiences.

Nor was Eighth Army's victory as decisive as those of the Japanese. Certainly Rommel had suffered the heavier casualties, 2,300 killed, 6,100 wounded and some 29,000 prisoners, but nearly two-thirds of his losses had been among the Italians, while a surprisingly high proportion of the German casualties had been of administrative personnel. More important, his army had not been destroyed, even temporarily, as a fighting force. Churchill at least appreciated this, lamenting that 'the bulk of' the enemy divisions had 'got away'. He was not consoled by Auchinleck's assurance that these were 'divisions only in name'.

For its part, Eighth Army had incurred 17,700 casualties, some 15 per cent of the troops involved. Both these figures would prove higher than those in Eighth Army's decisive victory at El Alamein in October 1942, though the fatal casualties in CRUSADER were less. Some 2,900 officers and men were dead, 7,300 wounded and the rest prisoners. Moreover the bulk of these losses had fallen upon the fighting soldiers, including a large proportion of veterans who would not be easy to replace.

In addition, simply because CRUSADER was a victory, the lessons that it taught were not learned; the warnings that it gave remained unheeded. Auchinleck's practice of controlling Eighth Army indirectly through a compliant Army Commander was not questioned. The lack of co-operation between different formations was not corrected. The use of 'Jock Columns' and the consequent dispersal of the artillery was not checked. As a result, the disasters in the Far East would be followed by, indeed accompanied by, disasters in North Africa as well.

Notes

1   See *British Intelligence in the Second World War: Its Influence on Strategy and Operations Volume II* by F.H. Hinsley with E.E.Thomas, C.F.G. Ransom and R.C.Knight. This has provided the basis for all information about 'Ultra'.
2   At this time Carver was a major on Norrie's staff. He had represented Norrie at the mid-day conference on 23 November.
3   It will be remembered that every Indian brigade contained a British battalion. The Royal East Kent Regiment was descended from a company of the London Trained Bands that had worn buff-coloured jerkins.
4   This was only just in time. Benghazi had to be evacuated by the Germans on the night of the 23rd.

4

COUNTER-STROKE

The great expansion of the Army meant that formations arriving in the Middle East were very inexperienced, and there was no method by which they could be introduced gradually to the battle. In the last war, new divisions could be placed first in quiet sectors, and thus gradually worked up till they found their feet. There was no means of doing that this time, and these new formations found themselves plunged straight into a big battle.

Colonel Jacob's Diary.
6 August, 1942.

The scene for the first disaster was already being set. 'It requires no hindsight', declares Ronald Lewin, 'to observe that for both sides Malta was the key to a sound strategic posture in the Mediterranean.' It had certainly been observed by Hitler. He had come to appreciate that when Malta was under pressure, the Axis cause in North Africa prospered, but when Malta was strong, the Axis forces were invariably in difficulties. Accordingly, while Eighth Army was completing the defeat of Rommel, his Führer was already taking the steps which would bring about a dramatic reversal of fortunes.

In late October, even before CRUSADER began, twenty-five U-boats were diverted from the Atlantic to the Mediterranean, scoring their first success on 13 November by sinking the famous aircraft-carrier HMS *Ark Royal*, which incidentally had just delivered a batch of Hurricane fighters to strengthen the air defences of Malta. On 2 December, Fliegerkorps II, previously conducting operations on the Moscow front, was ordered to Sicily, joining with Fliegerkorps X in the Balkans to form Luftflotte (Air Fleet) 2. Its commander, Field Marshal Albert Kesselring, a soldier turned airman, who would later turn soldier again in Italy, had already reached Rome from

Russia on 28 November. Shortly afterwards, he was appointed C-in-C, South with authority over all German naval and air forces in the Mediterranean. This enabled him to call on the Luftwaffe forces in Libya if necessary. Add the Italians' Regia Aeronautica, and Kesselring had 2,000 warplanes under his control.

Hitler's orders to his C-in-C South were admirably precise. He was to 'ensure safe lines of communication' with North Africa. 'The suppression of Malta' Hitler correctly considered, was 'particularly important in this connection'. In addition, Kesselring was to prevent any further supplies from reaching the island. 'The Germans', declares Major General John Strawson in The Battle for North Africa, 'had hit on the very formula' which could give them the victory. 'It remained to be seen whether they could apply it.'

Starting on 22 December, Kesselring set out to apply that formula to the utmost of his considerable ability. In the last week of that month over 200 aircraft attacked Malta and during January and February, 1942, the attacks steadily and relentlessly increased. The handful of RAF Hurricanes on the island still inflicted casualties and at least reduced the damage caused, while on 7 March fifteen Spitfires – the first such fighters to operate outside the United Kingdom – joined the defenders, having flown off the aircraft-carrier HMS Eagle. But by the end of that month hardly a single Spitfire was fit for combat and the number of raids had doubled the number in February.

The people of Malta faced the seemingly unending air attacks on their island, and the consequent privations they suffered, with astonishing fortitude. On 15 April King George VI took the unprecedented step of awarding the George Cross 'to the Island Fortress of Malta to bear witness to a heroism and devotion that will long be famous in history.' It was the first occasion – and would remain the only occasion – on which such an award was made to a community as a whole. During April, large numbers of Spitfires arrived in the island, the United States fleet carrier Wasp flying in forty-seven on the 20th. But during April also, twenty-three Spitfires and eighteen Hurricanes were destroyed, fifty-seven Spitfires and thirty Hurricanes were put out of action and the number of raids had all but doubled the number in March.

Under cover of Kesselring's bombardment, Axis convoys were able to resume the delivery of supplies to Rommel. During April, for example, he received 150,000 tons of equipment. None of the convoys though, had such dramatic consequences as the one which broke through to Tripoli on 5 January 1942. This carried twenty armoured cars, a batch of anti-tank guns, a stock of fuel, and fifty-four tanks (together with their crews), all of them being Mark IIIs strengthened with the additional plate on the front of the hull. Even after their arrival, Rommel could muster only eighty-four tanks in the Afrika Korps plus eighty-nine more in Ariete, but as von Mellenthin relates, the reinforcements had given him his chance – 'the opportunity of delivering an effective counter-stroke.'

Rommel was the more eager to grasp this opportunity because wireless interceptions had provided 'a fairly clear picture' of Eighth Army's dispositions – which were not very impressive. After the conclusion of CRUSADER, Auchinleck had resolutely begun planning for an Eighth Army advance to Tripoli, which was code-named Operation ACROBAT. Pending this, as the Official History points out, he had to consider whether it would be better 'to maintain active contact with the enemy about El Agheila and accept the risk of the British light forces in that area being driven back, or, alternatively, to yield some 150 miles of desert and develop his strength in the neighbourhood of, say, Msus and Benghazi.'

Auchinleck was convinced, continues the Official History:

> . . . that the policy must be to keep up such pressure as was possible rather than break away altogether. The risk of a reconnaissance in force must be accepted. General Ritchie, knowing his Commander-in-Chief's wishes, was not the man to act otherwise than with energy and enthusiasm in giving effect to them.

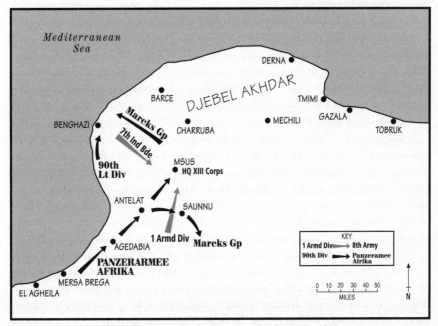

Map III: Rommel's Counter-stroke, January, 1942.

43

The unhappy result was that XIII Corps which, it will be recalled, had conducted the pursuit after CRUSADER, was not mustered at Msus or Benghazi, or even at Agedabia, forty miles north-east of El Agheila, as some of its own officers had suggested, and though its headquarters was at Msus, only supply units were stationed there.

Auchinleck's decision, in the words of Field Marshal Carver, placed 'Ritchie, Godwin-Austen and their subordinates in a fundamentally unsound position'. Had XIII Corps been concentrated further back, Carver believes, 'Rommel would probably never have chanced his arm.' As it was, the widely scattered British formations provided an open invitation for an Axis assault.

Nearest to the enemy was the under-strength 1st Armoured Division which had but recently reached the front and had been entrusted to Major General Messervy in the absence of Major General Lumsden, who had been wounded in an air attack . Furthest forward of its units was 200th Guards Brigade,[1] of which one half was stationed on the coast road near Mersa Brega where it had been split up into 'Jock Columns', and the other, minus any artillery, all of which had been allocated to the columns, was still at Agedabia. The weak 1st Support Group, new to the desert and also divided into columns, was established in difficult country around the Wadi Faregh, protecting the Guards' left flank.

Of the two armoured brigades placed under Messervy's direction, the 22nd had withdrawn to Tobruk to re-equip after the casualties it had suffered in the concluding stages of CRUSADER, while the 2nd, under Brigadier Raymond Briggs, was positioned between Antelat and Saunnu, a further thirty miles north-east of Agedabia. This brigade too was inexperienced in desert warfare and had received no training since leaving England in the previous September.

Further back still was Messervy's former command 4th Indian Division, now led by Major General Francis Tuker. His 11th Brigade was still in the Tobruk area – as incidentally was 7th Armoured Division – his 5th Brigade was in Barce, north-east of Benghazi, where it was virtually immobile for lack of transport, and only his 7th Brigade was likely to be able to take part in any coming action. This was stationed at Benghazi under the command of another Briggs, in this case Brigadier Harold.

Auchinleck and Ritchie were not unaware of the potential risk to their scattered forces; in fact it was the subject of some discussion between them. On 4 January, for instance, the former advised his subordinate that there was 'a possibility that Rommel might stage a counter-offensive with the object of throwing us back and possibly recapturing Benghazi', although personally he did not 'think it is likely' or that Rommel 'would get very far with it' if he tried.

This was a shrewd estimate at this time but, of course, on the following day, the arrival of the convoy radically altered the situation. Both Churchill and Auchinleck were made aware of the change of circumstances by 'Ultra' and the Prime Minister, though rarely noted for his caution, felt compelled on 11 January to send to his Commander-in-Chief, Middle East a query that was also a warning: 'How does all this affect ACROBAT? I am sure you and your armies did all in human power but we must face facts as they are.'

Auchinleck's response - which will be described shortly – was astonishing and one which throws an interesting light on his character. It may be of course that he was misled by his Director of Military Intelligence, Brigadier 'John' Shearer – his real names were Eric James – who does seem to have been continuously over-optimistic when assessing the enemy's resources and capabilities. Certainly Shearer had been at fault during the last part of the advance to El Agheila, for although 'Ultra' had warned that tanks were on their way to Rommel, Shearer had advised both Auchinleck and Ritchie that damage to the port facilities would prevent any armour being unloaded at Benghazi and accordingly the Axis supply ship which had docked there could only be carrying petrol. He must therefore bear much of the blame for the maulings received by the luckless 22nd Armoured Brigade in December 1941.

On the other hand, when summarizing the situation to Ritchie on 4 January, Auchinleck had reminded him that Rommel was not an opponent whom anyone could 'afford to under-estimate' and had even criticized Godwin-Austen as being 'a little apt to take too rosy a view of a situation'. It seems unlikely therefore that he would have accepted Shearer's estimates at face-value and that another reason must be sought for his reaction to Churchill's enquiry.

Since he had taken up his exacting office, Auchinleck had been bombarded with a constant stream of messages from Churchill, warning, encouraging, questioning, complaining. All were well-intentioned, by no means all were well-advised and it is easy to see how they must have proved a burdensome ordeal to their recipient. Nonetheless it was an ordeal which had been suffered by his predecessor and would in due time be suffered by his successor, but it affected neither of them so much as it did Auchinleck – who found Churchill's criticism not only worrying but deeply wounding.

It would appear that by this time Auchinleck had become so unhappy about Churchill's interference that he had determined, probably unconsciously, to reject on principle any suggestion that the Prime Minister might make, and the stronger that suggestion might be, the more firmly would it be resisted. Whether this was so or not, the fact remains that whereas before Rommel had received his reinforcements Auchinleck had retained a prudent degree of caution in his assessments, after the reinforcements – and

Churchill's enquiry – had arrived, Auchinleck seemingly rejected all the reservations he had previously held.

Accordingly, when he replied to the Prime Minister on 12 January, the Commander-in-Chief, Middle East contemptuously dismissed the Axis troops as 'much disorganized, short of senior officers, short of material', with their morale 'beginning to feel the strain'. He declared that he was 'convinced the enemy is hard-pressed, more than we dared think perhaps' and that therefore he was equally 'convinced that we should press forward with ACROBAT.' A week later Auchinleck told Ritchie: 'My present intention is to continue the offensive in Libya and the objective remains Tripoli.' Two days after that, Auchinleck's official Despatch relates how at dawn on the 21st 'the improbable occurred, and without warning the Axis forces began to advance.'

In the prevailing mood of over-optimism, Rommel's assault achieved complete surprise, made all the greater because this time it was the Desert Air Force's forward base at Antelat which had been flooded by heavy rain. This was just as well for Rommel since he would receive little support from the Axis air forces. For that matter he would get little assistance from his five Italian infantry divisions either, while the Ariete (Armoured) and Trieste (Motorized) Divisions played only a supporting role. The fighting was left almost entirely to 15th and 21st Panzer and to 90th Light which had now become fully mechanized. So much was this the case that when, on 23 January, General Ugo Cavallero, Chief of Staff of the Italian Armed Forces, arrived from Rome with instructions from Mussolini to halt the operations, Rommel curtly informed him that the German troops were the ones bearing the brunt of the action, so the only person who could stop him was Hitler.

Rommel's initial attack was made both along the Via Balbia and through the open desert some twenty miles away in the area of the Wadi Faregh. The former move was spearheaded by a mobile German infantry group with artillery support led by Lieutenant Colonel Marcks, but it was backed by the remainder of 90th Light commanded by Major General Veith and its right flank was protected by the Italian XX Corps – Ariete and Trieste. Crüwell, now a full general, took care of the latter move with his Afrika Korps – though he was considerably handicapped by bad going.

In fact the attacks made little progress on the first day, but it was scarcely to be expected that the advanced British troops, inexperienced and dispersed in their 'Jock Columns', could hold them up for long. On 22 January, Rommel's men, who this day formally received the ringing name of 'Panzerarmee Afrika', broke through the Allied defences. By 1100, Group Marcks had captured Agedabia. Then, followed by the Afrika Korps, it raced north to Antelat which fell at 1530. The fighters on the airfield, Hurricanes and the new Kittyhawks – similar but superior to Tomahawks – had to be man-handled to the only area not waterlogged to enable them to take off. Two damaged Hurricanes and four damaged Kittyhawks were destroyed on the ground but all the remaining machines made good their escape, the last as German shells began falling on the airfield. Group Marcks then swung eastward towards Saunnu, which it captured that evening.

This move cut off 2nd Armoured Brigade and the remaining advanced infantry units which were still south-east of Antelat. Rommel hoped to destroy them on the 23rd, but German planning went badly wrong. Group Marcks headed out of Saunnu to the south-east, intending to attack the eastern flank of the trapped forces, but the German armour which was supposed to take its place in Saunnu did not do so, thereby leaving an escape route open for the British. Covered by artillery fire, the remains of 1st Armoured Division fought its way northward to safety. Though 2nd Armoured Brigade lost a number of tanks in the process, the 10th Hussars being reduced to only eight, Crüwell also had his losses – about twenty in all.

There were no Axis successes on 24 January either. Messervy pulled his troops still further north towards Msus while Rommel hunted for them in vain south of Antelat. On this day the Axis air forces made their only real contribution to the battle, but they too fared badly, thanks mainly to the Hurricanes of 274 Squadron which intercepted a Stuka raid, destroying four dive-bombers plus three escorting fighters for the loss of one of their own number, which crash-landed.

Already, however, Godwin-Austen had become alarmed for the safety of Messervy's weakened 1st Armoured Division which he feared would be unable to hold Msus, and for that of 7th Indian Brigade, which might easily be outflanked at Benghazi. He therefore asked Ritchie for permission to withdraw eastward to Mechili if this proved necessary. Ritchie instructed him to cover Benghazi and Msus if possible but did give him discretion to retire if compelled. Ritchie also wisely ordered Norrie's XXX Corps up from the frontier to prepare a reserve defensive line running south from Gazala to protect Tobruk.

Then on 25 January, Rommel struck north for Msus. 1st Armoured Division was routed by Major General Gustav von Vaerst's far more experienced 15th Panzer Division – Rommel had again divided his armour it may be noticed – and driven back to Charruba some seventy miles east of Benghazi. A number of British soldiers were taken captive, among them Lieutenant John Ballingal of 11th Hussars. That night he managed to bluff the German guards, who were already uncertain of their location, into taking a route which led them towards the British positions to the north-east. Early next morning they encountered South African armoured cars – whereupon prisoners and escort exchanged roles.

The German guards were not the only ones who were becoming confused. On learning of the fall of Msus, Godwin-Austen ordered Messervy to retire to Mechili, while 7th Indian Brigade evacuated Benghazi and followed him. It was a decision which met with the approval of Messervy and Tuker – but not of Auchinleck. On the afternoon of the 25th, he flew to Ritchie's HQ at Tmimi where he remained until 1 February to give his Army Commander the benefit of his 'advice'.

Auchinleck as he notified his senior staff officer, Major General Smith, in a letter written on the following day, was 'very averse' to abandoning Benghazi. When he reached Tmimi therefore, states the RAF Official History[2] (on the authority of Tedder who again accompanied Auchinleck), the C-in-C, Middle East 'pressed Ritchie to cancel XIII Corps' orders for a general withdrawal.'

The Eighth Army Commander loyally complied. Tuker's 4th Indian Division – which in practice meant 7th Indian Brigade – was ordered to hold Benghazi and at the same time attack to the south-east in the direction of Antelat against Rommel's communications, using for this purpose, as Auchinleck would tell Smith, 'small mobile columns with artillery'. Meanwhile 1st Armoured Division was to protect Tuker's left flank and also block any Axis advance from Msus. Neither Godwin-Austen nor Messervy nor Tuker was happy about the new plans, the XIII Corps Commander in particular declaring bluntly that these were 'unsound'. Their warnings were over-ruled and to ensure that Auchinleck's wishes were met, Ritchie took 4th Indian Division under his own direct command.

Unhappily the warnings proved justified. As Liddell Hart points out, the new directions 'resulted in the British becoming spread out and static in trying to cover the 140 miles stretch between Benghazi and Mechili, while Rommel from his central position at Msus, was allowed time and freedom to develop his action, as well as a choice of alternative objectives.'

Rommel's activities had to be postponed on the 26th, when the bad weather which had hampered the Desert Air Force over the last few days, lifted, allowing strafing attacks by Hurricanes, Tomahawks and Kittyhawks that destroyed or damaged about 120 enemy vehicles. Next day though, the clouds were thicker than ever. By a cruel misfortune the only enemy move spotted from the air was the one Rommel wanted to be seen – a feint by a re-united Afrika Korps in the direction of Mechili.

While this distracted the attention of 1st Armoured Division, Rommel thrust towards Benghazi. 90th Light headed north along the Via Balbia, the Italian XX Corps to its east moved north from Antelat, and the Marcks Group, accompanied by Rommel in person, pushed north-west from Msus. 7th Indian Brigade, preparing for an attack on Rommel's communications, was not at all well placed to meet this threat, the more so since it had been separated into mobile columns as Auchinleck had urged. During the 28th, it became dangerously isolated and received reluctant permission from Eighth Army Headquarters to retreat. As darkness fell, the Marcks Group cut the coastal road north of Benghazi, but Brigadier Harold Briggs, leading his men across the open desert to the south-east, broke out of the trap, to reach Mechili with very few casualties.

Eighth Army now had no choice but to fall back to the defences at Gazala, which it did in good order, assisted by the fact that Rommel was becoming desperately short of petrol. Moreover on 5 February the Desert Air Force was again able to intervene, destroying or damaging another 100 Axis vehicles.

By 6 February the conflict had died down. All Allied troops were back behind the Gazala Line. Godwin-Austen, disgusted by the way his instructions had been countermanded and control of his subordinate formations taken out of his hands, had resigned, to be replaced by Gott. And the British were left to reflect bitterly that Rommel had twice now launched a counterstroke from El Agheila to catch them by surprise. As General Sir David Fraser points out in his history of the British Army in the Second World War, *And We Shall Shock Them*:

> The past achievements of CRUSADER – and they were real – were less apparent than the ignominy of the present hour. Once again the British had been through much for nothing. It had all gone wrong.

Somehow it quite failed to measure up to Blenheim or Waterloo.

It was now that the astonishing determination and enthusiasm with which Eighth Army had gone into CRUSADER and which had enabled its men to fight on throughout that confused and bloody encounter until success had been achieved, began to be replaced by a cynical scepticism. One aspect which this took was an increasingly ardent admiration for the enemy general. The German historian Paul Carell in *The Foxes of the Desert*, proudly notes that to the British as well as to his own men, Rommel had become 'the personification of the bold ruse, the lightning attack, the wild chase across the desert'. 'Rommel' declares Virginia Cowles in *The Phantom Major*, a biography of David Stirling, founder of the SAS Regiment, 'was regarded by both British and Germans alike as the only brilliant soldier in the Middle East.'

That such a belief was extremely unhealthy was rightly recognized by Auchinleck. There was, he declared, a 'very real danger' that Rommel might become 'a kind of magician or bogey-man to our troops'. Unhappily, the only way in which he attempted to counter the danger was by issuing instructions to his officers – ineffective and unenforceable – not to mention Rommel by name but to refer only to 'the Germans', 'the Axis powers' or 'the enemy'.

Alongside the cynicism, an even more alarming attitude began to spread slowly but steadily through Eighth Army, eating away at its morale – the haunting fear that victory was a mirage that would always disappear when it seemed within Eighth Army's grasp; that successes would always be but temporary ones; that the Eighth Army was doomed to fight up and down the Western Desert for all time. It was of course brought about by that sequence of advance followed by retreat which had so far characterized the war in North Africa and which became known by numerous sardonic expressions: 'The Annual Swan up the Desert', 'The Gazala Gallop', 'The Benghazi Handicap', 'The Djebel Stakes'. . . . It was put into words by no less a personage than Major General Francis Tuker:

> *Yearly we've ridden the Djebel Stakes,*
> *Yearly fought back on our course,*
> *Yearly we've made the same silly mistakes,*
> *Over-ridden a failing horse,*
> *At a fence too stiff for his strength to leap,*
> *With a rotten take-off, unfirm, too steep,*
> *Heavily breasted the top of the bank,*
> *Pawed, gasped and struggled, then hopelessly sank,*
> *Shocked, hurt and surprised at the toss we took –*
> *Rolling back adown the ditch at Tobruk.*

Notes

1 This was the old 22nd Guards Brigade which had been re-numbered to avoid confusion with 22nd Armoured Brigade.
2 Volume II: *The Fight Avails* by Denis Richards and Hilary St G. Saunders.

5

PAUSE FOR REFLECTION

The discipline of the Army is no longer what it used to be, and in the last resort it is discipline which counts.

Colonel Jacob's Diary.
6 August, 1942.

It was clearly essential that the problems of Eighth Army so vividly related in Tuker's poem 'The Djebel Stakes' should be rectified as soon as possible. This was the task of the Commander-in-Chief, Middle East and while it was certainly an unenviable one, he was at least granted a pause of three-and-a-half months before the next major conflict in which he could make the attempt.

General Sir Claude Auchinleck had come to Cairo with a fine reputation which was thoroughly deserved. As C-in-C, India, he had shown not only great ability as an administrator but also a genuine interest in and knowledge of the different races that peopled the sub-continent. As a result he had become virtually a father-figure to his Indian soldiers – a powerful factor in ensuring that, despite civil discontent, they never wavered in their loyalty to the King-Emperor.

On his arrival in Cairo, Auchinleck had won further golden opinions which again appeared entirely justified. He was a tall, well-built, distinguished man who possessed a natural dignity and charm of manner which inspired the affection as well as the respect of those who met him. He was immensely conscientious, concerned for the welfare of the men under his command and anxious only to fulfill the duties of his high office, to which, it should always be remembered, he had not asked or wished to be appointed.

Yet curiously enough, there somehow always seem to have been reservations about Auchinleck. Alan Moorehead relates that he was 'scarcely known to his men'; that there was a 'strange contradiction' about him; that he remained throughout 'something of a mystery'.

The last place in which to find the solution to that mystery is the massive official biography produced by John Connell. Connell was a novelist, and to judge from *Auchinleck*, an exceptionally good one. There is the handsome hero, 'capless', his hair 'ruffled by the desert wind'. He is 'quick, unorthodox and bold; he could apprehend a situation – and its complex implications – with speed and certainty and act with decision and promptitude.' He is 'realistic and far-seeing', 'clear-headed and calm'. He is 'cheerfully courteous' yet 'subtle and supple' in argument. He shows an 'unfailing positive reaction to every new experience'. He possesses 'guts', 'flair', a profound 'critical faculty', 'moral and spiritual stamina', a 'trained and educated brain', 'buoyancy, alertness and penetrating interest'. His very presence is 'a tonic and inspiration in the field'.

Confronted with this catalogue of virtues, it seems reasonable to enquire how it was that their possessor did not sweep the enemy from North Africa, bring about the surrender of two Axis armies, and then invade southern Europe, thereby ensuring the fall of Mussolini – as would happen after his departure. Connell, of course, has his answer ready. As in any good novel, there is a colossal conspiracy afoot, directed against the C-in-C, Middle East. Disappointingly, Connell does not tell us who the conspirators are and the sole piece of evidence he offers is a letter to Auchinleck from a former Brigadier, General Staff of Eighth Army, telling him that he had received blame that should really have fallen on others. This was Major General Sir Francis de Guingand – but when he came to describe his wartime experiences under the title of *Operation Victory*, not only did he not repeat but he implicitly contradicted his previous statement. It seems therefore that our curiosity must remain unsatisfied.

For his part, Auchinleck would offer a different reason for his lack of success – one which he had already offered in respect of an earlier campaign when he had commanded Allied forces in northern Norway in May 1940.[1] On the 17th of that month, the 1st Battalion, Scots Guards under Lieutenant Colonel Trappes-Lomax was holding an isolated position at Mo, some 200 miles south of Narvik, under-strength and short of equipment. Here it was attacked by five German infantry battalions, heavily supported by artillery and by an air force which had complete command of the skies. By the afternoon the Guards had been outflanked. Considering the enemy's superiority, this was neither surprising nor reprehensible; it surely deserved better than the comment from Auchinleck: 'Why our soldiers cannot be as mobile as the Germans I don't know but they aren't, apparently.'

After blowing up bridges to cover their retreat, the Guards fell back thirty miles northward to the valley at Krokstrand. Here on 20 May, Trappes-Lomax received a signal from Auchinleck, assuring him that he had 'reached a good position for defence' and it was 'essential to stand and fight.'

Unfortunately while Krokstrand – of which Auchinleck had no personal knowledge – may have seemed a good defensive position on the map, the reality was very different. The valley was too wide to be defended adequately as well as being very vulnerable to air-attack, while the surrounding ridges could easily be crossed by the experienced German mountain-troops.

Nonetheless despite their difficulties the Guards did hold firm until the evening of the 22nd, when they retreated to avoid certain destruction. By the 23rd they were at Viskiskoia, and here Trappes-Lomax learned that he had been dismissed from command of his battalion for disobeying Auchinleck's order to stand fast at Krokstrand. 'This crushing blow' states the Regimental War Diary, 'took place in the middle of an enemy attack, and it is hardly to be wondered at that the morale of both officers and men was still further shaken by the loss of a commanding officer for whose personality and ability everyone had the highest respect and in whom everyone had the greatest confidence.'

Had this been an isolated incident, it could be dismissed as an error of judgement, easily excusable in the stress of combat. Yet in his official Despatch on *Operations in Northern Norway*, Auchinleck would denigrate his British troops in general, comparing them unfavourably with the French forces under his command but ignoring the facts that, unlike the British, the French were operating in close proximity to their base, were supported throughout by the guns of the Royal Navy, and during the latter part of the campaign were protected by two RAF squadrons, No 263 flying Gladiators and No 46 with Hurricanes, the only modern single-engined fighters in the combat-zone. Furthermore, while the British faced the main German forces pushing up from central Norway. The French, who numbered five battalions, aided by four battalions of Poles and one of Norwegians, were opposed only by the isolated German garrison in Narvik. This was just 4,000 strong and although about half were tough Austrian Alpine troops, the rest were not even soldiers but survivors from sunken German warships.

None of these considerations prevented Auchinleck from reporting that:

> By comparison with the French, or the Germans for that matter, our men for the most part seemed distressingly young, not so much in years as in self-reliance and manliness generally. They give an impression of being callow and undeveloped which is not reassuring for the future.

Among the soldiers thus stigmatized were those of the 1st Battalion, Irish Guards. In the early hours of 15 May the troopship *Chobry* on which they were embarked was attacked by Junkers Ju 87 Stuka dive-bombers. Though the vessel was left blazing uncontrollably and threatening to explode at any moment, and though all their officers above the rank of captain were dead, the Guards formed up on deck carrying their arms and equipment as if on parade; awaiting their turn to be rescued by the escorting destroyers with such calm and disciplined courage that not a single man except for those killed in the actual attack was lost.

When events in North Africa also started to go wrong, Auchinleck was comparatively mild at first. Even so the set-backs to 22nd Armoured Brigade during the advance to El Agheila, for instance, prompted an order that Ritchie must determine whether the British tank commanders were blame-worthy; if any were, they should be considered as 'expensive luxuries'.

After the success of Rommel's counter-stroke, Auchinleck's strictures grew louder. He wrote to London as well as to subordinates such as Smith and Ritchie, criticizing not merely the leaders but the men of the armoured formations, declaring them unable 'to compete with the enemy satisfacto-rily' and 'incapable' of meeting him 'in the open, even when superior to him in number'. Nor were the advanced infantry units forgotten; they had, Auchinleck complained, been 'disconcerted' by Rommel's attack and too easily 'pushed aside'. Certainly the whole episode had been an ignominious one but when it is recalled that it was as a result of Auchinleck's own de-cisions that inexperienced units of the Eighth Army had been left in dangerously over-extended positions and that the infantry had been further weakened by being dispersed into 'Jock Columns', then it does seem that he might have been more sparing in his castigation of others.

It may be that Auchinleck's asperity was sharpened by a knowledge that he too was not considered blameless. In November 1941, his friend Dill had been succeeded as Chief of the Imperial General Staff by General Sir Alan Brooke, who was in every sense of the word a much more formidable figure. According to General Fraser, in his biography *Alanbrooke*, Rommel's counter-offensive prompted an entry in Brooke's Diary for 30 January: 'Nothing less than bad generalship on the part of Auchinleck'.

Brooke also disapproved of the hapless Brigadier Shearer and he pressed Auchinleck strongly to replace his Director of Military Intelligence. Again it is interesting to note the reaction of the C-in-C, Middle East. Though it had been Shearer's assurances that Axis tanks could not be unloaded at Benghazi that had really brought about the misfortunes of 22nd Armoured Brigade, Auchinleck insisted that he had 'found John Shearer's estimates of enemy strength and intentions consistently good and with a high degree of accu-racy.' He did not, he said, want to part with Shearer 'on any account'.

That was on 14 February. On 23 February Auchinleck decided that it would be better to part with Shearer after all, since he had 'lost the

confidence of the Army and especially of certain formation commanders.'
Shearer was therefore summarily removed to be succeeded by de Guingand
– he retired from the Army to follow a successful business career.

Brooke also felt that Smith, who by now was exhausted from his long
service in the Middle East, should be replaced as Auchinleck's Chief of Staff.
Again he had his way but this time with less happy results. He suggested that
Smith's successor should be Lieutenant General Sir Henry Pownall who had
recently been serving as Chief of Staff to Wavell in the Far East. This had
scarcely proved a successful time for the British cause, but at least Pownall
did have experience in managing a complex staff organization. Auchinleck,
however, insisted on appointing Lieutenant General Thomas Corbett, a
distinguished cavalry general in the Indian Army whom he described as 'an
educated soldier with great energy and drive' but who had never held a
senior staff appointment at such a high level. It is perhaps little wonder therefore that Corbett proved a complete failure in his new, unaccustomed role.

It should be stated that Brooke's attitude was by no means a negative one.
At this same time, Major General Richard McCreery was sent to the Middle
East. Brooke, who believed McCreery to be 'one of our best armoured
divisional commanders', intended he should act as the tank expert at
Auchinleck's Headquarters. It was not a move which Auchinleck welcomed.
Brooke would later reflect, somewhat indignantly, that McCreery had been
'practically ignored and never referred to by the Auk on the employment of
armoured forces.'

These actions by Auchinleck may perhaps provide the key to the mystery.
It is usually stated that Auchinleck's greatest fault was an inability to select
capable subordinates, but this is to over-simplify. Auchinleck was able to
build up an extremely efficient group of staff officers at Eighth Army
Headquarters who were later highly valued by his successors. Some of his
selections, in fact, appear little short of inspired, notably his choice of de
Guingand first as his Director of Military Intelligence, then as the Brigadier,
General Staff of Eighth Army, and later his appointment of Major General
Savory as Director of Military Training in India.

Whatever their different abilities or personalities, however, Auchinleck's
favoured subordinates all had one characteristic in common – a fierce
devotion to their chief. Corbett, Ritchie and de Guingand possessed this to
an almost notorious degree, and it would be de Guingand who would later
come to realize that Auchinleck had had a 'desperate need' for 'loyal
courtiers'.

This need arose because, despite a certain rather charming shyness,
Auchinleck was intensely vain. He was not the only senior officer of whom
this could be said, nor is the fault limited to any one profession, but in
Auchinleck's case it took an unusual form. He appears to have had an almost

feminine streak in his nature and though it is surely not true that he was homosexually inclined as some uncharitable critics have hinted, even one of his most slavish admirers[2] has confirmed that he was 'fond of his own appearance'. And his vanity was so easily wounded. He was intensely sensitive to criticism, which disturbed and distressed him to a quite unreasonable extent.

Hence Auchinleck's preference for 'loyal courtiers' who would do his bidding without question, over the most talented subordinates of an independent frame of mind. It accounts for his failure to make full use of the forceful, outspoken McCreery. Or of Wilson. Or of the able but acerbic Tuker. Or of Major General William Slim, later Commander of Fourteenth Army in Burma, whom Auchinleck saw depart to the Far East without regret, describing him as 'wanting in reputation, personality and experience'.

Hence also Auchinleck's hatred of Churchill's constant complaints, and of his distant attitude to Mr Richard Casey, who became the Minister of State, Middle East in April 1942. In *Operation Victory* de Guingand relates that although Casey was always 'wise and very accessible', Auchinleck did not 'make the best use' of him. 'I believe' de Guingand adds revealingly, 'that he thought, possibly unconsciously, that the politician was critical of his handling of the situation.'

Hence again perhaps, Auchinleck's readiness, as in the case of Shearer, to sacrifice the most loyal of his followers if this would divert criticism from himself, and his readiness also to load the blame for mishaps onto the shoulders of the men who were doing the fighting. In this connection it may have been a disadvantage that until he reached the rank of brigadier, Auchinleck had led only Indian troops whose unquestioning devotion naturally won the hearts of their British officers. Auchinleck might refer to his men's 'lack of self-reliance and manliness generally' but it seems that what really upset him about 'these damn British' – as he would describe them as late as July 1942 – was their tendency to lack respect for 'top brass'. It may also be that he felt similarly uneasy about the still more disrespectful soldiers from the Dominions. Perhaps this was why, after CRUSADER, the two finest divisions in the Middle East, 9th Australian and 2nd New Zealand, were kept uselessly in Syria – despite Churchill's protests – until it was almost too late.

Nor were these the only unhappy consequences of Auchinleck's almost obsessive dislike of criticism. As this increased with Eighth Army's mounting problems, so Auchinleck's self-confidence steadily wilted. Eventually he became, as de Guingand laments, reluctant ever to make a 'definite decision'. In the meantime his vanity and his sense of duty combined to tempt him to direct the fighting in the Desert which was the only active front in his command, but his lack of self-confidence urged him to do so through 'advice' to willing subordinates who could take responsibility should events turn out badly. 'He believed' says Alan Moorehead, 'that he could control the battle from Cairo.' He did not realize that 'the Desert is not geared to remote control.'

Auchinleck's self-confidence was scarcely encouraged by the obvious doubts entertained by Churchill and Brooke. These tended to drive him into a resentful remoteness just when he should have been directing all his energies towards rectifying the defects in Eighth Army. Yet it must be said that Auchinleck had only himself to blame for the attitude of his political and military superiors.

At this time Auchinleck was much concerned for the safety of his beloved India which he believed was threatened by a Japanese invasion. He was also worried about a possible collapse of Russian resistance which would enable the Germans to strike southwards from the Caucasus into Iraq and Iran. He urged that troops should be despatched from the Desert to protect both the sub-continent and what was called the 'Northern Front'.

This suggestion infuriated Churchill and with some reason. Neither of the supposed dangers was very imminent in May 1942. The Japanese had no intention of invading India. As for the threat from the Caucasus, during the winter of 1941–42, the Russians were slowly but relentlessly pushing the invaders back and it is now clear that only Hitler's stubborn determination not to yield an inch of ground without a fight prevented a more catastrophic retreat than that of Napoleon. It was not until 19 May, 1942, that the Russian advance was finally halted. It was not until 22 June, the anniversary of their original assault, that a new German offensive began – by which time Auchinleck had been forced to turn his attention to matters nearer to hand.

Undoubtedly Auchinleck's concerns about the Northern Front were prompted by a realization that the oil-fields of Iraq and Iran were absolutely vital to the Allied cause. These, however, could be invaded from a conquered Egypt just as well as from the Caucasus and it was the defence of Egypt that was Auchinleck's own immediate responsibility. Moreover the key to the defence of Egypt was the retention of Malta and that island was now in greater peril than ever.

It is true that by early May the possibility that Malta would be crushed by air-attack alone had passed. 'Hitler' in the unkind words of the RAF Official History, 'with that improvidence characteristic of the master-plotters of war, was short of aircraft.' The bulk of Kesselring's forces had to be transferred to the Russian front or to North Africa and in the lull that resulted, on 9 May, forty-seven more Spitfires were flown off USS *Wasp*, seventeen off HMS *Eagle*. All except three reached Malta safely.

The siege of the island, however, was in no way lifted. On the contrary, the capture by Rommel's counter-stroke of the Martuba airfield complex just south of Derna had meant that the British were no longer able to provide fighter protection for the convoy-routes to Malta. These accordingly became increasingly dominated by the Axis airmen. Malta's ordeal by starvation had begun in earnest.

The prospect, 'all too close ahead', as the RAF Official History puts it, that 'failing the arrival of a convoy, the last reserves of fuel, food and ammunition' on Malta would be exhausted, naturally filled Churchill with dismay. He repeatedly urged Auchinleck to recapture those vital Martuba airfields but Auchinleck as repeatedly ignored him. By a rather horrible irony, the one person on either side who failed to appreciate the value of Malta's strikes against the Axis supply-lines was the man who gained the most benefit from them. As early as August, 1941, the Prime Minister had written delightedly to his C-in-C, Middle East of the difficulties that Malta's attacks would make for the maintenance of Rommel's army. As late as August, 1942, Auchinleck would refuse to stage a diversionary move to draw attention away from a convoy making for Malta, then reduced almost to the point of surrender. The island's retention, he stated, was not absolutely necessary to his plans.

By 8 May, Churchill's patience was exhausted. On that day, the Prime Minister warned Auchinleck that the loss of Malta 'would be a disaster of first magnitude to the British Empire and probably fatal in the long run to the defence of the Nile Valley.' He stated bluntly that Eighth Army should be prepared 'to attack the enemy and fight a major battle, if possible during May, and the sooner the better.' When this brought no response, Churchill, with the full consent of the Chiefs of Staff who shared his views, told Auchinleck on 10 May that: 'We are determined that Malta shall not be allowed to fall without a battle being fought by your whole army for its retention' – such battle to begin in June at the latest.

These requirements, Churchill tells us, amounted to 'definite orders which Auchinleck must obey or be relieved'. For nine days he did nothing. Then, after a further demand for a decision, he reluctantly agreed to attack in mid-June. Preparations for the new offensive were put in hand but before they could be completed, the 'Ultra' Intelligence revealed that Rommel intended to attack first on 26 May.

This of course meant that the enemy would hold the initiative and it seemed clear to many that Eighth Army's freedom of movement would be further hampered by the steps which had already been taken in connection with its own proposed advance. In particular, an immense supply dump, known as No 4 Forward Base, containing among other items a million-and-a-half gallons of petrol, had been built up at Belhammed, to which the rail link from Egypt had recently been extended. The need to protect this would

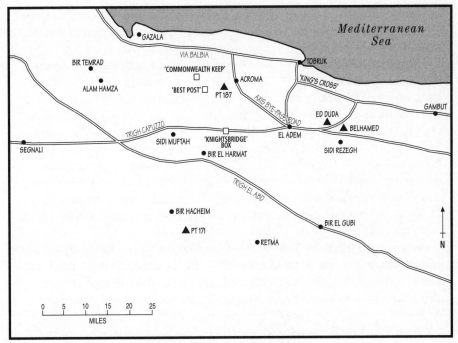

Map IVA: The Gazala Battlefield.

Map IVB: The Cauldron.

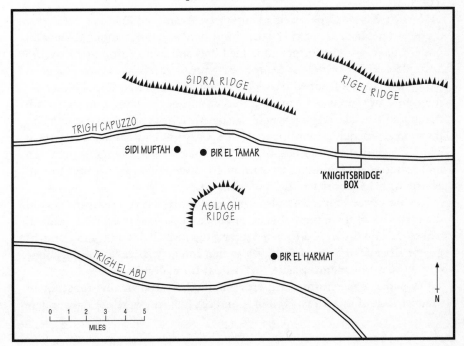

be a constant source of anxiety to the British for it was well within range of a sudden swoop by Rommel – indeed he would direct 90th Light to just this area.

Nonetheless Auchinleck awaited the coming attack with some confidence. The Gazala Line was held by Gott's XIII Corps, stationed in strong defensive positions. Pienaar, now a major general, guarded the northern section with the three brigades – 1st, 2nd and 3rd – of 1st South African Division. On his left were 151st and 69th Brigades from Major General Ramsden's 50th (British) Division. There was then a gap of five miles, filled with minefields, to Ramsden's third brigade, 150th Brigade under Brigadier Haydon, located near Sidi Muftah between the Trigh Capuzzo and the Trigh el Abd. The South Africans were supported by 32nd Army Tank Brigade; 50th Division by 1st Army Tank Brigade. Together these contained 110 Matildas and 167 Valentines.

South of the Trigh el Abd came another ten miles of minefields, at the end of which was the fortified position of Bir Hacheim (pronounced and sometimes spelt Bir Hakim). This was held by the Free French Brigade of Brigadier-General Marie-Pierre Koenig. Tobruk was secured by 2nd South African Division, now under Major General Klopper, containing 4th and 6th South African Brigades, and also 9th Indian Brigade detached from 5th Indian Division. Another of 5th Indian's Brigades, the 10th, was in reserve at Gambut, while 11th Indian Brigade from 4th Indian Division was moving up to the front-line and would in due course replace 9th Indian Brigade in Tobruk.

Norrie's XXX Corps was made up of 1st Armoured Division, now once more under Major General Herbert Lumsden, and 7th Armoured Division under Messervy. The former contained 2nd and 22nd Armoured Brigades and also 201st Guards Motor Brigade[3] which was stationed at 'Knightsbridge', a fortified position or 'box' on the Trigh Capuzzo behind the centre of the Gazala Line. Messervy's armour was to be found in 4th Armoured Brigade led by Brigadier Richards. When its tanks were added to those in Lumsden's two brigades, XXX Corps had a total strength of 257 Crusaders, 149 Stuarts and 167 of the new American Grants, of which more shortly. In addition, 1st Armoured Brigade was on its way to join Norrie with 145 more tanks, 75 of them Grants.

Koenig's Free Frenchmen also came under Messervy's command, as did the garrisons of three more 'boxes' stretching eastward from Bir Hacheim. These were in order, 3rd Indian Motor Brigade at Point 171, 7th (British) Motor Brigade at Retma, and 29th Indian Infantry Brigade, the backbone of the Oasis Force during CRUSADER, at Bir el Gubi.

On paper, Panzerarmee Afrika contained six Italian divisions but in practice four of these, two each in X and XXI Corps, were not only under-strength but lacked motor vehicles which meant they could play only minor roles in the coming mobile battle. Commanded by Crüwell and stiffened by the German 15th Rifle Regiment detached from 90th Light, these troops were detailed to make holding attacks against the northern part of the Gazala Line. The main assault was to take place in the south. The Afrika Korps, now under Lieutenant General Walther Nehring, accompanied by the Italian XX Corps – Ariete and Trieste – would outflank the Free French at Bir Hacheim before turning north to engage the Gazala Line from the rear, while Major General Kleemann the new leader of 90th Light would take his division, accompanied by Reconnaissance Units 3 and 33, north-east towards Tobruk to menace Allied supply-dumps.

Rommel cheerfully assumed that the destruction of the defenders, followed by the capture of his main objective, Tobruk, would take just four days. It was an incredibly optimistic estimate, for Rommel controlled only 332 German tanks, of which 50 were Mark IIs, plus 228 Italian ones. He also had only 77 more German tanks in reserve, though the not very efficient Italian Littorio (Armoured) Division would arrive at the front in the final stages of the fighting.

Admittedly the Panzer divisions presented a considerably more formidable picture than at the time of CRUSADER. Not only did all their tanks now boast the additional frontal protection but new Mark III or Mark IV Specials had also made their appearance. These had 50mm front hull armour, though the Mark III Specials normally had only 30mm turret armour and both had only 30mm side plates. They also both had long-barrelled high-velocity guns – 50mm in the Mark III Specials, 75mm in the Mark IV Specials.

Thus all German tanks were now superior to the Crusaders or Stuarts in hull armour, though not in turret armour; they were still inferior, however, to the heavy 'I' tanks. The standard Mark IIIs or IVs remained of course inferior to all Allied tanks in gun power but the new Specials could out-gun all those types that had previously been in use. Fortunately there were only nineteen Mark III Specials on hand when the Battle of Gazala began; only twenty-seven by 10 June. As for the Mark IV Specials, there was at first no ammunition available for them and their numbers had still not reached double figures by as late as the end of July. They would only become a threat at a subsequent date.

Any progress made by the Germans moreover was completely over-shadowed by the appearance in strength on the battlefield of the American Grant tanks. These had a thickness of armour at least equal to and in most respects superior to that of their German rivals – 50mm on the front of the hull, 38mm side plates, 57mm on the turret. They thus had little to fear from the standard German tanks even at close range. Ronald Lewin in his study of the Afrika Korps describes its men watching 'with horror the shot from the German 50mms bouncing off the Grants' armour'. Major General 'Pip' Roberts in his memoirs, *From the Desert to the Baltic*, reports that during the early exchanges at Gazala, in which he commanded 3rd Royal Tanks, his own Grant was hit eight times without a shell penetrating it, while another Grant resisted twenty-five hits successfully.

Roberts also points out that the Grants' armament was at this time 'superior in anti-tank capability to any guns mounted in the German tanks'. Grants carried both a 37mm in the turret and a 75mm in a sponson on the side of the hull. This could fire either high-explosive shells at non-armoured targets or armour-piercing shells with a greater penetrative power even than those of the new long-barrelled Mark III Specials. Not that the Grant was perfect either. The 75mm, in its sponson, had only limited traverse and gave the Grant an undesirably high silhouette. It was also somewhat slower than the German tanks. These defects though did not prevent it being more than a match for any opponent it had to face before the Mark IV Specials began to arrive in large numbers.

Nor was the Grant the only new weapon gained by Eighth Army. It had also received 112 of the new 6-pounder anti-tank guns which possessed a considerable superiority over the German 50mms and were approximately equal to the captured Russian 76mm anti-tank guns that were now reaching Rommel. The German 88mms remained the most deadly guns on the battlefield but, fortunately for Eighth Army, Rommel had only forty-eight of these.

In theory, the opposing air-arms were roughly equal in strength. Coningham's Desert Air Force contained some 380 fighters or fighter-bombers, 160 bombers and 60 reconnaissance machines. At the expense of abandoning his sustained raids on Malta, Kesselring had sent sizable re-inforcements of fighters and Stuka dive-bombers to North Africa, bringing the Axis strength there to some 350 fighters, 140 bombers and 40 recon-naissance machines. In practice though, the Italians, whose aircraft made up about half of this total, played a very small part in the coming struggle. Coningham had also received improved types of aircraft. The Kittyhawks, of which there were six squadrons, were steadily replacing the older Tomahawks, of which only two squadrons now remained. Both the Kittyhawks and the Hurricanes, of which Coningham could use six squadrons in varying roles, were being adapted so as to carry a 250-lb bomb under each wing, though only about a third of them had been so converted by the time the battle began. 55 and 223 Squadrons now flew Martin Baltimore bombers. The first Spitfire squadron, No 145, saw action as from 1 June – Spitfires had been used in the reconnaissance role even earlier – while seven days later, No 6 Squadron, flying Hurricane IIDs armed with two 40mm armour-piercing guns, also joined in the fighting.

All of which looked fine on paper but concealed a number of weaknesses on the British side. As General Jackson explains, Auchinleck had decided to implement certain 'changes which had been advocated for some time in India but found little favour in England'. In particular he felt that the infantry divisions were too unwieldy. He therefore determined to use, as his basic infantry formations, brigade groups operating independently of their parent division. These he believed would be more flexible but he rightly realized they might also be more vulnerable. To guard against this danger the brigade groups were usually stationed in the 'boxes' previously mentioned, which were designed to resist attack from any direction, being protected by mines and barbed wire and well supplied with guns.

Unhappily, the scheme did not prove very successful. It inevitably weakened the integrity of the infantry divisions, it encouraged the already existing tendency to disperse the artillery, but, if anything, it made Eighth Army rather less flexible than before. The trouble was, as Field Marshal Carver points out, the brigade groups in their 'boxes' remained 'static' and since they were often widely separated, they were unable to support each other and 'could only influence the battle within range of guns sited within the position.' This was true even of those brigade groups which were mechanized and so theoretically more mobile, because their transport vehicles were usually sent away from the 'boxes' to save them from becoming easy targets for enemy shellfire. Thus, for example, Carver reports that 201st Guards Motor Brigade remained motionless in its 'box' at 'Knightsbridge' 'from 26 May to 13 June, and, although it served a useful purpose as a rallying point for the armoured brigades, it took no other part in the battle' – which for almost the whole of that period was raging all round it.

The British positions at the southern end of the Gazala Line were also highly vulnerable. In correspondence with Ritchie, Auchinleck informed him that 3rd Indian Motor Brigade at Point 171 was 'fit for battle' if 'not absolutely fully equipped'; in reality it was without most of its supporting units including more than half its allotted quota of anti-tank guns. 7th Motor Brigade had been split up into 'Jock Columns' and sent out of its 'box' at Retma to support the British and South African screen of armoured cars. And although Auchinleck was confident that 29th Indian Infantry Brigade at Bir el Gubi would present a threat to 'any wide turning movement from the south against Tobruk or from the west against Sollum, unlikely as this may seem to be', in practice, as Carver curtly remarks, 'an infantry brigade, dug into a defensive position in the desert' could scarcely be expected to 'threaten anything beyond the range of its guns'.

Auchinleck's comments confirm a later statement by de Guingand that both before and during the coming battle, the Commander-in-Chief, Middle East had:

> . . . a lot to say regarding the major decisions within Eighth Army. If he was not up there himself, frequent signals would be exchanged. In addition he would send up one of his principal staff officers every day or two to convey his views to the Army Commander.

On 20 May for instance, Auchinleck wrote a lengthy letter to Ritchie setting out the conclusions he had reached regarding Rommel's plans – for while 'Ultra' had provided warning of the impending offensive, it had given no details of the form this would take. Auchinleck believed that there were 'two main courses open to the enemy'. The first was 'to envelop our southern flank, seizing or masking Bir Hacheim en route and then driving on Tobruk' while at the same time creating a diversion in the north. The second was to deliver an attack on 'the centre of the main position, with the object of driving straight on Tobruk', accompanying this with 'a feint against Bir Hacheim in which the Italian tanks might well be used with the aim of drawing off the main body of your armour to the south, and so leaving the way open for the main thrust.' In either case he thought that the offensive would be reinforced by a seaborne landing to the east of Gazala – which in reality was at least one problem that Eighth Army would not have to worry about.

'I feel myself' Auchinleck declared, 'that the second course' – the attack on the centre of the Gazala Line – 'is the one he will adopt and that it is certainly the most dangerous to us.' He did add that Eighth Army must 'be ready to deal with the enemy should he adopt the first course', and that Ritchie had to be careful 'not to commit your armoured striking force until you know beyond reasonable doubt where the main body of his armour is thrusting.' Clearly though, Auchinleck was not really concerned with the first alternative for the bulk of his letter thereafter dealt with 'the method I think he is likely to adopt to put the second course into effect' and the actions to be taken to oppose this – chiefly the concentration of the British armoured divisions astride the Trigh Capuzzo. He also suggested later that Ritchie should consider withdrawing the troops in the probable vicinity of the attack from their forward positions, thereby 'reducing the effect' of any artillery bombardment – though also, as Carver notes, 'giving up the commanding high ground'.

Ritchie by contrast had always believed that Rommel would try to outflank the Gazala Line to the south. Three days before Auchinleck's letter was written, he had so advised his Corps Commanders. Three days after it was written, Ritchie replied firmly that he still felt that Rommel 'will try to go round our southern flank.' He was of course quite correct. Von Mellenthin tells us that Rommel never considered an attack on the British centre for one moment, believing it 'would have had no chance whatever'. He adds that he is 'rather surprised' that 'such an eminent soldier' as Auchinleck could possibly have suggested this.

Ritchie was also rightly worried that keeping his armour too far north would dangerously expose the weak Allied formations in the south and his logistic units, in particular the vast, vital No 4 Forward Base. Auchinleck reminded him that an advance by Rommel in this area would 'very soon expose his supply lines to your attack' but Ritchie was well aware that if Rommel reached No 4 Forward Base he would not need to bother further with any supply lines. Auchinleck declared that any concentration of armour on the Trigh Capuzzo did 'not look from the map to be too far north to meet the main attack, should it come round the southern flank, instead of against the centre as I anticipate' but Ritchie was concerned with the protection of his men and equipment, not the markings on a map in Cairo.

Wisely therefore, Ritchie did not concentrate his armour on the Trigh Capuzzo. Indeed his armour was not concentrated at all. This latter decision is more open to criticism for there is no doubt that Auchinleck's advice that it should be was excellent – in theory. In practice there were objections. If the armour was concentrated it might become the target for Axis air attack. It was likely at best to be spotted by Axis reconnaissance aircraft, enabling Rommel to choose a line of advance deliberately avoiding it. Finally wherever it was concentrated it might well be unable to intervene in time if isolated units such as the 'boxes' in the south, 150th Brigade or the Free French should come under attack from the Afrika Korps.

Accordingly Ritchie, after consulting with Norrie, established the armoured brigades in positions where they should be able to go quickly to the aid of any formation that might be threatened and though separated should also be able to come to each other's support in a comparatively short time. 4th Armoured Brigade was stationed some twelve miles east of Bir Hacheim, 22nd Armoured fifteen miles to the north-west at Bir el Harmat just north of the Trigh el Abd, and only 2nd Armoured on the Trigh Capuzzo a further eight miles to the north-east of the 22nd between 'Knightsbridge' and El Adem. It has been suggested that Auchinleck was not aware of this decision but his letter of 20 May had been brought to Ritchie by Corbett who then stayed for two days at Eighth Army Headquarters. It is inconceivable that Corbett did not discuss the matter with Ritchie during that time and report back to Auchinleck. Indeed after Corbett's return to Cairo, Auchinleck wrote to Ritchie on 23 May specifically confirming that he was now 'quite happy about the positioning of the armoured divisions', to which Ritchie replied on the 25th: 'I was sure that you would be once you were in possession of the correct facts.'

Nonetheless Auchinleck's constant interference, which was intended only to help his Eighth Army Commander, had a different and unfortunate effect. As the Official History indicates, Ritchie became 'accustomed to consult the Commander-in-Chief, not because he had not the strength of character to make decisions for himself but possibly because he continued to think more as a staff officer than as a commander.' General Jackson is less polite. 'Ritchie' he says, 'became progressively more like a puppet, acting on the instructions passed on to him by Auchinleck in a voluminous shower of letters and signals.' 'Ritchie' says Field Marshal Carver, should 'have demanded either that he should be allowed freedom to command his army in his own way, or be replaced. But he was too decent, loyal and traditional a soldier to put his superior, whom he liked and admired, in such a difficult position. He was to suffer for it.'

He was indeed – both at the time and later. It might seem unfair to describe Ritchie as a 'puppet'; after all he did query Auchinleck's prediction as to Rommel's line of attack and his suggestions as to the actions that should therefore be taken. Yet the fact remains that, with admirable loyalty but far less wisdom, Ritchie passed on Auchinleck's prediction to his own subordinates. They readily accepted it because while at this time 'Ultra' was of course a closely guarded secret, it was known in Eighth Army that Auchinleck had access to a particularly good Intelligence source. In consequence, Norrie, Lumsden and Messervy all issued orders based on the assumption that the enemy assault would be delivered in the north and any sweep round the southern flank would be no more than a diversion.

From this followed all the troubles of the next few days. In the first place when Rommel's offensive did come in from the south, it achieved complete surprise and the warning which would have allowed the armoured formations time to concentrate was simply not given. Worse still as General Fraser relates in *And We Shall Shock Them*, Auchinleck's supervision had already tended to 'diminish the standing' of Ritchie in the eyes of his own command. The realization that Ritchie had tamely forwarded views with which he personally disagreed virtually ruined his standing.

As a result, the coming battle would be marked by what Fraser calls 'indiscipline at the top. Orders were received, doubted, questioned, discussed. Formation commanders were sceptical of Ritchie's wisdom and independence of judgement. Was he not still, some thought, a staff officer of Auchinleck's?' Field Marshal Carver is even more direct. Norrie and Gott, he states, were constantly 'ganging up against' Ritchie 'because they felt he was merely the mouthpiece of Auchinleck, far away in Cairo.'

Indeed when the Corps Commanders were querying the decisions of the Army Commander, when the Army Commander was passing on advice which he correctly believed was wrong, when the Commander-in-Chief was offering guidance from afar after lengthy staff meetings that, according to de Guingand who attended them, 'used to go on sometimes for hours' by which time the situation at the front would probably be entirely different; then well may it be asked who was really directing Eighth Army during the Battle of Gazala? The only proper answer would appear to be: No one.

Notes

1   Detailed accounts of the events here described can be found in *Norway 1940* by Bernard Ash and *Scandanavian Misadventure: The Campaign in Norway 1940* by Air Commodore Maurice Harvey.
2   Philip Warner: *Auchinleck The Lonely Soldier*.
3   The former 200th Guards Brigade, renumbered once again when it was mechanized.

6

CAULDRON

The Army was broken into a thousand fragments. Whether or not this flexibility-run-wild was responsible, it is undoubtedly true that we showed ourselves incapable of concentrating superior force and of utilising the whole of our resources simultaneously. This showed itself in the dismal recurrence of the same event, namely the over-running of brigade after brigade by an enemy in superior force, while the rest of the Army appeared powerless to assist.

Colonel Jacob's Diary.
6 August, 1942.

The battle of Gazala began with Rommel's initial assault achieving complete surprise. When air reconnaissance sighted the Axis striking force in the early evening of 26 May, this was heading due east, thereby apparently confirming Auchinleck's prediction of an attack in the vicinity of the Trigh Capuzzo. It was only as darkness was falling at about 2100, that Rommel swung round to the south-east.

During the night, the enemy's advance was monitored by Lieutenant Colonel Newton-King's 4th South African Armoured Cars, the reports of which were seconded by those of Brigadier Renton's 7th Motor Brigade – but their warnings were disregarded. Field Marshal Carver (who was then a major on the staff of XXX Corps) relates that he personally 'had become increasingly convinced during the night that these movements represented the main threat' but when he contacted Messervy's chief staff officer, Lieutenant Colonel Pyman, the latter, reflecting Messervy's own views, considered that the armoured cars were exaggerating and it would be premature to jump to conclusions. Carver also tried to persuade Norrie to order

1st Armoured Division to be ready to move south but Norrie declined, believing 'the movement reported could be the feint that everybody had predicted.' Major General Roberts reports that when his 3rd Battalion, Royal Tank Regiment was finally ordered into action, 4th Armoured Brigade advised him that the 'enemy movement' was a 'sort of SINBAD' – code-name for a reconnaissance in force – 'we don't think it's anything very serious.'

By the time that dawn on 27 May had enabled the British reconnaissance aircraft to discover the true situation, it was too late. Rommel's three German divisions plus Ariete had all outflanked the Gazala Line and were preparing to fall upon the weak and divided Allied units in the south.

At 0715, Ariete Division, supported by part of 21st Panzer, duly assaulted 3rd Indian Motor Brigade at Point 171. Despite the shortage of anti-tank guns, the defenders put up a gallant fight before falling back to Bir el Gubi at about 0800. They had knocked out fifty-two tanks, unfortunately almost all of them Italian, but had lost eleven officers and 200 men killed and thirty officers and 1,000 men prisoners, including an Admiral, no less. This was seventy-two-year-old Sir Walter Cowan, who had insisted on being in the front line in the guise of naval liaison officer and who was only captured after defiantly emptying his revolver at an enemy tank.

Meanwhile, at almost the same time that Point 171 was attacked, von Vaerst's 15th Panzer engaged 4th Armoured Brigade which had just begun its move southward. Confronted unexpectedly with not a reconnaissance in force but, says Roberts indignantly, 'a whole ruddy Panzer division', the brigade still inflicted very heavy casualties on it. Unhappily, both 3rd Royal Tanks and 8th Hussars suffered severe losses in their turn, not in the main from the enemy tanks, which they outclassed, but from von Vaerst's 88mms, whose shells did not bounce off the Grants' armour. Though his remaining unit, 5th Royal Tanks, was still virtually intact, Brigadier Richards decided it would be best to retire, ultimately to the vicinity of El Adem.

On Rommel's right at about 0845, Kleemann's 90th Light Division engaged the 'Jock Columns' of 7th Motor Brigade which had retreated to their Retma 'box' but had had no chance to organize a defence of it after their activities on the previous night. Three-quarters of an hour later, Brigadier Renton fell back to Bir el Gubi with the loss of eight of his brand-new 6-pounder anti-tank guns.

By now Norrie, for one, had appreciated the true position and he ordered Lumsden to send 22nd Armoured Brigade to Messervy's aid. Lumsden, however, as General Jackson tells us, 'objected on the grounds that an attack might still come in the centre along the Trigh Capuzzo.' 22nd Armoured did eventually move south but by that time, having left Ariete to attack Bir Hacheim, 21st Panzer, under its brilliant new young commander, Major

General Georg von Bismarck, was already pressing northward. At 0907, it caught 22nd Armoured by surprise, forcing the British to retire with the loss of some thirty tanks. As a final misfortune, at about 1000, Reconnaissance Unit 33 attacked Headquarters 7th Armoured Division, capturing both Messervy and Pyman, though both were later able to escape, having hidden their badges of rank.

However, by no means all Rommel's early moves were successful. A diversion by Crüwell's Italians against the northern part of the Gazala Line had little effect. Trieste, as a result of conflicting orders, ran into the minefields in the area between 150th Brigade and the Free French. The assault by Ariete on Bir Hacheim was a failure.

Finally, at about 1330, Ritchie, alarmed by the advance of 90th Light, which was threatening No 4 Forward Base, ordered 4th Armoured Brigade to intervene. Brigadier Richards promptly obliged, forcing Kleemann to retire and thereafter so harassing him that he did not finally re-join Rommel until the night of the 28th–29th.

Rommel would later comment scathingly on the 'dispersal of the British armoured brigades', which he described as 'incomprehensible'. His criticism has been echoed in numerous British accounts but in retrospect it seems not so much unfair as largely irrelevant – especially bearing in mind that for much of the battle Rommel himself would disperse his own armoured units. It was the separation of the British infantry into brigade groups and 'Jock Columns' that was mainly responsible for the initial losses on 27 May. 3rd Indian and 7th (British) Motor Brigades would have been mauled just the same had the British armour been concentrated. Indeed, had it been concentrated on the Trigh Capuzzo, additional misfortunes would probably have occurred before the British tanks could have intervened.

Of course, if the armour had been united, 4th and 22nd Armoured Brigades would not have had to face the enemy on their own. Paradoxically, however, their prompt and unexpected appearance probably proved more effective than a 'set-piece' attack by a stronger armoured force later in the day would have done. 'Encounter battles' like those fought early on 27 May tended to give the British better prospects of engaging the enemy armour to which their own tanks were superior, while allowing the Germans fewer opportunities for preparing a defence based on their trump cards, the 88mms.

Moreover, the very fact that he had been opposed by the British armour so early on 27 May led Rommel into a serious error. His Intelligence reports had greatly underestimated the number of tanks available to Eighth Army. Believing that he had already disposed of the bulk of these, he therefore ordered a rapid advance northward regardless of risks. He was to pay dearly for this rash action.

By the early afternoon of 27 May, 22nd Armoured had reorganized near 'Knightsbridge'. It now encountered 15th Panzer which in its hurry had neglected to co-ordinate its artillery support and suffered heavy losses from Brigadier Carr's Grants. At about 1400, 2nd Armoured Brigade joined in the fighting with a flank attack on 15th Panzer's 115th Motorized Infantry Regiment causing still heavier casualties. Meanwhile, on the other flank of the Afrika Korps, an attack by 44th Royal Tanks from 1st Army Tank Brigade fell on 21st Panzer's 104th Motorized Infantry Regiment, so decimating one of its rifle battalions that this had to be disbanded. The British losses were eighteen Matildas.

Rommel had now been deprived of one-third of his precious tanks as well as large numbers of German infantrymen. To make matters worse, Coningham's Hurricanes and Kittyhawks were by this time savaging his vulnerable supply vehicles as these made the long haul south of Bir Hacheim. The chief results of their efforts were felt by 15th Panzer which had run out of fuel by the evening of 27 May; nor could its tanks be replenished until the following evening.

On the 28th therefore, 21st Panzer moved northward alone at about 0800. It was opposed by 8th Royal Tanks from 1st Army Tank Brigade which put up a spirited resistance, symbolized by the action of Major Sutton who, though wounded and left on foot between the opposing forces when his tank was destroyed, continued to cheer on his men until he was picked up. Eventually, however, his squadron was forced to retreat, leaving nine of its fifteen Valentines behind. Von Bismarck then pushed on to the escarpment overlooking the coast road, capturing a South African strongpoint at 'Commonwealth Keep' just south of this on the way. Having reached the escarpment, he halted, and next day was recalled by Rommel who had finally realized the seriousness of his position.

Ironically, Rommel would have to rely for his salvation on the allies he so often disparaged. The most conspicuous Axis success on 28 May was achieved by Ariete. Summoned from Bir Hacheim to Bir el Harmat to cover the right rear of the Afrika Korps, the Italians beat off attacks by 2nd Armoured Brigade throughout the afternoon, their supporting 88mms, virtually without loss, destroying almost all the Grants of the 10th Hussars. At dawn on the 29th, the Italian Sabratha Infantry Division made a gallant attempt to help Rommel by attacking the Gazala Line near Alam Hamza, but this failed, leaving 400 prisoners in South African hands. At about the same time, Crüwell was also taken prisoner when the Fiesler Storch light aeroplane in which he was trying to contact Rommel was shot down by AA fire as it flew over 150th Brigade's position. His pilot was killed but miraculously the aircraft, in Crüwell's own words, 'made a perfect crash-landing' on its own, leaving him unhurt but on his way to Cairo as a captive. His place was taken by Kesselring, who happened to be on a visit to the front. Amidst all these excitements, few on either side will have noticed that by the 29th, the Trieste Division had succeeded in clearing a path through the minefields along the Trigh el Abd.

It was on 29 May in fact, that the tide began to turn back in Rommel's favour – in circumstances which make nonsense of those criticisms usually levelled at Eighth Army. On the one hand, though 90th Light was back in the fold, Rommel's tanks were still widely scattered, for the bulk of 21st Panzer, having again been engaged, this time by 7th Royal Tanks, was unable to re-join him until late in the day. By contrast, on the British side, 2nd and 22nd Armoured Brigades had already combined their strengths and 4th Armoured Brigade, despite the delays caused by sandstorms and the need to refuel, joined them that afternoon.

The concentrated armour all came under the command of Lumsden, by whom it was launched in a whole series of attacks. Further tank losses were suffered by the Germans and von Vaerst, among others, was badly wounded. However, the Axis army was at its most dangerous when forced onto the defensive, for then its anti-tank gunners had their greatest opportunities.

On the 29th, the Axis anti-tank gunners, particularly those of Ariete and 90th Light, duly inflicted heavy casualties. Next day, Lumsden resumed his assaults, though only with 2nd and 22nd Armoured, 4th Armoured having been diverted against some twenty-five damaged German tanks wrongly reported to be in the vicinity of Bir Hacheim. Lumsden again suffered crippling casualties from the anti-tank guns, so much so that the two brigades were forced for the time being to combine their remaining tanks in one composite formation. Heavy raids by Coningham's fighter-bombers, aided by the Bostons of 12 and 24 Squadrons SAAF, were much more successful but inevitably the greatest injuries they inflicted were on Rommel's 'soft-skinned' vehicles.

Meanwhile, on the night of the 29th–30th, Rommel had fallen back slightly, linking up with Trieste to take advantage of the gap which the Italians had cleared in the minefields. His new positions were protected to the north by the Sidra Ridge which lay just north of the Trigh Capuzzo, and to the south and east by the Aslagh Ridge north-west of Bir el Harmat. To the west, however, he was faced with the 'box' manned by the British 150th Brigade. It was an area which would become known, appropriately if rather obviously, as 'The Cauldron'.

Later, vastly exaggerated suggestions would be made that Rommel was now in a desperate state, bereft of supplies and contemplating surrender. It can only be said that his actions do not support such contentions. Certainly Rommel's logistic situation was far from good but throughout 30 May he was taking steps to rectify this; his empty motor vehicles streaming back through the gap in the minefields to pick up fresh supplies, the first of which were already reaching him during the night of the 30th–31st. During the afternoon of the 30th also, Rommel personally drove back through the gap to confer with Kesselring and Hitler's adjutant, Major von Below. He made no mention to them of any thought of surrender or even of withdrawal. On the contrary, he stated his intention to hold off the British attacks on the Cauldron and build up his forces there ready for a resumption of his offensive.

Nonetheless, the initiative was very much with Eighth Army and had the British attacked the Cauldron at once, while Rommel was still too weak to deal with 150th Brigade and to resist a simultaneous assault from the east, it seems almost impossible to doubt that they would have completed a decisive victory. They did not do so and their failure gives a graphic illustration of the problems which were bedeviling Eighth Army at this time.

First and foremost was the absurd command structure which prevented Eighth Army from being commanded. When Rommel's initial attack was delivered in the south, Auchinleck at first made a gracious response. At 1545 on 27 May, he signalled to Ritchie: 'You were right and I was wrong.' Unfortunately, he then added 'but watch out for favourite pincer movement possibly tonight against extreme north flank and coast'.

At 1650, he put the same point more strongly:

> In view our estimate total enemy strength would not, repeat not, rule out second attack by tanks etc. against front one SA Div this evening or tonight coupled with attempted landing on coast east of Gazala. This would be in accordance with pincer principle and he may hope to have drawn off all our tanks far to south.

As a result, the South Africans, the main part of 50th Division and most of 32nd Army Tank Brigade, continued to prepare for an action that was never to be fought, while Eighth Army's formation commanders in general were reluctant to commit their forces until the situation had become more clear.

On the morning of 29 May, a letter from Auchinleck arrived at Eighth Army's Headquarters at Gambut. In this incidentally, Auchinleck listed Eighth Army's resources, among which he mentioned '1st Armoured Brigade Group complete', though in practice this was still moving forward from Egypt and its advanced units would only reach the front on 3 June. Unhappily, despite this clear evidence of his chief's lack of knowledge of the true situation on the battlefield, Ritchie, as misguidedly loyal as ever, at once turned his attention to implementing the plan which Auchinleck's letter suggested.

This, code-named Operation LIMERICK, had a double intention.

Auchinleck wished Eighth Army to move round Rommel's flank south of Bir Hacheim, the 'immediate objective' being Segnali, Rommel's main base, due west of the centre of the Gazala Line. At the same time Ritchie was told that 'to pin the enemy farther north, we should put in a secondary attack, preferably with 50th Div and heavy tanks against Temrad.' – Bir Temrad being situated west of 1st South African Division. As late as 3 June, Auchinleck would continue to urge not an assault on Rommel in the Cauldron but 'an offensive directed towards Temrad so as to threaten his bases, coupled with threats from Segnali and the south against his lines of supply' – this despite the fact that, two days earlier, Rommel's intention of renewing his own offensive had been revealed by 'Ultra' and that, one day earlier, his preliminary moves had already taken place.

The inevitable consequence of this interference, as General Jackson points out, was that 'Ritchie was less concerned with liquidating Rommel's force in the Cauldron than with mounting LIMERICK.' It also resulted in a singular display of 'indiscipline at the top' as Eighth Army's senior commanders argued over the action that should be taken.

Neither Pienaar nor Ramsden nor Harold Briggs, now a major general commanding 5th Indian Division, which had been brought up to support XIII Corps, believed that an offensive towards Bir Temrad could succeed. Later, 50th Division would break out in this area but that was a desperate move in a desperate situation which caught the enemy by surprise. At this time the Axis commanders were ready for such an action and probing attacks in the area had achieved little, though one on 3 June did earn a Victoria Cross for South African Sergeant Quentin Smythe who, though wounded and with his officer killed, led his platoon to capture an enemy strongpoint and then brought his men back to safety in the face of enemy counter-attacks.

According to von Mellenthin, Auchinleck's proposed offensive in this area 'would have been too risky in view of Rommel's commanding position in the Cauldron' since the vulnerable infantry plus all the supplies needed for it would have had to be assembled within easy reach of another strike northward by the German armour. Similar considerations spoke against the wide sweep round the south of Bir Hacheim which Briggs, at least, did favour. This would have had to have been accompanied by Norrie's tanks if 5th Indian Division was not to be at risk from a swift move back by Rommel through the gap in the minefields. Yet if the armour was thus redeployed there would be nothing to prevent Rommel thrusting eastward towards the British supply depots, in particular No 4 Forward Base.

The need to consider all these factors inevitably caused delays which were made worse by other problems. Ritchie, though reserving his main efforts for LIMERICK, did also wish to mount further assaults on the Cauldron. However, the experiences of 29 and 30 May had convinced Lumsden that it would be futile to deliver these with armour alone; he wished to bring up infantry to deal with the Axis anti-tank guns. This, of course, took time and, as a result, no pressure was put on Rommel on the 31st. Ritchie then planned an attack for that night but Gott and Norrie asked for another postponement of twenty-four hours in which to assemble and prepare their forces. They have been roundly condemned for their hesitation but they had some excuse in that the close co-operation between armour, infantry and artillery which they were trying to achieve had never been properly tested. It was asking for trouble to introduce this in the middle of the Battle of Gazala. It should have been tested, practised, developed and, with luck, perfected in the long lull prior to that battle. This should have been the concern of the Middle East Command, rather than considerations of remote possibilities in India or the Caucasus.

On the Axis side there were no such inhibitions. Panzerarmee Afrika's leader made several mistakes but he was on the spot and his orders were obeyed promptly and without argument. On 31 May, Rommel attacked 150th Brigade with 15th Panzer, 90th Light and Trieste, supported by heavy Stuka raids. He again achieved complete surprise because reports of the supply vehicles moving back through the minefields had led to a general belief that he was bent only on retreat. Moreover poor communications prevented the news of his advance becoming known to the main body of Eighth Army.

Brigadier Haydon's three battalions, 4th East Yorkshires and 4th and 5th Green Howards, were therefore left to fight it out, supported only by the guns of 124th Field Regiment and thirty Matildas of 42nd and 44th Royal Tanks from 1st Army Tank Brigade which had joined Haydon on the 29th. All day the defenders resisted every assault but by nightfall only thirteen tanks remained, most of the guns had been destroyed and the infantry had all but exhausted their ammunition. At dawn on 1 June, Rommel personally led in a final attack. Haydon was killed. Some 3,000 men and 124 guns were captured.

Rommel had now secured his position in the Cauldron. On 2 June, he struck out from it, sending 90th Light and Trieste to engage the Free French at Bir Hacheim, and 21st Panzer on a raid to the north. This first dispersed the sixteen Valentines of 8th Royal Tanks, then routed 4th Armoured Brigade which, taken unawares, lost twenty-one tanks. 5th Royal Tanks suffered particularly severely, losing its CO, Lieutenant Colonel Uniacke. As usual though, misfortunes were partially redeemed by individual actions of great courage, and also of great unselfishness, such as that of Trooper Barton who won a DCM for a valiant though vain attempt to save the life of a wounded companion.

By 3 June Ritchie had rightly, if belatedly, determined to ignore

LIMERICK in favour of an all-out assault on the Cauldron which was planned for two days later. Auchinleck to his credit accepted this decision, urging his Eighth Army Commander to 'strike hard and at once' and to launch his offensive 'immediately the tactical situation on your front permits'. He also warned him that 'there must be thorough reconnaissance and preparation even at the cost of delay' – which rather contradicted his previous 'advice'.

The plan for Operation ABERDEEN, as Ritchie's offensive was called, appeared a good one. It envisaged a holding attack against the Sidra Ridge on the north of the Cauldron by 69th Brigade from 50th Division, supported by 32nd Army Tank Brigade. Meanwhile the main assault would be delivered against the Aslagh Ridge on Rommel's eastern flank by 5th Indian Division. Its 10th Indian Brigade would seize the Ridge with the aid of the Valentines of 4th Royal Tanks. Then 22nd Armoured Brigade, now transferred to Messervy's command, would move on Sidi Muftah (once held by 150th Brigade). The ground won would be secured by 9th Indian Brigade, after which 22nd Armoured would thrust northward to attack the Sidra Ridge from the rear. The Desert Air Force was requested to render as much assistance as was possible and, despite reports to the contrary, the RAF Official History makes it clear that 'most of the available air support' did operate in the area of the Cauldron, while Luftwaffe reports confirm clashes there with Allied fighters, bombers and fighter-bombers throughout 5 June.

Sadly though, in the event, ABERDEEN proved a total calamity. The attack on Sidra Ridge was thwarted by a combination of minefields and 21st Panzer's anti-tank guns. 32nd Army Tank Brigade lost fifty Matildas out of the seventy with which it began the engagement. The survivors were withdrawn safely by Lieutenant Colonel Foote of 7th Royal Tanks who had been forced to leave his own tank when this was disabled by a mine but who had continued to direct his men amidst heavy machine-gun fire – an action that earned him a DSO as a prelude to a still greater award soon afterwards.

Elsewhere, 10th Indian Brigade captured all its objectives with ease but the reason for this was that the main Axis defences lay just to the west of the Aslagh Ridge; a powerful artillery bombardment in support of the Brigade had fallen mainly on empty desert. When 22nd Armoured and the leading battalion of 9th Indian Brigade, 2nd West Yorkshires, pushed forward from the ridge they encountered fierce resistance. At about mid-day, the infantry were thrown back with loss by Ariete, while the tanks yet again suffered crippling casualties from the Axis anti-tank guns. Next they were assaulted by 21st Panzer, by now freed from concern for the Sidra Ridge area, and were driven out of the Cauldron with the loss of sixty of their number. 21st

Panzer then fell upon one of 10th Brigade's battalions, 2nd Highland Light Infantry, at Bir el Tamar, north-west of the Aslagh Ridge, so mauling it that it had to be withdrawn from the battle to reorganize.

The crowning catastrophe, however, occurred in the south. On the previous night the enemy had fortuitously made a gap in the minefields south-west of Bir el Harmat in order to salvage some abandoned tanks. Colonel Crasemann, commanding 15th Panzer in the absence of the wounded von Vaerst, now led his men, urged on by Rommel, through this gap. Overwhelming the weak 1st Battalion, Duke of Cornwall's Light Infantry, guarding the British left flank without any artillery support, 15th Panzer knocked out the headquarters of Briggs, Messervy, and Brigadiers Fletcher and Young commanding 9th and 10th Indian Brigades respectively.[1] Control of the battle understandably broke down completely and as an example of the resultant confusion, 2nd Armoured Brigade, which Norrie had brought up to assist Messervy, was directed away from the combat-zone by a mistaken order.

Crasemann's manoeuvre trapped the remnants of 10th Brigade, much of 9th Brigade, the motor battalion from 22nd Armoured and four artillery regiments in the Cauldron. Throughout 6 June these were attacked from all sides, while attempts by 2nd Armoured Brigade to interfere – 22nd Armoured had not recovered from its battering on the previous day – were held off by 21st Panzer. By nightfall it was all over. Another 3,000 men had been taken prisoner. 133 guns were lost.

While the main body of Eighth Army concentrated on Operation ABERDEEN or was distracted by Operation LIMERICK, the garrison at Bir Hacheim had been holding off attacks by 90th Light and Trieste, backed by the full weight of Kesselring's airmen. Luckily for Koenig's Free Frenchmen – 'Fighting Frenchmen' as they were re-christened early that month – the Desert Air Force, in its commander's words, had been ordered to 'adopt' the fortress. While Coningham's Bostons and fighter-bombers attacked enemy troops or supply vehicles, his fighters grappled furiously with the Luftwaffe. On 3 June for instance,the Tomahawks of 5 Squadron SAAF claimed ten Stukas – though this figure is not confirmed by enemy records – losing five of their own number to the escorting enemy fighters.

Further vicious combats took place on 4 June.[2] During the next two days both air forces turned their attention to the Cauldron, but on 7 June they resumed their fight for Bir Hacheim with even greater intensity. On the 8th, Rommel, leaving 21st Panzer and Ariete to guard against a renewed attack by Eighth Army, sent strong detachments from 15th Panzer, led by Lieutenant Colonel Baade, the commander of 115th Motorized Infantry Regiment, to reinforce the ground attacks on the fortress. Eighth Army, still recovering from its losses in ABERDEEN, was quite unable to interfere, though the South Africans had attempted a diversion on the 7th by attacking the Italian infantry positions fronting the Gazala Line – an action that cost them 280 casualties for very little in exchange.

Once more the Desert Air Force provided magnificent support for Bir Hacheim, engaging the enemy on the ground as well as in the air and dropping supplies to the Fighting Frenchmen. On 8 June, the Hurricane IIDs of No 6 Squadron (which, it will be recalled, carried 40mm anti-tank guns) made their first successful sortie, destroying a number of German vehicles including four tanks and three half-tracked troop-carriers. By the evening of the following day, however, 115th Regiment had captured Point 186 to the north of Bir Hacheim from which Baade was able to bring the fortress under continuous artillery fire. At 1700 Koenig requested permission to withdraw. He personally was able to leave but it proved impossible for the bulk of the garrison to be taken out at such short notice. Under Koenig's second-in-command, Colonel Amilakvari, the defenders held out all through 10 June. That night, leaving behind only the wounded and a small rearguard, some 2,700 men plus two female staff-car drivers turned volunteer nurses broke out of the trap, having done much to restore the reputation of their country's armed forces.

Freed from this thorn in his flesh, Rommel struck northwards. First 21st Panzer and Ariete were sent on a feint to the west of 'Knightsbridge'. This produced a clash with 6th Royal Tanks, illuminated by the courage of Captain Raymond Powell who left his disabled tank under fire to rescue a wounded man and thereafter remained outside it to affix a tow-rope enabling it to be brought to safety – he won a Military Cross. Then, under cover of this diversion, at 1500 on 11 June, 15th Panzer, with Trieste on its left flank, really did advance to the east of 'Knightsbridge', while 90th Light, accompanied by Reconnaissance Units 3 and 33, headed north-eastward for El Adem.

The enemy made little progress at first. 90th Light was opposed by 'Jock Columns' from 7th Motor Brigade which, as usual, proved only of nuisance value, but it found El Adem strongly held by 29th Indian Brigade. Kleemann, whose division had been greatly reduced in numbers, could make no impact on its defences either on the 11th or on the following days and was ordered to withdraw on the 13th. 15th Panzer had little success either in the face of resistance by 4th Armoured Brigade and spent the night of the 11th–12th south-east of 'Knightsbridge'.

Next day, 12 June, the Battle of Gazala reached its climax – in the air as well as on the ground, though with very different results. The biggest air-action of the battle took place that evening when four squadrons of Hurricanes met a huge enemy formation in the area of El Adem. 33 and 213

Squadrons lost five machines between them though they destroyed two German fighters, but 274 Squadron, soon to convert to 'Hurribombers', shot down four enemy fighters without loss, while 73 Squadron broke through to the German bombers, downing six of them, again without loss. This perhaps marked the moment when the Desert Air Force gained a command of the skies which, with one tragic exception, it would retain from then onwards.

It was just as well, for on the ground the story was one of disaster – and it is more than a shade ironical that on 12 June Rommel's panzer formations were separated as usual whereas Norrie's three armoured brigades plus 32nd Army Tank Brigade were all concentrated to the north and east of 'Knightsbridge'. Indeed 12 June gave graphic proof that concentrating the armour did not solve Eighth Army's problems, particularly if it was concentrated too far to the north, leaving more vulnerable targets unprotected.

The day began with high hopes. Norrie placed 2nd Armoured Brigade under Messervy's command for a joint assault with 4th Armoured on 15th Panzer while this remained isolated; 22nd Armoured and 32nd Army Tank Brigade being left to watch the troops in the Cauldron. 'Indiscipline at the top' now intervened. Messervy had wished to take 4th Armoured south to join 7th Motor Brigade on Rommel's outer flank. Instead of obeying orders, he set off to see Norrie in an attempt to impose his own views. Near El Adem, his party encountered Reconnaissance Unit 33 and was forced into hiding in a dry well, 'leaving his brigades' says Ronald Lewin, 'without direction or control'. At 1200, Norrie, realizing that Messervy was out of action, transferred command of those brigades to Lumsden, but it was not until 1525 that that officer was able to take charge, by which time 4th Armoured had already suffered from 15th Panzer's anti-tank guns, handled, as was so often the case, more aggressively than the German tanks.

This delay was fatal. Rommel, having learned of 15th Panzer's initial encounters, ordered von Bismarck to thrust eastward from the Cauldron with 21st Panzer to engage the British armour from behind. Von Bismarck's move duly struck the rear of 4th Armoured, achieving complete surprise. Brigadier Richards lost twenty tanks in short order, and when Lumsden ordered 22nd Armoured to his assistance, it too suffered heavy losses to von Bismarck's anti-tank guns. At the same time, 15th Panzer attacked both 4th and 2nd Armoured Brigades. The former was so mauled that Richards withdrew northward right out of the battle area; the latter, also hard hit, joined 22nd Armoured in the area north of 'Knightsbridge' and south of the Rigel Ridge – which was the western extremity of that First Escarpment mentioned so often in the course of the CRUSADER fighting. During 12 June Eighth Army lost altogether some ninety tanks. It was a catastrophic defeat.

Notes

1   Brigadier Desmond Young was taken prisoner. After the war he was to write a biography of Rommel.

2   Kesselring, who despite his nickname of 'Smiling Albert', was in his way just as aggressive a leader as Rommel, personally flew on one Stuka raid against Bir Hacheim on this date. He had a narrow escape when the dive-bomber carrying him crash-landed.

7

DIVIDED COUNSELS

In the later stages of the battle, the co-operation between the infantry and the armoured formations deteriorated. The infantry had had heavy losses in attacks in which they had not been supported by the tanks.

Colonel Jacob's Diary.
6 August, 1942.

The British commanders now had to determine the best ways of mitigating the ill-effects of their defeat. It was not a simple task but one step that they might have taken had already been foreseen by their enemy. After the fall of Bir Hacheim, Rommel tells us, they 'ought to have realized that there was nothing more to be gained by holding on to the northern part of the Gazala Line.' They should therefore have moved the two divisions there 'into the Acroma-Gazala area for mobile defence against the expected advance of my motorized forces.' He was very apprehensive of such a move, which he believed 'would have tilted the scales heavily in the British favour.'

Rommel's anxieties could well have been justified, for by 12 June Ritchie, as the Official History confirms, was already rightly alarmed that his enemy might 'advance north and cut off the 1st South African and 50th Divisions.' Unfortunately, in de Guingand's words, Ritchie 'was not entirely master in his own house.' On 12 June Auchinleck had arrived at Eighth Army Headquarters at Gambut.

Two days earlier, the C-in-C, Middle East had been warning Churchill of the serious threats to Syria, Iraq and Iran, but it seems that he felt matters in the Desert, at least, were well under control. He sent a report to the Prime Minister which, as Ronald Lewin states, was one of 'inexplicable confidence' and before he flew back to Cairo on the 13th, he issued firm orders that the divisions in the Gazala Line should stay where they were. He thereby not only put them in a situation of the gravest danger but ensured that when they were finally withdrawn this would have to be done in such a great hurry that there would be no time to plan the best way of redeploying them.

On 13 June, 21st Panzer seized the western end of the Rigel Ridge north-west of 'Knightsbridge' after a resolute defence by 2nd Battalion, Scots Guards, supported by the guns of 6th South African Field Battery. Lumsden ordered 2nd and 22nd Armoured Brigades to assist the defenders but this only resulted in yet more losses to the enemy anti-tank guns as well as leaving the way clear for a thrust by 15th Panzer east of 'Knightsbridge'.

The 'Knightsbridge' 'box' was still held by 201st Guards Brigade which had recently received an interesting reinforcement in the form of a pair of 3.7-inch heavy anti-aircraft guns converted to the anti-tank role in the hope that they would have the same effect as the Germans' redoubtable 88mms. Unfortunately the general opinion at the time did not consider these a great success. They proved impossible to conceal, they possessed very poor sights and when they fired they blew a huge cloud of dust into the air which provided a splendid target for the enemy. Although some 3.7-inch anti-tank guns were later used in the defence of Tobruk, the experiment was then discontinued and it is a matter of regret in some quarters that no attempts were made to cure the faults just described.

Even ignoring the new guns, the Guards could undoubtedly have put up a stout defence of 'Knightsbridge' had it been subjected to a direct attack but as a fixed, isolated position it was now in great danger of being cut off, particularly since Lumsden's battered units were no longer able to support it. Gott therefore ordered that it be evacuated on the evening of 13 June while 32nd Army Tank Brigade, under the command of Lieutenant Colonel Foote of 7th Royal Tanks, successfully held off the German armour. Foote's own Matilda was the last to leave the field, by which time his gallantry had won a Victoria Cross.

More resolute courage was displayed on the 14th as Rommel urged his tanks on towards the Via Balbia to cut off the divisions in the Gazala Line. 2nd and 22nd Armoured Brigades fought a desperate delaying action, symbolized by the exploit of Corporal Newman who, when his tank was set on fire, first beat out the flames then, though in agony from serious burns on his legs and lesser injuries to hands and face, continued firing his gun until another hit put it out of action. He survived to receive a DCM.

The courage of the infantry matched the courage of the armour. To break through to the Via Balbia the Germans had to overcome a series of defences stretching eastward from the Gazala Line to Acroma on the Axis Bye-Pass south-west of Tobruk. The key Allied positions were Point 187, five miles south-west of Acroma, held by 1st Worcesters, and 'Best Post', further west, held by a South African detachment under Lieutenant Colonel Bester from whom it took its name. The Worcesters resisted attacks from 15th Panzer until 1700 when they finally fell back towards Tobruk. The South Africans defied 21st Panzer all day, only retiring under cover of darkness. Though Rommel ordered his men to resume their advance that night, they were much too exhausted to comply.

Equal courage, though of a different kind, was demonstrated by Eighth Army's leaders. It was now clear to both Ritchie and Gott that the enemy was on the point of cutting the coast road, thereby trapping the South Africans and 50th Division. Their withdrawal could not be delayed any longer. Despite Auchinleck's commands therefore, Ritchie gave orders that they must be prepared for a retreat on the night of 14–15 June.

It was already almost too late. The only apparent escape route was the Via Balbia, a 'bottle-neck' threatened by Rommel's armour, horribly vulnerable to air-attack and unable to carry two divisions in a short space of time without becoming impossibly congested. To make matters worse, although Ritchie and Gott did not know it, 32nd Army Tank Brigade, which was supposed to keep the Via Balbia open, had misunderstood its orders and retired to Tobruk at dawn on the 15th, leaving the infantry unprotected.

In these circumstances, the fact that the divisions in the Gazala Line did escape would seem to reflect great credit on all concerned. Ritchie and Gott decided that only Pienaar's South Africans should fall back along the coast road while the remaining two brigades of Ramsden's 50th Division should break out through the Italian positions opposite to them and thereafter make the long march south of Bir Hacheim to rejoin the Allied lines.

It was also decided that both divisions would retire all the way to the Egyptian frontier. This would cause some heart-searching later but seemed then to be entirely reasonable. In the case of 50th Division there was little choice in any event. Ramsden's men would have swung well away from the combat-zone, could not possibly reach any defensive positions for some time and would have been of little use when they had done so, since they had been forced to abandon most of their equipment in the Gazala Line. Far better that they should stay clear of the fighting and be given the opportunity to re-arm and reorganize. Ritchie could probably have retained 1st South African Division in defences west of the frontier but he cannot be blamed for not having considered such an action in the short time available to him. Long before the battle started, a plan, oddly code-named Operation FREEBORN, had been drawn up to deal with a possible retirement from Gazala to the frontier, and as this was already in existence, Ritchie and Gott wisely put it into effect when they needed to get the South Africans to safety at short notice.

Operation FREEBORN was in existence because Auchinleck had

repeatedly made it clear that if the Gazala Line was broken there would be no second siege of Tobruk and the enemy's advance would be stopped at the frontier defences. As late as 13 June he had written to Ritchie confirming that in the 'worst possible case', that is if Eighth Army was defeated, then it would hold 'the frontier position as a rallying point'. It is not surprising then that Ritchie not only took advantage of a previously prepared plan but never considered that this might not be in full accord with his superior's wishes.

Unfortunately, however, despite all his previous instructions, Auchinleck now decided that he did not want Pienaar and Ramsden to withdraw to the frontier after all. In fact he considered it would be 'undesirable' for them to make any withdrawal whatever since 'the tactical advantage' of having their two divisions in the Gazala Line would then be lost. What that advantage might have been at this time is not particularly clear but in any case it seems that what really concerned Auchinleck was that he had received a signal from Churchill early on the morning of 14 June stating bluntly: 'Retreat would be fatal.'

Accordingly at 1115, Auchinleck signalled to Ritchie: 'Even if you have to evacuate Gazala you should hold Acroma, El Adem and to the south, while I build up reinforcements on the frontier. . . . Are you able to do this?' A quarter of an hour later, he sent definite instructions: 'Tobruk must be held and the enemy must not be allowed to invest it. This means that Eighth Army must hold the line Acroma-El Adem and southwards and resist all enemy attempts to pass it. Having reduced your front by evacuating Gazala and reorganized your forces, this should be feasible, and I order you to do it.'

Had Auchinleck shared Ritchie's fears for the safety of Pienaar's and Ramsden's men and issued orders for their redeployment on 12 or 13 June when the danger to them was not so great, then perhaps the necessary arrangements could have been made in time. As it was, his second signal did not even reach Eighth Army HQ until 1520 on the 14th. Ritchie was then away visiting his Corps Commanders; he returned only at 1600. The retirement of the Gazala Line divisions was then due to begin in just two hours time and Ritchie rightly considered that it was far too late for the plans to be altered to comply with Auchinleck's new instructions and that any attempt to do so would only result in the sort of confusion which had so harmed Eighth Army in the past.

As already indicated, the retirement went surprisingly well. Ramsden's move westward on the night of 14–15 June was quite unexpected by an enemy whose attention was fixed on the coast road. Most of 50th Division was therefore able to break out successfully, though the troops were still arriving at the frontier as late as the evening of the 16th. Only the very last battalion to leave, 9th Durham Light Infantry, found its way barred by a finally alerted foe. Lieutenant Colonel Percy thereupon doubled back to join the rearguard of the South Africans.

The South African retreat was also more successful than could have been hoped. Daylight found much of the division still on the Via Balbia, 'bunched together and pouring back along a single narrow ribbon of communication – a situation' relates the RAF Official History, 'such as might present itself to ardent young commanders of ground attack squadrons in their dreams.' Yet such was the magnificent protection afforded by the Desert Air Force that just six soldiers were lost to strikes by the Axis airmen. Indeed the retirement was so well organized that Rommel quickly accepted he would not be able to cut off the bulk of Pienaar's men. Dividing his armour as usual, he sent his main force eastward, leaving only 15th Panzer to press on to the north. It reached the coast road at 1100, but by that time could trap only rearguard detachments. Even then the indomitable Percy managed to escape nearer to the coast with his battalion, accompanied by a number of stragglers.

1st South African and 50th Divisions were saved – but they could not be used to hold 'the line Acroma-El Adem and southwards' either. Moreover despite later suggestions to the contrary, it is clear that Auchinleck was well aware of this, at least by the evening of the 14th. Ritchie had sent a signal as early as 1030 – it crossed with those to him from Auchinleck – stating that he was 'building up as strong an armoured and infantry force as possible in the desert west of the frontier' but that he was withdrawing the South Africans and 50th Division 'into Army Reserve'. This surely indicated that these formations would not be among those held 'west of the frontier'; the only reason why Ritchie did not say this in so many words was because when the signal was sent, he saw no need to spell out the details of a move which had been envisaged for several months. Other signals followed, and at about 1730 Brigadier Davy, Auchinleck's Director of Military Operations, who had been at Eighth Army Headquarters almost all day, arrived back in Cairo, bringing with him, as the Official History confirms, all 'the latest information'.

Nonetheless Auchinleck remained adamant that 'the line Acroma-El Adem and southwards' should still be held, and Ritchie and Gott had in fact already intended to do so if possible; indeed before he received Auchinleck's orders, Ritchie, in his 1030 signal, had indicated that he hoped to make a stand in much this same area. Both Ritchie and Gott, however, were only too well aware that the new 'line' might not be able to hold firm for long. Ritchie's signal warned his superior of this and continued: 'Alternatives therefore are (a) to accept risk of temporary investment in Tobruk or (b) to go the whole hog, give up Tobruk and withdraw to the frontier. I am at any rate clearing all non-essentials out of Tobruk and making preparations for demolitions. Do you agree to me accepting the risk of investment in Tobruk?'

The wording of the signal shows that Ritchie did favour accepting the risk of investment in Tobruk. He did not want to lose the vast amounts of supplies there if this could be avoided. Neither did Gott, and their views were made still clearer in later signals on the same day. But of course the decision had to be that of Auchinleck as the superior officer. It was not an easy one to make, particularly as Ritchie had indicated that Auchinleck's own preferred alternative of holding on to Tobruk but without its being invested, was unlikely to prove possible. Understandably Auchinleck did not reply until 2040, but then he stated expressly that: 'On no account will any part of Eighth Army be allowed to be surrounded in Tobruk and invested there.' In which case surely Eighth Army should 'go the whole hog, give up Tobruk and withdraw to the frontier.'

Unhappily there was one more in this spate of signals still to come. It was from Churchill and it reached Auchinleck late that evening: 'To what position does Ritchie want to withdraw the Gazala troops? Presume there is no question in any case of giving up Tobruk. As long as Tobruk is held no serious enemy advance into Egypt is possible. We went through all this in April 1941. Do not understand what you mean by withdrawing to "old frontier".'[1]

It is difficult not to sympathize with Auchinleck's feelings when this message arrived, but it was clearly his duty to disregard Churchill's wishes if he thought they were ill-judged; he had after all done so often enough in the past, sometimes mistakenly. Perhaps though, that was just the trouble. It may be that Auchinleck was unwilling to risk any more adverse criticism from the Prime Minister.

Whatever the reason, at 1135 on 15 June Auchinleck informed Churchill that he hoped to hold the Acroma-El Adem Line and 'although I do not intend that Eighth Army should be besieged in Tobruk, I have no intention whatever of giving up Tobruk.' Next day the Prime Minister, who clearly wished there to be no room for doubt, replied: 'We are glad to have your assurance that there is no intention of giving up Tobruk. War Cabinet interpret your telegram to mean that, if need arises, General Ritchie would leave as many troops in Tobruk as are necessary to hold the place for certain.' To which, at 1515, Auchinleck confirmed: 'War Cabinet interpretation is correct. General Ritchie is putting into Tobruk what he considers an adequate force to hold it even if it should become temporarily isolated by enemy.'

Auchinleck, early on the morning of the 16th, had already signalled to Ritchie: 'Although I have made it clear to you that Tobruk must not be invested, I realize that its garrison may be isolated for short periods until our

1. General Sir Claude Auchinleck

2. Brigadier Jock Cambell VC with Lieutenant General Gott.

3. Rommel with some of his staff.

4. Kesselring and Rommel confer.

5. Stuart tank being prepared for action.

6. Matilda tanks moving up.

7. German Mark III with short 50mm gun.

8. The real tank killer: the German 88mm mobile gun.

9. Operation CRUSADER: British troops pass through the wire fence marking the Cyrenaican frontier.

10. Members of the Tobruk garrison and the New Zealanders meet at Ed Duda.

11. Crusader tank under repair.

12. British armoured cars on patrol.

13. German 8-wheeled heavy armoured car.

14. Boston bomber, just back from a raid.

15. Ritchie and his Corps Commanders. On his right, Norrie; on his left, Gott.

16. New weapons: the Grant tank.

17. New weapons: a British 6-pounder anti-tank gun.

18. New weapons: German Mark III Special, with long 50mm gun.

19. British infantry attacking.

20. British Valentine tanks advancing towards the 'Cauldron'.

21. Hurricane IID with 40mm anti-tank guns. These aircraft were first in action
in the fight for Bir Hacheim.

22. Junkers 88 Stuka dive-bombers setting out to attack Tobruk.

23. British prisoners captured at Tobruk.

24. Major General von Bismarck, Commander 21st Panzer Division, watching the assault on Tobruk.

25. British artillery falling back from the frontier.

26. General Freyberg wounded at Mersa Matruh. Despite the bandage round his head, his most serious wound was to his neck, just missing his jugular vein.

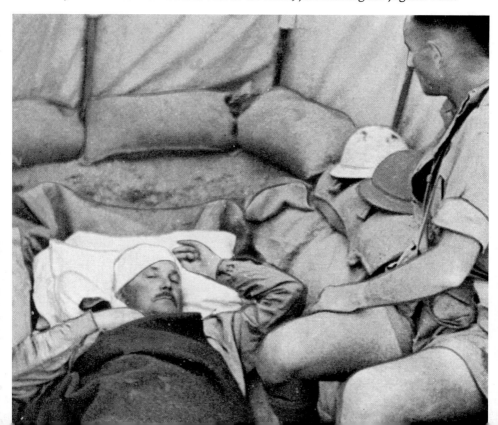

27. An Australian 25-pounder crew in action.

28. Australian infantry at Alamein.

29. Auchinleck at Alamein. He spent 'long hours staring through binoculars at the distant void horizon.'

30. Change of command. (Left to right) Alexander, Churchill, Montgomery and Brooke.

counter-offensive can be launched. With this possibility in mind you are free to organize the garrison as you think best.' Since no one has ever been able to explain the practical difference between 'isolation' and 'investment' – Auchinleck's staff at the time used both terms without distinction – in reality the first of the alternatives offered by Ritchie on the 14th had now been adopted and the risk of Tobruk being invested accepted by all concerned. And that risk had now become a near-certainty for the 'line Acroma-El Adem and southwards' had already been broken.

As mentioned earlier, Ritchie had always hoped to establish such a 'line' except that he preferred to base its north-western boundary not on Acroma but on the already prepared and garrisoned western perimeter of Tobruk – though a South African company under Captain French would hold Acroma as an outer bastion until the night of 18–19 June. The 29th Indian Brigade was still at El Adem, and the 20th Indian Brigade, which had recently been brought up to the front, was stationed on Eighth Army's old battle ground around Sidi Rezegh, though, as so often, in widely scattered positions.

Ritchie had also attempted to provide a strong force of tanks in the shape of an enlarged 4th Armoured Brigade to which were sent the remains of 2nd and 22nd Armoured together with the survivors of 1st Army Tank Brigade which had been all but destroyed in the early part of the battle. Brigadier Richards now commanded ninety tanks but as many of these badly needed maintenance he had retired temporarily to the area of Gambut. In addition, on 14 June, Auchinleck had urged that 'our tanks should be husbanded as a reserve of striking power and, therefore, should not engage enemy tanks unless at a great advantage.' There had already been instances where the infantry had not been properly supported by the armour and this decree would mean that in future 'our tanks' would often not engage at all – with catastrophic consequences.

While Churchill, Auchinleck and Ritchie had been sending out signals, Rommel had been acting. Early on 15 June he directed 21st Panzer, 90th Light and strong artillery units eastward. They were harried by the Desert Air Force, a particularly determined raid by No 6 Squadron's Hurricane IIDs destroying five tanks, five lorries and an anti-tank gun. In the course of this action, Flight Lieutenant Hillier pressed home his attack to such close range that his Hurricane struck a tank, knocking off its tail-wheel and the bottom of its rudder.In spite of this, Hillier returned safely to base. He later became the first anti-tank 'ace' with a score of at least nine destroyed before he was killed on 6 September, when, by a sad irony, he was demonstrating his technique to senior Army officers.

Such actions, however, could not halt the enemy advance. Though the main body of 29th Indian Brigade held firm at El Adem, a detached battalion, 3/12th Frontier Force Rifles, located to the north-west on the Axis bypass, was over-run in the late afternoon with the loss of 700 men as prisoners of war. That night, von Bismarck followed the road eastward to the old CRUSADER battle-ground, capturing Ed Duda early on the 16th. Rommel then ordered 15th Panzer and Trieste to 21st Panzer's aid, while Ariete moved south of El Adem to hold off any attempts by Eighth Army to counter-attack from that direction.

Thereafter the scattered British garrisons suffered a series of blows. By 1900 on the 16th, 21st Panzer had driven 1/6th Rajputana Rifles, detached from 20th Indian Brigade, out of Sidi Rezegh. 29th Indian Brigade still held out at El Adem, but Ariete had thwarted attempts by 7th Motor Brigade to go to its aid. Though Brigadier Reid wished to continue his gallant defence, Messervy, under whom both 20th and 29th Brigades had been placed, was now convinced that El Adem could not endure for more than another twenty-four hours. He therefore persuaded Ritchie and Norrie, despite their initial reluctance, to authorize Reid's retirement, which took place successfully on the night of the 16th–17th.

Meanwhile the main body of 20th Indian Brigade, though in a far less isolated position at Belhamed, was in even greater danger. On the afternoon of 17 June, 4th Armoured Brigade tried to move up to its assistance but was met by both 15th and 21st Panzer and lost thirty-two tanks, the majority it seems as a result of mechanical failures. Richards, short of fuel, then retired southward in accordance with his instructions that the armour should be 'husbanded'. That evening the Desert Air Force was compelled to withdraw from its advanced airfields at Gambut. Deprived of the support of both the armour and the airmen, 20th Brigade evacuated Belhamed at 2135, but next morning its luckless troops were attacked by German tanks and most of them were taken prisoner.

The withdrawal of 29th Brigade had almost certainly saved the majority of Reid's men from a similar fate, but, welcome though this was, it was not men but material that had constituted the principal Allied losses since 15 June. Though Auchinleck assured Ritchie on 17 June, that Rommel must have 'great anxiety over his fuel situation', the Germans had now broken into that area of supply dumps that had so crippled Eighth Army's freedom of movement since the start of the battle; all their reports refer gleefully to the 'extraordinary size' of the depots captured – full of food, ammunition, vehicles and petrol. With his maintenance problems temporarily solved and his morale uplifted, Rommel swung his forces north-eastward. On 18 June he cut the Via Balbia near Gambut and Tobruk was now unquestionably isolated.

Even so there still seemed every reason for hoping that Tobruk, as Auchinleck informed Field Marshal Smuts of South Africa, was 'only temporarily isolated'. Next day he offered a similar opinion to his superiors in London, reporting that: 'Tobruk should be able to hold out until operations for relief are successfully completed after resumption of our offensive.'

Though Auchinleck's belief that 'the enemy is exhausted and weakened and would give anything for a period of rest and reorganization' was premature, he did have justifiable reasons for his confidence. Tobruk was garrisoned by 2nd South African Division, its 4th and 6th Brigades holding the western and south-western perimeter of the defences. Though these units had seen little action, they could be relied upon to offer a resolute resistance in their well-protected positions, and in the event the blow would fall not on them but on the south-eastern part of the perimeter. This was secured by Brigadier Anderson's 11th Indian Brigade from 4th Indian Division. Its three battalions were 2nd Camerons, 2/5th Mahrattas and 2/7th Gurkhas, all veteran soldiers under very experienced leaders.

A number of other, chiefly South African, units added to the strength of the defenders, but the main reserve formation was 201st Guards Brigade under Brigadier Johnson. Though only 3rd Coldstreams was truly a Guards unit, its other battalions, 1st Sherwood Foresters and 1st Worcesters, were both redoubtable units though the last-named had lost all its heavy weapons in the course of its splendid defence of Point 187 on 14 June. Three field regiments and two medium regiments provided artillery support and there were sixty-nine anti-tank guns – though only eighteen of these were 6-pounders – and also it appears a few of the converted 3.7-inch AA guns. The armour consisted of some sixty Valentines and Matildas, mainly the former, in 32nd Army Tank Brigade. Its commander, Brigadier Willison, was a veteran of the previous siege and he had very capable subordinates including Eighth Army's latest VC, the valiant Foote. As Auchinleck informed Smuts, the defenders were also 'well supplied with necessities' – food, water, petrol, ammunition – sufficient for three months at the very least.[2]

The garrison's senior officer was the South African Major General Klopper, who unfortunately did lack experience, for he had only commanded his division for about a month, having previously been its chief staff officer. It would be highly unjust to put too much blame on the hapless Klopper, but it must be a matter of regret that Gott, who if he had recommended that Tobruk be invested should that prove necessary, was at least willing, indeed eager, to share its dangers, was not permitted to take control of the fortress. Had he done so, the story might well have been different.

Rommel began his preparations for the assault on Tobruk on 19 June. 90th Light, which captured Bardia on that day, and the newly-arrived Littorio Armoured Division, were left to hold off any British threat from the frontier. The Italian infantry divisions were ordered to make diversionary moves against the western perimeter. The Afrika Korps, with Ariete and

Trieste on its left, pushed forward opposite the positions held by 11th Indian Brigade. This was the area in which 70th Division had broken out during the CRUSADER fighting and the minefields there had been much reduced at that time and again at a later date when many of their mines had been used to strengthen the fields protecting the Gazala Line.

The assault began at 0520 on the 20th, the first blow coming not from the Axis Army but from the Luftwaffe. A few hours earlier, Ritchie had signalled to Auchinleck that it appeared that Rommel was about to 'turn his main attention to Tobruk' and warned him that the enemy had 'removed our air threat from Gambut group of aerodromes.' It is probable that his superior was not too concerned, since on the 16th he had informed Churchill that the Desert Air Force could 'operate fighter aircraft over Tobruk even if use of Gambut landing grounds should be temporarily denied to us.'

Unhappily though, this was just what could not be done. With the Gambut airfields gone, the Desert Air Force was compelled to fall back to Mersa Matruh, almost 200 miles further east. Though light bombers could still reach Tobruk from there, fighters or fighter-bombers could not without long-range tanks, only a few of which were readily available. The loss of Gambut really doomed Tobruk, for Kesselring had massed some eighty Junkers Ju 87 Stuka dive-bombers to blast a way through the remaining minefields as well as to strike at the hapless 2/5th Mahrattas on whom the assault of the Afrika Korps would fall. Three Stukas were shot down by AA fire but this was the only opposition they had to face. As the German accounts at the time note succinctly: 'They flew without interference, for the RAF had been driven off Gambut airfield, and the Luftwaffe had no Huren-kähne to harass them.'[3]

Under cover of this raid, which von Mellenthin describes as 'one of the most spectacular attacks I have ever seen', and which was reinforced by every gun that Rommel could bring to bear, the Afrika Korps broke through the Mahrattas' defences at about 0820. A counter-attack by the Gurkhas was also thrown back. Though the Gurkhas continued to hold their own positions at the extreme eastern end of the perimeter, while the Camerons were able to beat off the attacks of Ariete, the fatal breach had already been made.

Now the inexperience of Klopper and his staff proved calamitous, though in fairness to them it should be remembered that they were not helped by having their headquarters attacked repeatedly by the Stukas which, throughout the day, were in constant action as 'flying artillery' for their ground-troops. It was rightly realized that a counter-attack by 32nd Army Tank Brigade and the Guards Brigade was desperately needed, but muddled orders resulted in the execution of this being delayed, the infantry and the armour failed to co-operate with each other, and the two armoured regiments involved were brought into action separately. Only after 4th Royal Tanks, the first to engage, had been destroyed soon after mid-day, did 7th Royal Tanks come up; it had suffered a similar fate by about 1400.

Though the enemy armour undoubtedly suffered losses also – Rommel would have only forty-four German and fourteen Italian tanks available when he resumed his advance to the frontier – its progress was hardly checked, let alone halted. By 1400, both panzer divisions had reached 'King's Cross' as the junction between the coast road and the road south-west to El Adem was called. There they separated. 21st Panzer, with the aggressive von Bismarck leading his tanks in the sidecar of a motor-cycle, thrust northwards to the town proper of Tobruk, which was entered at about 1900, the area commander, Brigadier Thompson, being captured on a roof-top where he was personally manning a machine-gun.

Meanwhile, on von Bismarck's left, 15th Panzer, still led, in von Vaerst's absence, by Colonel Crasemann, accompanied by the Afrika Korps Commander Nehring – whose efforts were to be rewarded by promotion to full General – fell on 1st Sherwood Foresters and 3rd Coldstream Guards, who were forced to surrender by 1900, apart from one Guards company under Major Sainthill which withdrew westward to join the 1st Worcesters. 15th Panzer's advance had also threatened Klopper's headquarters. Believing, wrongly as it transpired, that this was about to be over-run, Klopper retired to the headquarters of the 6th South African Brigade in the north-west of the perimeter, after ordering the destruction of all documents, equipment and wireless-sets. This was the final misfortune as it ended Klopper's ability to control the battle. In consequence, no counter-attacks, which might still have proved embarrassing to Rommel, since he was very weak in infantry, were delivered that night.

Nor had any help been received from the main body of Eighth Army. Auchinleck had urged the launching of a major counter-offensive on 20 June against the German forces attacking Tobruk. Field Marshal Carver calls this scheme 'ambitious and, in the circumstances, totally impractical' but as the message did not reach Eighth Army HQ until 2120, it was in any case irrelevant. Ritchie had already given orders at about mid-day to bring as much pressure as possible on the enemy, but since the only unit in a position to do so, 7th Motor Brigade, was still operating in 'Jock Columns', its efforts, as might have been expected, had virtually no effect.

Accordingly, Ritchie could only suggest to Klopper that he break out towards the frontier with as many troops as he could muster. Klopper at first made preparations to do so, but by about 0600 on 21 June, feeling that such an attempt could only result in 'terrible casualties', he changed his mind. Soon afterwards, a white flag was raised above the fortress which the year before had been the symbol of British resistance to the Axis powers, though the Gurkhas did not surrender until that evening or the Camerons until early on the 22nd. A few brave individuals did not surrender at all. Lieutenant Bailie and Sergeant Norton brought small parties of South Africans to safety, while Major Sainthill, remarking that the Coldstream Guards did not know how to surrender as they had never practised such a manoeuvre, led 199 of his own men and 188 South Africans in a successful break-out to the south-west. A handful of stragglers from the Coldstreams, under the command of Sergeants Brown and Turner, refused to surrender either, and they too ultimately made good their escape to the Allied lines.

Such acts of gallantry could scarcely disguise the extent of Rommel's success. He had captured 19,000 British soldiers, nearly 9,000 white and over 1,700 black South Africans,[4] 2,500 Indians, guns, ammunition, 5,000 tons of food, 2,000 serviceable vehicles, 1,400 tons of petrol – and he had won his Field Marshal's baton. It was a triumph from which he would never fully recover.

Notes

1   It is not clear how Churchill received this information. The Minister of State, Mr Casey, had certainly warned him that the divisions in the Gazala Line were retiring but he had made no mention of 'the old frontier'. Nor was information to this effect sent to Churchill by Eighth Army; it would not indeed have been proper for Eighth Army to have done so. The Prime Minister therefore can only have learned of it from Auchinleck's headquarters in Cairo, which would appear to provide further confirmation that Auchinleck was well aware of the true situation at least by the evening of 14 June.

2   The garrison might have been still larger had the main strength of 20th Indian Brigade attempted to retire to Tobruk instead of heading for the frontier – and destruction by the panzers – as previously described. Since, however, it seems most unlikely that such a course of action would have brought about Tobruk's salvation, the brigade's fate would merely have been postponed.

3   Heinz Werner Schmidt: *With Rommel in the Desert*. Schmidt was at this time a captain in 15th Panzer's 115th Motorized Infantry Regiment.

4   The black South Africans were line of communications troops only; it was the white South Africans who fought and if necessary died. It should be remembered, however, that, black or white, all the South Africans were volunteers.

8

FALSE DAWN

There is a need for new blood, and a more rapid interchange between the Middle East and home, and particularly among the commanders. All spoke in the highest terms of 'Strafer' Gott, but he had been two years in the desert without a break, and had gone through the hardest fighting from beginning to end. His experience would have been invaluable at home, but everyone said that he would not last much longer unless he had relief from the strain. The same is true of many lesser men.

Colonel Jacob's Diary.
6 August, 1942.

It would appear that Rommel was so dazzled by attaining the objective that had so long eluded him that he forgot that if the Axis powers were to conquer first North Africa, then the Middle East, the great prize was not Tobruk but Malta. Its capture would secure the Axis supply lines and so make an Axis victory certain – or at least as certain as anything in war ever can be.

Of course there were other possibilities. Rommel might be able to over-run Egypt even without Malta falling. He might be able to hold the Martuba airfields for so long that Malta would be starved into surrender. These roads to success would remain open for some time to come – the first until September, 1942, the second until November, 1942. But neither could compare with the prospects offered by a direct attack on Malta, and it was just this which Hitler was planning.

On 30 April, Mussolini and Cavallero had been summoned to the Führer's presence to hear an exposition of what Hitler called the 'Great Plan'. The first part of this had been achieved by 21 June with the capture of Tobruk. It had, however, been Hitler's intention that Panzerarmee Afrika would then halt on the Cyrenaican-Egyptian frontier while he mounted Operation HERCULES.

This was an assault upon Malta originally destined to take place on 10 July. It is difficult to see how it could have failed for by this time attacks by U-boats and by Italian midget-submarines, together with the need to send reinforcements to counter the Japanese threat in the Indian Ocean, had greatly reduced the strength of the Royal Navy in the eastern Mediterranean. It possessed, for instance, not one single battleship or aircraft carrier fit for action. Moreover Rommel's most recent conquests had given Axis bombers new bases from which to raid Alexandria. The Navy therefore evacuated it, sending some vessels to the Red Sea through the Suez Canal and others to rearward bases in Palestine, from which they would have found it difficult to interfere with the planned seaborne invasion of Malta, though, in any case, the Italians had agreed to provide a heavy naval escort. Further assaults would be made on Malta from the air by a German parachute brigade and the equivalent of three Italian parachute battalions. In all 35,000 Axis soldiers would take part in Operation HERCULES and they would be supported by every fighter and bomber that Kesselring could muster.

These bright prospects were now wantonly thrown away by Rommel. Intoxicated by the supplies that had fallen into his hands in or around Tobruk, he felt that all his logistical anxieties had been solved. Acting on his own initiative, he appealed directly to Hitler:

> The morale and condition of the troops, the quantity of stores captured and the present weakness of the enemy make it possible for us to thrust onwards into the heart of Egypt. Therefore request that the Duce be prevailed upon to remove the present restrictions on movement and that all troops now under my command be placed at my disposal to continue the offensive.

It was not a suggestion that was well received in many quarters. Westphal, Rommel's prudent Chief Operations Officer, warned him that supplies would never last until the Suez Canal was reached. Bastico, Rommel's official superior, on 22 June actually commanded him to halt. The Italian General Staff, the German Naval Staff and General von Rintelen, the German military attaché in Rome, all voiced their opposition. On the 21st, Field Marshal Kesselring flew to meet Rommel. He pointed out that forces from Malta were again menacing the Axis convoys. To counter this threat he must withdraw the bulk of his units to Sicily; they would thus be unable to support Rommel's advance. 'Kesselring maintained' says von Mellenthin who was present at this conference, 'that the only sound course was to stick to the original plan and postpone an invasion of Egypt until Malta had fallen.'

But, as Kesselring would later complain in his *Memoirs*, 'at that period Rommel exercised an almost hypnotic influence over Hitler, who was all but incapable of appreciating the situation objectively.' The German dictator strongly supported the views of his latest Field Marshal. Mussolini, with still less excuse, for even now he pointed out that the success of an attack on Egypt depended principally on the safe passage of supplies to North Africa, also went with the tide. 'And so' says General Jackson, 'the fatal decision which was to lose the North African campaign for the Axis was taken. Malta was spared, and Rommel was authorized to advance into Egypt.' 'Three opportunists' declares Ronald Lewin, 'the Führer, the Duce and the Axis field commander, had in effect destroyed the last chance of retaining a presence in Africa.'

In fact, from the Axis point of view, it was not quite as bad as that. There was after all, a chance that Malta might still be starved into submission or that Rommel might still be able to conquer Egypt even if Malta did not fall. His prospects of so doing, however, would only become good at a later date when he had received heavy reinforcements of men and material. For the present it is worth pointing out that even after the capture of Tobruk, Eighth Army still had many more men, tanks, guns and supplies than did Rommel, while every mile he advanced into Egypt would ensure that his supply line would become more dangerously stretched. It did not seem to occur to him that the booty of Tobruk offered false promises: that without spare parts his captured vehicles would quickly become unserviceable; that once his captured ammunition had been fired his captured guns would be useless. Or perhaps it did, but he meant to take the risk anyway; he later called his move 'a plan with a chance of success – a try-on'.

Rommel's 'chance of success' was further reduced when Ritchie, on Gott's advice, decided not to fight on the frontier after all but to fall back all the way to Mersa Matruh, thereby aggravating the enemy's supply problems. This again could be construed as contrary to Auchinleck's orders and that officer, as he remarks in his official Despatch, 'was by no means happy at the decision.' Nonetheless, at a meeting of the Middle East Defence Committee on 21 June, the other members, Casey, Tedder and the new naval C-in-C Mediterranean, Admiral Sir Henry Harwood, victor of the Battle of the River Plate, all supported Ritchie – an attitude which presumably did not make Auchinleck any more happy.

On 25 June, Auchinleck reported to Brooke that Ritchie was 'apt to be slow' – a fault unlikely to be cured by bombarding him with directions from Cairo – that Eighth Army had 'to some extent lost confidence' in Richie as its leader, and that he, Auchinleck, would take personal command of the

Army that afternoon. Probably he had little choice in the matter. Churchill, Brooke, Casey and Tedder had all been urging this step for some time and Brooke and Tedder had made clear their rejection of Auchinleck's alternative suggestion that he appoint Corbett in Ritchie's place. There appears little doubt that had Auchinleck not assumed direct responsibility, he would have been compelled to resign, and this, quite naturally and understandably, he had no desire to do.[1]

It seemed that Auchinleck had at least chosen a good moment on which to take over. On the late afternoon of 26 June, the Battle of Mersa Matruh began in circumstances which greatly favoured the Allies. The folly of Rommel's 'try-on' was already becoming apparent. His Italian troops, who in any case numbered only 6,000 men and some forty tanks of little value, were still making their way up to the front-line. Only his three German divisions were immediately available and they were at last nearing exhaustion after their continuous activity since 26 May. Moreover they contained a mere 2,500 infantrymen between them and 15th and 21st Panzer together had only sixty tanks, of which about a quarter were Mark IIs. Rommel was also getting very short of transport vehicles which, ever since he had crossed the frontier on 23 June, had been subjected to sustained attacks by Coningham's Bostons, Hurribombers and Kittybombers.

The Desert Air Force, which as well as its British units contained two Australian and no less than ten South African squadrons, was the more effective because the Axis air-arm, now commanded by Lieutenant General Otto von Waldau, had been left well behind Rommel's ground forces and was further handicapped by being given a low priority for supplies. The consequences were well demonstrated on 26 June. The men of the Desert Air Force flew literally from dawn to dusk – and indeed thereafter for Flight Sergeant Joyce, a Hurricane pilot of No 73 Squadron, shot down a Junkers Ju 88 that night. The two Australian Kittyhawk squadrons were particularly hard-worked – No 3 Squadron RAAF flew ten missions either as bomber-escorts or on fighter-bomber raids but lost its CO, Squadron Leader Barr, shot down to become a prisoner of war; No 450 Squadron RAAF flew eight missions, mainly to provide fighter-cover for the Bostons.

Also on the 26th, the Axis airmen made a valiant attempt to aid their own troops – but to little effect. The Hurricanes of 213 Squadron had an especially good day, shooting down five enemy fighters without loss in one combat and destroying three Stukas and damaging four more, again without loss, in a later encounter. By the end of the day, not only were the German pilots physically exhausted but their fuel supplies were exhausted as well. As a result, one fighter Gruppe[2] was able to fly only a single mission with four aircraft on the 27th, while another was grounded entirely on the 28th.

By contrast, Eighth Army was supported by a dominant air force, was of

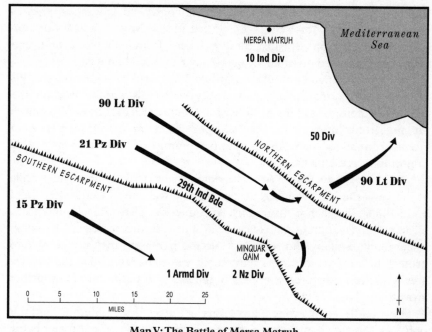

Map V: The Battle of Mersa Matruh.

superior strength and contained new fresh formations. Norrie's XXX Corps had retired a further 120 miles to prepare the defences in the 'bottle-neck' at El Alamein, but to replace it Auchinleck had finally and reluctantly, with many reminders of the 'grave risk of internal trouble' that he was running, been persuaded to bring forward from Syria the 10th Indian Division and the 4th and 5th Brigades of the 2nd New Zealand Division. 10th Indian formed part of X Corps, commanded by Lieutenant General William Holmes, to which the two remaining brigades of Ramsden's 50th (British) Division were now transferred. The Indians held Mersa Matruh while 50th Division was stationed to the south-east, both being protected by mine-fields. Together they covered the area between the coast and an escarpment some ten miles to the south.

A further ten miles or so southward was a second larger escarpment, the gap between the two being protected by more minefields. Behind these were positioned detachments from 29th Indian Brigade, the bulk of which was to be found on the southern escarpment. This brigade formed part of Gott's XIII Corps, as did Freyberg's New Zealanders who were stationed at Minquar Qaim to the east of 29th Brigade. South of the southern escarpment was Lumsden's 1st Armoured Division, now made up of both 4th and

22nd Armoured Brigades, which together controlled 159 tanks, sixty of them Grants. 7th Motor Brigade and 3rd Indian Motor Brigade were on Lumsden's left flank. Against these defences Rommel's weak, tired and largely unsupported divisions should really have stood no chance.

Late on 25 June, Auchinleck notified his Corps Commanders of his tactical and strategical aims – they would be his watchwords for the remainder of his time in the Middle East. With regard to tactics, Auchinleck announced his intention 'to keep all troops fluid and mobile, and strike at enemy from all sides. Armour not to be committed unless very favourable opportunity presents itself.'

It is not clear how Eighth Army was supposed to strike from all sides while at the same time 'husbanding' its armour, but the crucial words were 'fluid and mobile'. In order to ensure this, Auchinleck as General Jackson reports, 'ordered the creation of mobile battle groups within each brigade based on the available artillery and transport. No more infantry than was needed to protect the guns and could be kept mobile was to be retained in the forward area' – the rest was to be sent back to the Alamein position or even further away to the Nile Delta.

These battle groups were really larger, stronger 'Jock Columns' and not only was it unwise to make such changes in organization when a major battle was clearly imminent but their introduction naturally weakened the infantry formations. Freyberg refused point-blank to consider breaking up his brigades in this way, claiming his responsibility to his own government as his justification, but 29th Brigade was less lucky and would suffer accordingly.

'Fluidity and mobility' also tended to encourage a still greater dispersal of the British artillery. Auchinleck did appreciate the danger of this and hoped to counter it by an increased co-operation between the various units. Unhappily such problems as dust-storms, bad going, air attack or communications failure meant that in practice a concentration of artillery fire would only be achieved when Auchinleck's subordinates or Auchinleck's successors abandoned his 'fluid and mobile' tactics.

As for Auchinleck's future strategy, his message to his Corps Commanders on 25 June stated that he 'no longer intended to fight a decisive action at Matruh' but would engage the enemy over the whole area between 'Matruh and the El Alamein gap'. 'At all costs' Auchinleck declared, 'and even if ground has to be given up, intend to keep Eighth Army in being and to give no hostage to fortune in shape of immobile troops holding localities which can easily be isolated.' In particular, as he would later confirm in his official Despatch, 'in no circumstances was any part of the Eighth Army to be allowed to be shut up in Matruh, even if this involved abandoning the position entirely.'

'As a result of Auchinleck's new policy' states Field Marshal Carver bluntly, 'everybody assumed that withdrawal was planned.' Auchinleck's 'firm decision not to allow an investment of Matruh' reports Ronald Lewin, 'combined with his declared policy "to keep the Eighth Army in being", tended to make his subordinates look over their shoulders and, rather than fight today, prefer withdrawal and the hope of fighting some other day.' Von Mellenthin confirms this from the enemy's point of view, adding severely: 'A battle cannot be fought in this fashion; if Auchinleck did not feel strong enough to fight at Matruh he should have gone back to Alamein. If he did want to fight at Matruh – and his forces were ample for a successful defence – then he should not have given his subordinates the idea that this was only a delaying action. As a result of Auchinleck's hesitation, the British not only lost a great opportunity of destroying the Panzerarmee but suffered a serious defeat.'

As was mentioned earlier, Rommel began his attack on the afternoon of 26 June, once again separating his armoured divisions for this purpose. 15th Panzer attacked south of the southern escarpment but was easily checked by 1st Armoured Division. By sheer ill-luck, both 21st Panzer and 90th Light attacked the weakest part of the defences between the escarpments, routing the mobile columns from 29th Brigade stationed there. They continued to advance next day, the 27th, and at dawn 90th Light came into contact with 50th Division, falling on the isolated 9th Battalion, Durham Light Infantry which it also routed, taking 300 prisoners. In the course of this encounter, Private Wakenshaw had his left arm blown off by a shell. In spite of this, he continued to fire his 2-pounder anti-tank gun, destroying at least one enemy gun before another shell killed him outright. He was awarded a posthumous VC.

Meanwhile 21st Panzer had engaged 2nd New Zealand Division. This attack was thrown back, but during the afternoon the Germans began to outflank the New Zealanders. At about 1700, Divisional Headquarters was heavily shelled, Freyberg being seriously wounded in the neck.[3] The German tanks, eager as usual for easy victims, also managed to scatter the New Zealand transport. Yet still the defenders held firm. In fact it was 21st Panzer which was now in a dangerous situation. It could make no progress against the New Zealanders, was threatened by counter-attacks from units of 1st Armoured Division and had no possibility of linking up with 15th Panzer, which was also pinned down, very short of both fuel and ammunition. 90th Light was in even greater danger. It resumed its advance during the afternoon of the 27th, cutting the coastal road east of Mersa Matruh soon after dark. This looked serious, but 90th Light contained only 1,600 men who were now fifteen miles away from support. It could easily have been destroyed before help could reach it.

'Concerted attacks by the greatly superior British forces' von Mellenthin informs us, 'could have terminated the existence of Panzerarmee Afrika.' 'We should have obliterated the lot' lamented Lumsden afterwards. According to Field Marshal Carver, if 'Eighth Army had delivered a resolute and properly organized counter-attack either on 27 or 28 June, the subsequent battles on the El Alamein line might never have been necessary.'

Instead the British commanders were 'looking over their shoulders' and their tendency to do so was increased when just before mid-day on the 27th, Auchinleck signalled to both Gott and Holmes that if they had to withdraw, their corps should fall back together to Fuka some thirty miles to the east. Hardly surprisingly this message seemed to them a confirmation that Auchinleck 'no longer intended to fight a decisive action at Matruh.'

As a result, Gott, who had observed the rout of the New Zealand transport and erroneously believed that the division had been over-run, ordered his corps to disengage at 1920. 1st Armoured Division and the remnants of 29th Indian Brigade duly retired towards Fuka but the latter formation was overtaken by the German tanks and dispersed on the following evening. The New Zealanders were cut off but broke out successfully on the night of 27–28 June, inflicting very heavy losses on their enemy in the process.

Despite later accusations to the contrary, Gott did advise Auchinleck of his decision to withdraw and his superior promptly notified Holmes. More ill-luck now intervened for communications problems prevented the message from reaching X Corps until 0430 on the 28th. Auchinleck then instructed Holmes to 'slip out tonight with whole force on broad front' – not an easy feat considering that the lagging Italians were at last arriving to re-inforce 90th Light. Holmes had to fight his way clear, which he did on the night of the 28th–29th, though at the cost of some 6,000 men and numerous supplies. Rommel had won another incredible – and frankly undeserved – victory. It convinced him that he should follow his star onwards to Alexandria and Cairo.

On 1 July, Rommel thrust into 'the El Alamein gap'. Liddell Hart calls this 'the most dangerous moment of the struggle in Africa', but it is difficult to support this contention, especially since he then admits that in reality 'the British situation was never so desperate as it outwardly appeared.' For a start, Rommel was outnumbered even more heavily than usual. His Italian troops were again unable to assist him for, as at Mersa Matruh, they had fallen well behind and were still moving up along the coast road. This left him with only some 1,500 German infantrymen with which to face an Eighth Army that had just been reinforced by two more infantry brigades, and with only fifty-five tanks, no more than fifteen of which were the new Mark III

Specials, with which to oppose a British armoured force that as late as 3 July after two days of fighting would still contain in 1st Armoured Division alone 119 tanks, thirty-eight of them Grants.

Rommel's soldiers were not only few in number, perhaps more important they had, as Alan Moorehead relates, 'reached the limit of physical despair.' Von Mellenthin declares that both the panzer divisions and 90th Light were by now 'very weak and utterly exhausted'; 'exhausted and attenuated' is Field Marshal Carver's description. Even in its War Diary 90th Light laments that it was not allowed 'to have a swim in the sea and to sleep its fill' after its victory at Mersa Matruh but was hounded on ever eastward. Now the strain suddenly became too much to bear. As Moorehead openly admits, the German advance was halted:

> . . . not because Rommel made a mistake, or because Auchinleck achieved an eleventh-hour miracle, but because the German army was exhausted. It could do no more. The German soldiers were wearied to the point where they had no more reserves either of body or of will-power.

By contrast, says von Mellenthin sadly, the Axis soldiers 'were compelled to tackle fortifications manned by resolute troops in good physical condition.' Not all the Allied troops were in fact in fortifications but certainly most of them were comparatively fresh. Some, such as 6th New Zealand Brigade and 18th Indian Brigade, had taken no part at all in the recent fighting, having only just arrived at the front. 1st South African Division had had a week's rest strengthening the defences at El Alamein. 4th and 5th New Zealand Brigades had only re-joined Eighth Army shortly before seeing action at Mersa Matruh. They may not have benefited from that experience but they were much less tired than the German soldiers who had been in virtually continuous action for about a month.

Eighth Army's companion-in-arms, the Desert Air Force, had also received reinforcements. A second Spitfire squadron, No 601, had joined No 145, flying its first sorties on 27 June. Tedder – who on 1 July was promoted to Air Chief Marshal – had also sent forward two squadrons of Hurricanes previously defending the Canal zone, together with the equivalent of two more from Operational Training Units. Moreover Tedder had other aircraft readily available in Egypt which were not part of the Desert Air Force as such, and proportionally far more Allied machines than Axis machines were serviceable. To assist Eighth Army, Tedder could at any given moment find 65 Wellingtons, 30 Bostons, 30 Baltimores, 170 Hurricanes, 60 Kittyhawks and 20 Spitfires.[4] Whereas, even in theory, Rommel could expect the aid of only forty bombers and fifty-five fighters and these were again lagging far behind their ground forces and were often simply not there when required. On 30 June for instance, the Allied pilots did not encounter a single enemy aeroplane.

As if these disadvantages were not enough, Rommel's supply line, which had been stretched too far and was highly vulnerable to the superior Allied air strength, was on the point of breaking down completely. While Eighth Army was so close to its bases that its every need could be met, Panzerarmee Afrika was desperately short of petrol, ammunition, food and water. The problem was so serious that when Kesselring and Cavallero – who had now also been promoted to the rank of Marshal – joined Rommel for a conference on 26 June, both insisted that he ought not to advance beyond El Alamein whatever happened in view of the serious supply difficulties which must be expected; so serious that Rommel could not spare the fuel for a reconnaissance of his enemy's positions; so serious that Rommel's choice of attack-routes was restricted still further than the already limited choice imposed on him by geography.

The Eighth Army's defences at El Alamein at this period did not really form a 'line' at all but were a series of separate strongpoints guarding the El Alamein 'gap'. This was thirty-eight miles in width, its boundary-markers being, to the north the little ridge of Tell el Alamein, the hill of twin cairns,

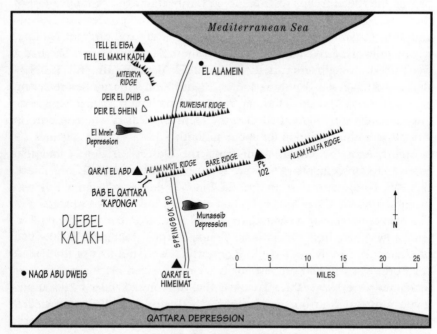

Map VI: The Alamein 'Line'.

and to the south, the 700-foot-high Qaret el Himeimat – Mount Himeimat. North of El Alamein was the Mediterranean; south of Himeimat was the Qattara Depression, a vast, chocolate-coloured quicksand lying 200 feet below sea-level through which no vehicles could pass, beyond which again was the almost equally impassible Great Sand Sea. If Rommel wished to reach Cairo and Alexandria he would have to do so through the 'gap'.

Better still from the British point of view, other geographical features within the 'gap' allowed Rommel just three possible lines of advance. From the railway station on the El Alamein Ridge, level ground ran away to the south – though the long, low Miteirya Ridge lay to the south-west – until some eight miles away the rocky Ruweisat Ridge rose threateningly ahead. The first avenue of advance was north of this. The second lay between the ridge and another series of high points some seven miles further south. This began in the west with the peak of Qaret el Abd, continued with the Alam Nayil Ridge, became the Bare Ridge and finally rose triumphantly to the ridge of Alam el Halfa – or plain Alam Halfa, as the soldiers called it. The final means of advance was between these features and the great Qattara Depression. North and north-east of Qaret el Himeimat, vehicles could find plenty of good going, but to the north-west, steep escarpments restricted an attacker to a narrow funnel north of Djebel Kalakh.

Some two months later, by which time this funnel was already in his hands, Rommel would deliver his last attempt to reach the Nile – it would be called the Battle of Alam Halfa – through this southern route. On 1 July he had neither the time nor the petrol to consider such a move. This may have been fortunate, for XIII Corps, which held the southern half of the Alamein defences, did not enjoy much protection from 'fortifications'. 4th and 5th New Zealand Brigades held a natural fortress at Deir el Munassib – the Munassib Depression – between Alam Nayil and Himeimat, from which they could cover both the central and the southern avenues of advance. To the west were two isolated 'boxes' – one at Bab el Qattara, a pass lying close to Qaret el Abd; the other at Naqb abu Dweis, south-west of Djebel Kalakh and some fifteen miles from Himeimat. The former, called 'Kaponga' by its defenders, 6th New Zealand Brigade, helped to guard the central route, but the Naqb abu Dweis position, held by 9th Indian Brigade, was too remote to have much practical value. In addition the Corps was supported only by armoured cars since all the British tanks had gathered further north.

In the north, where Rommel did attack, the 'fortifications' protecting Norrie's XXX Corps were much more worthy of the name. The most secure was the 'box' at El Alamein, where 3rd South African Brigade sheltered behind sizable minefields. 1st and 2nd South African Brigades were stationed between this and the Ruweisat Ridge, while to the south of them

Norrie had hastily prepared a further 'box', also partially protected by mine-fields, at Deir el Shein, a shallow depression near the western end of the Ruweisat Ridge, which was manned by 18th Indian Brigade. 1st Armoured Division guarded the South Africans' flanks, its 4th Armoured Brigade between the Alamein 'box' and Pienaar's other two brigades, its 22nd Armoured Brigade astride the Ruweisat Ridge covering the South Africans' left rear and in a position from which it could block either the northern or the central routes of advance. 50th Division – transferred to Norrie from X Corps – was in reserve, north of the eastern end of the Alam Halfa Ridge.

In these circumstances it would have been a miracle had Rommel's 'try-on' succeeded and this was already clear to the bolder spirits in Eighth Army. Brigadier Inglis, who had replaced the wounded Freyberg in temporary command of 2nd New Zealand Division, best summed up their attitude. To defeat Rommel, he maintained, 'all Eighth Army needed to do was face westwards and fight.'

Unhappily, not every senior officer was so confident. 'It may be thought' the Official History remarks with its usual restraint:

> . . . that General Auchinleck should have declared that it was now 'Backs to the Wall' and that the Army, reinforced by every possible man and gun from Egypt, and fully supported by the Middle East air force, would die where it stood. Certainly such an order would have cleared away much bewilderment and doubt.

It was not given. The best that Auchinleck could manage was a message to his Army on 30 June to the effect that Rommel was 'stretched to the limit', hoped to 'take Egypt by bluff' and should be shown 'where he gets off' – not a bad summary of Rommel's position but scarcely inspirational.

Auchinleck's attitude is understandable enough when the reason for it is realized. As the Official History explains:

> . . . he felt that although he had a good chance to stop Rommel and fully intended to try, it would be wrong to ignore the possi-bility that once more his own rather loosely-knit army might be outmanoeuvred or outfought. Above all, he decided, it must be kept in being. Therefore it might have to retreat again.

Though Auchinleck undoubtedly intended to retreat only as an unwelcome last resort, this was certainly not the impression he gave when late on 28 June he announced his intentions both to Brooke in London and to senior officers in Eighth Army by way of Middle East Headquarters in Cairo. He merely said that he would impose the 'utmost delay possible' at El Alamein and that only if it could be achieved 'without entailing encirclement or destruction of Eighth Army'. If 'withdrawal from El Alamein position' should be 'forced upon us', the South Africans would retire to Alexandria where they would join 9th Australian Division, then on its way up to the front, while the remainder of Eighth Army would fall back to Cairo. As if that was not dispiriting enough, on 1 July in the midst of the fighting, Auchinleck, as at Mersa Matruh, again reminded his Corps Commanders of his 'provisional orders covering a possible withdrawal eastwards, should this prove necessary.'

To make matters worse, as the Official History notes, Auchinleck took a number of measures which 'seemed to the men in the ranks inconsistent with a firm determination to fight.' In particular, it was certainly not the case that 'every possible man and gun' was being used to hold the Alamein positions. On the contrary, the remainder of X Corps apart from 50th Division had been sent all the way back to the Nile Delta, as had the 'surplus infantry' from Auchinleck's new battle groups. There was thus an appalling risk that, as at Mersa Matruh, everyone would feel that a delaying action only was to be fought. In which case Eighth Army might well be kept in being by the simple method of withdrawing it as fast as possible.

Indeed it is quite clear that both Corbett, whom Auchinleck had left in charge in Cairo, and Gott were convinced that this was the case, and the latter in particular was totally discouraged as a result. Major General Sir Howard Kippenberger relates in his memoirs, *Infantry Brigadier* – he commanded 5th New Zealand Brigade – that on 29 June Gott told him that 'a general retirement and evacuation of Egypt was in contemplation.' The sturdy Kippenberger protested that 'we were perfectly fit to fight and that it was criminal to give up Egypt' but that evening, he tells us, 'a provisional order for our retirement arrived from XIII Corps. It certainly envisaged the abandonment of Egypt.'

Yet by an extraordinary irony, this danger was to be averted by one of Eighth Army's greatest faults – 'indiscipline at the top'. Lieutenant General Willoughby Norrie is normally dismissed rather slightingly as brave, charming but not very decisive. It will be recalled, however, that earlier, especially during CRUSADER, he had put forward a number of valuable suggestions which his superiors had rejected to their cost. It may be that the memory of these now served to stiffen Norrie's resolve. In any event, unlike Gott, Norrie was not disheartened by Auchinleck's depressing 'provisional orders'. He simply ignored them.

He did more. He took the action that the Official History believes Auchinleck should have taken. In the words of General Jackson: 'Fortunately Norrie on whom Rommel's main blow was to fall, had made up his mind and had told his subordinates that this *was* the last ditch. XXX Corps would fight and die where it stood.' This attitude was also backed by

Pienaar, for though that officer – more irony – was personally all in favour of a retreat, he was equally determined that the South Africans should fight to the utmost at El Alamein so as to wipe out the stain of Klopper's surrender at Tobruk.

Having taken the first step, Norrie and Pienaar, the former in particular, then proceeded to carry their indiscipline a stage further. Rommel would later give high credit to the British tactics on 1 July. In fact it is difficult to feel that these were very impressive and it would seem that Rommel's praise was intended, consciously or unconsciously, to conceal the real cause of his misfortunes, his own strategic blunder in pressing deep into Egypt with an inadequate supply line. What is really interesting though, is that the tactics, whatever their quality, were not those of the Commander of Eighth Army. Auchinleck's wishes, it may be remembered, were to keep all forces 'fluid and mobile' and to 'give no hostage to fortune in the shape of immobile troops holding localities which can easily be isolated.'

These ideas were again ignored by Norrie and Pienaar. They were determined that Eighth Army should on the contrary remain static, 'anchoring its operations' says Field Marshal Carver, 'on the fixed defences of El Alamein and taking little account' of Auchinleck's 'concept of moving columns of artillery around' – thereby ensuring that for once the British artillery was fully concentrated. Norrie's determination to avoid a 'fluid and mobile' encounter also justified his crucial allocation of 18th Indian Brigade to the new 'box' at Deir el Shein. This brigade was not ready for 'fluid and mobile' operations since it had only recently arrived from Iraq and contained two battalions which had never been in action. On the other hand Norrie rightly considered that in fixed defences it would be capable of putting up an effective resistance.

As indeed it did, for when Rommel advanced on 1 July, it was on 18th Indian Brigade that the attack of Nehring's Afrika Korps was to fall. The two panzer divisions were admirably concentrated and promptly showed the dangers of such a course of action by becoming the targets of a heavy air-raid at 0615. This delayed their advance and caused considerable confusion which had not been fully resolved before the Afrika Korps collided unexpectedly with the Deir el Shein 'box', of the existence of which Rommel was quite unaware. Nehring called on the garrison to surrender, and when his demand was refused, attacked.

The 18th Indian Brigade consisted of the 2/5th Essex, 4/11th Sikhs and 2/3rd Gurkhas, all under the temporary command of the Gurkhas' CO, Lieutenant Colonel Gray. It had been reinforced by nine Matildas and was supported by sixteen 6-pounder anti-tank guns and twenty-three field guns from 97th, 121st and 124th Field Regiments. All day these troops kept up a fierce resistance which only began to flag at about 1600. Unfortunately, as with 150th Brigade in the Cauldron, poor communications prevented the remainder of Eighth Army from realizing the extent of Gray's peril until another hour had passed. By that time all the Matildas and many of the guns were out of action, but the infantrymen continued the fight until shortly after 1900, when they were finally overcome. Their sacrifice had not been in vain. The Afrika Korps had wasted an entire day – in practice, as it transpired, even longer – and had lost eighteen tanks – one-third of its strength.

On the coast, 90th Light Division, moving too far north, ran into, instead of avoiding, the Alamein defences. There it was thrown back by the fire of the 3rd South African Brigade. In the afternoon, it tried to circle south of the 'box' but was halted in short order by the artillery of all three South African Brigades and 1st Armoured Division. Next morning, 90th Light once more attempted to resume its advance but the South Africans continued to thwart all its efforts.

The Afrika Korps, probably exhausted by its clash with 18th Indian Brigade on top of all its other exertions and certainly harried by persistent attacks by the Desert Air Force, made no move at all on 2 July until the afternoon, when it advanced on the Ruweisat Ridge. Here it encountered 1st Armoured Division and since it was outnumbered by over three to one it is hardly surprising that it made no progress. In an attempt to find easier targets therefore, 21st Panzer joined 90th Light at 1630 in a series of attacks on 1st South African Brigade. All were beaten off but Pienaar, who had not forgotten *Totensonntag*, became alarmed and suggested that his threatened brigade should fall back that night. When Norrie refused, Pienaar appealed to Auchinleck who weakly told him that he 'must use his own discretion.' Pienaar then ordered 1st South African Brigade to withdraw but Norrie, resolute as ever, sent forward detachments from 50th Division with heavy artillery support to take its place and prevent any further Axis advance.[5]

By the end of the day, in any case, 15th and 21st Panzer Divisions could muster just twenty-six tanks between them and though they resumed their efforts on both the morning and the afternoon of 3 July, these were opposed both on the ground and from the air and, understandably, failed as well. Also on the morning of the 3rd, Auchinleck ordered the New Zealanders to attack northwards. Their assault fell on the artillery units of Ariete which had finally taken station on the German flank. The Italians collapsed with little resistance, losing forty-four guns and 350 prisoners – 'a clear sign' as Liddell Hart remarks, 'of overstrain'.

By 3 July, Rommel's airmen had also come up at last and at 1835 he made his final effort to break through, sending a large formation of Stukas against the El Alamein 'box', the defences of which he hoped they would shatter as they had done those of Tobruk. Once more the South Africans played a major role in saving the day. While the Hurricanes of No 274 Squadron RAF kept away the escorting enemy fighters, the Hurricanes of Major Le Mesurier's No 1 Squadron SAAF tore into the dive-bombers. Hopelessly trapped, these jettisoned their bombs, but the South Africans, for the loss of one of their own machines which force-landed, shot down nine of them, all confirmed from the ground, then pursued the survivors for miles, claiming to have destroyed at least four more. Air Vice Marshal Coningham hastened to send a congratulatory telegram.

Rommel had played his last card – for the time being at least. That evening, he sent a gloomy report to his superiors, complaining bitterly of 'the steadily mounting strength of the enemy, the low fighting strength of my own divisions which amounted by that time to no more than 1,200 to 1,500 men' and especially 'the terribly strained supply situation' – comments which must have brought a sardonic smile to the face of Kesselring, who ever since Tobruk, had vainly warned him that this would happen. He therefore called off his offensive, and three days later, by a last horrible irony, Norrie, the man most responsible for that desirable result, like Godwin-Austen before him, left Eighth Army at his own request, his place being taken by Ramsden.

Yet the ultimate responsibility for Rommel's repulse must surely rest with the officers and men of Eighth Army as a whole. Despite the lack of firm direction from their leader, they remained firm. Despite all they had been through, it was not they who suffered from 'overstrain'. They did face westwards. They did fight. It has been necessary to recount many instances of how they had been baffled, in more ways than one. It is perhaps time to repeat that they had also been very brave, and they went on being brave for a very long time.

Notes

1   It is true that on 23 June, Auchinleck had written to Brooke suggesting that he might 'consider the advisability of retaining me in my command' but in case Brooke took this as more than a formal gesture he had hastily added that: 'Personally I feel fit to carry on and reasonably confident of being able to turn the tables on the enemy in time.'

2   A Gruppe was roughly equivalent to a British squadron but of noticeably larger size.

3   Freyberg was called by Churchill 'the salamander of the British Empire' because he 'thrived in the fire'. Churchill relates that shortly after the First World War he had persuaded Freyberg to show his wounds. 'I counted twenty-seven' says Churchill, to which Freyberg would add three more in the later conflict. Admittedly, as Freyberg modestly pointed out, 'you nearly always get two

wounds for every bullet or splinter, because mostly they have to go out as well as go in.'

4 These figures are based on the detailed account to be found in *The Desert Air Force* by Roderic Owen, one of its former personnel.

5 A full description of this episode appears in Field Marshal Carver's autobiography *Out of Step*. It will be recalled that Carver was then an officer on Norrie's staff.

9

TACTICAL DISCUSSIONS

Everyone regards General Dorman-Smith as a menace of the first order, and responsible for many of the evil theories which have led to such mistakes in the handling of the Army. General Auchinleck thought Dorman-Smith had a brilliant brain, and also thought he could keep him under control. In this he was quite mistaken.

Colonel Jacob's Diary.
6 August, 1942.

The fighting in the first three days of July, 1942, is now generally known by the name of the First Battle of El Alamein. Few indeed of the men who fought in Eighth Army – or in Panzerarmee Afrika for that matter – would ever refer to it as such. For them the only battle worthy of the name of Alamein would not begin until late on 23 October 1942. Nonetheless 'First Alamein' will serve well enough for the action just described provided the title is restricted to this action and is not extended to include operations in the remainder of July which took place in different circumstances and had a totally different aim – and provided the title is not taken as giving some mysterious warranty that 'First Alamein' was at least as important as, if not more important than the later battle of the same name.

Remarkable claims have been made for 'First Alamein' which become the more extreme the farther one travels from the battlefield. Thus, for instance, John Wheeler-Bennett in his biography *King George VI* declares that:

The actual turning of the tide in the Second World War may be accurately determined as the first week of July, 1942. After Rommel was repulsed at El Alamein on 2 July and turned away

110

in deference to British resistance, the Germans never again mounted a major offensive in North Africa; while in Russia the summer offensive of the Red Army marked the beginning of their ruthless and remorseless progress from the Don to the Elbe.

It would be difficult to find a passage with more factual inaccuracies. To enable its reliability to be judged, it may be convenient to examine first what was happening in Russia during the first week of July, 1942. At that time and for some weeks thereafter it was in reality the Germans who were making progress. They captured Rostov on 27 July, then broke over the River Don to advance towards the Volga and the Caucasus. The wrecked, abandoned Maikop oilfields were occupied on 9 August and on the 22nd the swastika flag was hoisted on the summit of Elbrus, Europe's highest mountain. On 15 September, the Germans assaulted Stalingrad and it was not until a month later that their attacks petered out. The following month, the Russians counter-attacked, trapping the German Sixth Army, but even after its destruction Hitler was still able to embark on a further offensive in February, 1943, which would culminate in the recapture of Kharkov on 15 March.

Turning now to North Africa and ignoring the fact that Rommel temporarily abandoned his advance to the Nile on 3 July not 2 July, it can be seen that Wheeler-Bennett is equally ill-informed. The Germans did mount 'a major offensive' there after July, 1942. It began on the night of 30–31 August, it was called the Battle of Alam Halfa, and Rommel for one considered that this time it was very much more than a mere 'try-on'.

That this offensive took place at all demonstrates that 'First Alamein' was not a decisive encounter. It was not decisive because it solved neither of Eighth Army's major problems. It did not prevent Rommel from making another, and infinitely more dangerous attempt to conquer Egypt two months later. Nor did it rob him of his opportunity to win the campaign even if that attempt should fail by simply holding his ground long enough to ensure the fall of Malta.

It would be more correct to state that 'First Alamein' ought to have proved decisive and would have done so if only it had been followed up properly. Rommel's troops, as Liddell Hart notes, were now 'nearer to complete collapse than they had ever been to complete victory'. Paul Carell confirms that: 'Rommel's military strength was exhausted and his position more than dangerous. With his weakened forces, he lay day after day in front of the ever-increasing British might.' 'The fact was' says Ronald Lewin, who as a young artillery officer arrived in the Desert shortly after the events to be described, that Rommel's army 'should never have been allowed to break into Egypt; having made its entry it should have been expelled.'

There was ample cause for such opinions. Auchinleck's supply-line was secure; Rommel's was stretched to breaking-point. Auchinleck's numbers were already far greater than Rommel's, his men were comparatively fresh while Rommel's were exhausted, and he was receiving heavy reinforcements including a complete division, 9th Australian under Major General Leslie Morshead. Axis reinforcements were also arriving in North Africa but the shortage of motor transport made it impossible for most of them to get up to the front in time. The only substantial formation to reach Rommel was the 382nd Infantry Regiment from Major General Günther Lungerhausen's 164th Light Division,[1] the advanced elements of which arrived, though without any vehicles, on 10 July – in the nick of time as it turned out.

Auchinleck also enjoyed an immense superiority in equipment. On the only occasion when the Eighth Army artillery was properly concentrated, the German accounts refer to it as delivering the heaviest volume of fire they had so far experienced. By contrast the past months of continuous fighting had deprived both Germans and Italians of about half their anti-tank guns and much of their field artillery. The guns that remained were desperately short of ammunition which was only very slowly coming up the long, vulnerable supply-line. The British guns which Rommel had captured at Tobruk were even more of a diminishing asset, since once their captured ammunition had been fired, it could not be replaced at all.

The discrepancy in armour was even greater, for here again Auchinleck was being reinforced. His strength in tanks had increased to over 200 by 10 July, almost 400 by the 20th. The number of German tanks during this same period varied from under thirty to the stupendous total of about fifty, while the figures for the wretched Italian tanks were only marginally greater. No wonder that among the senior Axis commanders nerves were taut and there were profound anxieties as to how they could possibly resist an onslaught by their vastly more powerful enemies.

Nor was it only Auchinleck who was receiving reinforcements. So too was Tedder. They included thirty-two Halifaxes from 10 and 227 Squadrons, the first four-engined bombers to reach the Middle East; these flew their initial sorties on the night of 11–12 July. In any case, reinforcements of aircraft were of less significance than the fact that the Allied airmen by this time enjoyed a complete command of the skies. This may seem an exaggerated statement in view of the splendid performances of the German Messerschmitt Bf[2] 109 and Italian Macchi MC 202 fighters, both of which were faster than any of their Allied rivals, including, contrary to legend, the Spitfires. Fortunately, however, just as the British wasted their superior armour, so the Germans wasted their superior fighters.

The real problem was that the Germans had succumbed to an 'ace' complex. In their account of the air battles in the North African campaign, *Fighters Over the Desert*, Christopher Shores and Hans Ring state flatly that 'some pilots were clearly more interested in increasing their personal scores than inflicting the most telling casualties.' This attitude may best be illustrated by an incident which occurred slightly later, on 16 August. On that day, five 109 pilots claimed a total of seven Hurricanes and five 'Curtiss fighters' – the general name for Kittyhawks or Tomahawks. That the Allies suffered no such losses is not surprising for another pilot reported having seen these men firing their guns into the sand in mock combat.

Admittedly this was an extreme case. That it came to light shows the honesty of the man who reported it. That it was hushed up confirms only that the authorities rightly regarded it as discreditable. Nonetheless, it does indicate the extent to which purely individual achievement had become all-important among the German fighter squadrons.

This had innumerable ill-effects for their cause. While Allied fighter pilots flew constant missions against enemy ground forces, the 109s rarely even strafed British troops. Shores and Ring quote Oberleutnant (Flying Officer) Werner Schroer, the top-scoring pilot to survive the Desert fighting, as admitting: 'Like the RAF we should have concentrated on attacks on vehicles, tanks, forces, airfields etc, but we shirked this as often as possible.'

The 109 pilots also shirked engaging Allied bombers. They had many successes against the escorting fighters, tied down as these were by the need to protect their charges, but they rarely broke through to the really important targets. Schroer again is admirably honest: 'Perhaps we could have shot down more bombers, but it is possible that we were not too interested – they had tail gunners.' Yet Schroer also admits that 'the constant British air attacks' had a 'devastating effect on morale' in the Axis army.

On the other hand, the 109s frequently failed to protect their own bombers, especially the vulnerable Stukas, from interception by Allied fighters, though they sometimes inflicted heavy losses on these afterwards. Indeed it is difficult to avoid the conclusion that the Luftwaffe 'aces' preferred that the RAF aircraft should engage the German bombers, since the 109s could then attack from above with a better chance of success.

This was one more example of the way in which the German pilots were obsessed with their own achievements regardless of all other considerations. Their 'aces' might be the idols of the Luftwaffe, might receive their decorations from Hitler's own hands, might enjoy the personal congratulations of Kesselring, but the final judgement of Shores and Ring is that:

> Looking at the impressive personal scores of the top German pilots in the Desert, it is hard not to gain the impression that these men were sometimes conducting a private war of their own,

divorced almost entirely from the actions of the main forces in the sands below.

The Allied air arm was thus not only bigger than its opponent, it was infinitely more effective.

As if these advantages were not enough, Auchinleck enjoyed a precious insight into his enemy's thoughts – the vital 'Ultra' Intelligence which revealed clearly the desperate state to which Panzerarmee Afrika had been reduced. By contrast, Rommel, as will be related, would have to fight for most of July after having suffered, mainly by bad luck, a grievous blow to his own Intelligence service.

It is also worth noting that in his book *Alamein*, Brigadier C.E.Lucas Phillips who took part in the July battles as an artillery officer, declares firmly that Eighth Army now possessed a 'brilliant team' of staff officers. The Brigadier, General Staff at this time was 'Jock' – really John – Whiteley, a Royal Engineer who had served at Middle East Headquarters in Cairo before taking up his post. He was replaced towards the end of the month by de Guingand and has suffered by comparison with his successor – as would anyone. Nonetheless it should be recorded that de Guingand personally acknowledges a debt of gratitude to Whiteley who 'agreed to give me three days of his advice and help before I took over, and I must say I did not waste my time.'

Among Whiteley's distinguished subordinates were: Brigadier Brian Robertson who still wore the shoulder flashes of South Africa with whose soldiers he had served in Abyssinia but who was now the Senior Administrative Officer responsible for personnel and logistics; his assistant Lieutenant Colonel Miles Graham, whose talents were such that a later Eighth Army Commander would defy War Office instructions in order to retain them; Lieutenant Colonel Hugh Mainwaring, whose responsibility for Operations would sadly be terminated by his capture; the efficient, energetic, ruthless Lieutenant Colonel R.F.K. 'David' Belchem who acted as a reserve Chief of Staff; the extraordinarily versatile Lieutenant Colonel Charles Richardson, from whom we will hear shortly; and the young Captain Edgar Williams whose task it was to interpret the 'Ultra' interceptions but who would shortly rise to become head of Eighth Army Intelligence, a promotion that subsequent events would more than justify.

In the late evening of 4 July, these men and the Army in general learned of Auchinleck's aim:

> Our task remains to destroy the enemy as far east as possible and not to let him get away as a force in being . . . Eighth Army will attack and destroy the enemy in his present position.[3]

Attacks in plenty were made, and rightly so, but to quote a reasonably neutral authority, the RAF Official History, 'they somewhat improved our general position, but they signally failed in their main purpose of putting the enemy to flight' – let alone destroying him.

The sad fact is that the advantages enjoyed by Eighth Army were simply squandered. The benefits to be gained from superior Intelligence were lost because Auchinleck failed to make proper use of the information he received. For this there were two main reasons. In the first place Auchinleck was still C-in-C Middle East as well as Eighth Army Commander. Most unwisely he allowed his attention to wander from the conflict so close at hand to a future danger that might arise from German successes in Russia. Whatever the biographer of King George VI might believe, Auchinleck was too well aware that the enemy was biting ever deeper into the Caucasus. On 8 July he asked for guidance from London as to whether he should divert forces from the Desert to guard against a possible Axis offensive from the Caucasus towards the vital oil-fields of Iraq and Iran.

To which Churchill, who knew all about Rommel's perilous situation from 'Ultra', retorted four days later that he was confident the Russians would hold firm. Even if they did not, 'General Winter' should postpone an enemy assault on Iraq and Iran until the spring of 1943. But in any event, 'if you do not succeed in defeating and destroying Rommel, then there is no possibility whatever of making a sufficient transference' (of troops) 'to the north'.

In addition, Auchinleck proved unable to achieve the swift, co-ordinated reactions necessary to take advantage of the Intelligence with which he was provided. He had unwisely set up his Headquarters in that unpleasant fly-infested area near the Ruweisat Ridge which would later attract Churchill's acid comments. Auchinleck's biographer John Connell offers the excuse that Rommel 'fought and worked under just the same conditions' – a comment that reminds one of the tribal chief who believed that the way to defeat the British was to dress his warriors in red coats – but its discomforts were in any case the least of this Headquarters' unsuitability. It was danger-ously far forward, in an isolated piece of desert and with poor communications. In such a headquarters, Auchinleck and his advisers – mockingly known to the troops as 'The Short-Range Desert Group' – re-mained almost as out of touch with events as when they had tried to direct the fighting from Cairo.

Worse still, since the start of CRUSADER, the headquarters of the Army and the Desert Air Force had always been close together – it was, says the Official History, 'the first essential' and 'the basis' of 'all subse-quent successful co-operation between the Services'. Now Headquarters Eighth Army had been moved over forty miles away from Coningham, who had remained on the coast at Burg el Arab. 'This alone' reports de Guingand, 'produced great difficulties in the laying on of the best air support.'

Tragically, therefore, during the rest of July, at a time when the supremacy of the Desert Air Force was overwhelming, the Luftwaffe would be able to deliver a number of very effective raids against Eighth Army, while the Allied air operations would take place as it were in a vacuum for, like the activity of the German 'aces', they would be largely unconnected with the needs of the fighting on land. The relations between the Services quickly ceased to be cordial and the criticisms by the airmen grew steadily in volume and would one day be made very clear to Churchill.

If Auchinleck failed to make full use of his Intelligence or of his supporting air-arm, so he also failed to make full use of his staff. On 29 July Auchinleck's unsatisfactory relationship with his neglected tank expert Major General McCreery finally came to an end. The C-in-C, Middle East proposed to include an armoured brigade in each infantry division and to group all the Crusader tanks into a new light armoured division, 'not dissimilar from Rommel's famous 90th Light' according to John Connell who was presumably unaware that 90th Light was a motorized infantry division.

McCreery was unimpressed by these suggestions and while it is permissible to disagree with him, it must surely be acknowledged that it was not only his right but his duty to make his views known to his superior. Unfortunately Auchinleck did not want independent views; he wanted 'loyal courtiers'. He therefore dismissed McCreery forthwith, telling him that he was valueless if he was not prepared to 'fall in with his Commander-in-Chief's intentions'.

The real problem, however, as de Guingand relates, was that Auchinleck had brought with him from Cairo 'a sort of personal adviser' but one who 'carried no responsibility in Eighth Army.' This was Major General Eric Dorman-Smith, always known as 'Chink' from his prominent teeth, an Irishman of immense charm, ready tongue and consuming ambition, who had been appointed Deputy Chief of the General Staff on 18 May 1942.

At an earlier date, Dorman-Smith had been Auchinleck's Director of Military Training in India. Here he had become accepted as a 'loyal courtier' to such an extent that Field Marshal Carver in his autobiography *Out of Step* declares that Dorman-Smith 'mesmerized' his superior and came to exercise a 'sinister influence' over him. In London also, Brooke felt that Dorman-Smith's power was dangerous and that Auchinleck had 'allowed himself to fall too deeply under "Chink's" influence.'

'Too deeply' because Dorman-Smith's influence was to cause immense harm. On his arrival at Eighth Army Headquarters, he immediately began in effect to usurp Whiteley's position by issuing his own instructions. General Sir Charles Richardson in *Flashback: A Soldier's Story* reports that for the subordinate staff officers of whom, as already related, he was one, 'this duplication produced chaos.' Richardson had previously known and liked Dorman-Smith but he was quickly disillusioned. He remarks that he was immensely sorry for Whiteley who:

> . . . seldom knew which particular hare of 'Chink's' was running at the moment; and I felt sure he realized, as I did, that 'Chink's' intellectual dominance of the Auk was such that it was not possible to arrange the removal of this dangerous supernumerary adviser.

On the contrary the one who was to be removed would be Whiteley.

All this might have been bearable had Dorman-Smith's activity been beneficial but those who served in Eighth Army at the time are united almost to a man in declaring that the reverse was the case. Dorman-Smith's 'quick brain and fertile mind' states de Guingand:

> . . . produced appreciations and plans at a quicker rate than anyone I have ever met; he was perhaps too clever to be wise. . . . At first I sat up all night conscientiously working on these projects, but I soon found they took up too much of my time and, I regret to say, wasted a lot of it as well.

Others were less tactful. According to Field Marshal Carver; Dorman Smith was:

> a trenchant critic but not so good when it came to proposing a course of action. His principal motive seemed to be to suggest some startlingly novel solution, regardless of whether or not it had a hope of working.

Dorman-Smith's:

> vigorous, restless and inventive mind, [reports General Richardson], was continually looking for clever, unconventional and daring solutions to the dire battlefield problems with which Rommel confronted us. Few if any of these solutions were attuned to the capabilities of Eighth Army, which had recently been disastrously defeated. Moreover 'Chink' was seldom content with pursuing only one solution.

Major General Oswald, then a staff officer with 10th Indian Division but later on the staff at Eighth Army Headquarters, would go so far as to state that Dorman-Smith 'really was as near being a lunatic as you can get.'

The tactics which Dorman-Smith recommended are summed up by Major General Strawson as follows:

> To concentrate the army, to fight it in integrated battle groups, to mass the artillery, to husband the armour, to form a light armoured brigade for flank reconnaissance, to attack and wear down the Italian divisions.

The question of flank reconnaissance was not of great importance, especially since only one of Auchinleck's future offensives would be delivered on the desert flank, but the other ideas were fundamental and it is interesting to consider how far they were reflected in the initial fighting that took place in the first three days of July.

The fact is that they were hardly reflected at all. The army had not been concentrated; many units had been sent back to the Nile Delta while others, notably 2nd New Zealand Division and 9th Indian Brigade had held positions well to the south of the main scene of action in case Rommel advanced in those areas. The army had not fought in integrated battle groups, because Norrie and Pienaar had refused to keep it 'fluid and mobile' but had insisted instead that it anchor its operations 'on the fixed defences of El Alamein'. The artillery had been massed, but only because Norrie and Pienaar had taken 'little account' of Auchinleck's desire to move it about in columns. The armour had not been husbanded; it had engaged its enemy which happily it had greatly out-numbered. The bulk of the fighting had been with the Germans who had suffered almost all the Axis casualties. The only encounter with the Italians had been the New Zealanders' attack on Ariete, and the orders issued at the time show clearly that the intention had been to engage the Germans from the flank and Ariete had become involved only coincidentally because it had happened to come up on the panzers' right at the crucial moment.

All of which confirms the point made earlier that the tactics adopted by Eighth Army during the first three days of July had not been those of Auchinleck. For the remainder of the month, however, Auchinleck's tactics, as advised by Dorman-Smith, would be employed and although Strawson considers they 'were sound ones and were to persist' it is impossible to agree with him on either count.

For a start the tactics did not 'persist'. In Strawson's own words, 'Auchinleck's command . . . was characterized by inconsistency. There seemed always to be too much chopping and changing in methods of training and tactics.' That alone would suggest that the tactics were not 'sound' and when they are examined more closely it quickly becomes clear that they could not possibly have been sound if only because they were mutually contradictory.

Thus it was certainly a sound idea to 'concentrate the army' but the one way of guaranteeing that this could not be achieved was to 'fight it in integrated battle groups' because these were produced by what Lucas Phillips calls 'the fragmentation and dismemberment of divisions'. When an infantry brigade remained under the command of its parent division it benefited from all that division's other elements – field artillery, anti-tank guns, engineers, medical staff, signals staff and so on – which could readily be switched to support whatever formation most needed them. Once brigades began to operate independently this flexible strength was lost.

And battle groups were still weaker than independent brigades, consisting as they did of mobile artillery with just sufficient infantry as was necessary to protect it. Moreover, because they operated separately, they ensured that it would not be possible 'to mass the artillery', which on the contrary was thus dispersed even more widely than had previously been the case.

In a letter to his wife on 17 July, Rommel told her that Eighth Army's superiority in infantry numbers was 'enough to make one weep'. So too it might be thought was the failure to make use of this superiority. The battle groups not only made the Allied infantry less effective, they made it more vulnerable. There was a cynical saying in Eighth Army that the definition of a 'battle group' was 'a brigade group which has been twice over-run by tanks'.

Nor was this melancholy fate caused solely by the weakness of the battle groups. It was caused also by Auchinleck's desire 'to husband the armour'. It will be recalled he had first recommended this towards the end of the Battle of Gazala, with the result that the British tanks had tended to be held back just when the infantry had most need of them. The same consequence would be apparent to an even greater extent throughout the remainder of July and would cause more ill-feeling among the different branches of Eighth Army than any other single factor.

Finally the idea of opposing the Italians rather than the Germans was an excellent one in theory. It was not so easy to achieve in practice but surely the most obvious method of putting pressure on the Italians would have been to use the British superiority in armour against them, particularly since Auchinleck, though sharing the erroneous belief that British tanks were inferior to German ones, was well aware that in quality as well as quantity they vastly exceeded those of the Italians. Unfortunately Auchinleck's intention 'to attack and wear down the Italian divisions' proved impossible to reconcile with his other aim of 'husbanding the armour'.

No wonder then that neither Auchinleck nor any of his subordinates were able to apply these conflicting ideas successfully. No wonder that Auchinleck's offensives were, complains Lucas Phillips, 'terribly badly laid on from the top'; were 'the negation' confirms General Richardson 'of that careful "stage management of the battle" that was to be the hallmark of our next manager'; were 'costly, unsuccessful and from the tactical point of view extremely muddled' according to von Mellenthin. The price would be paid by the soldiers of Eighth Army who would again endure the anguish and humiliation of undeserved, unnecessary defeat – five such defeats in quick succession.

Notes.

1   This was a Saxon division, its emblem being the crossed swords familiar to many from Meissen porcelain.
2   'Bf' was short for *Bayerische Flugzeugwerke*:- Bavarian Aircraft Company. The abbreviation 'Me', though widely used, was not officially correct until 1944.
3   Quoted in Captain Liddell Hart's *History of the Second World War*.

10

FIVE FAILURES

The result of all this was that in the battle fought in July on the El Alamein front, at a time when the Italians were at the end of their tether, and the Germans were hard put to it to stop the gaps with their much reduced Panzer Divisions, our Army was unable to seize its opportunities and complete the local successes gained. The fundamental causes can undoubtedly be traced back to the faulty tactics already referred to.

Colonel Jacob's Diary.
6 August, 1942.

On the morning of 5 July, 1942, a detachment of the Special Air Service led by Major David Stirling was heading for the Qattara Depression at the start of a raid behind the enemy lines, when it sighted a British column moving westwards. Curious to know if this was taking part in an intended Eighth Army offensive which he knew had been code-named Operation EXALTATION, Stirling leaned out of his staff car and called out to the nearest vehicle: 'EXALTATION?'. 'Depression' answered its driver, apparently believing that Stirling was enquiring after his destination. It was a reply that delighted Stirling's men. 'A truthful bloke' commented one. A good prophet also, for if there was one word which would sum up Eighth Army's feelings at the end of July, it would be 'depression'.

In order to appreciate the reasons for this, certain facts must be established and a number of myths have to be pushed aside. In the first place, it is incorrect to refer to all the actions fought during July 1942 as if they were one battle, the First Battle of El Alamein. There were six battles fought around the Alamein Line during the month and if this label is to be affixed it should refer only to the action on 1–3 July which has already been described. The other five were quite separate battles from this and from each other, and some of them were given their own names by the men of Eighth Army and appear under those names in the Official History.

In addition the aims of the five later actions were quite different from those in the fighting on 1–3 July. Even in accounts written fifty years later, it is still possible to read dramatic slogans such as: 'The July Battles: Rommel's Advance Is Halted!' Rommel's advance was not halted by the July battles. Rommel's advance was halted – for the time being anyway – by the action of 1–3 July. Thereafter, apart from local counter-attacks, Rommel made only one forward move during the rest of the month and that, as will be seen, was only to follow up what he believed to be a British retirement.

Instead it would be Eighth Army that would be attempting to advance. In all five later battles Auchinleck's aim, as he had stated before the first one began, was not to halt Rommel's advance but 'to destroy the enemy as far east as possible and not to let him get away as a force in being'; to 'destroy the enemy in his present position.' Indeed as General Jackson points out, before each encounter, 'Auchinleck's orders were couched in terms that assumed a breakthrough and a pursuit of the Panzer Army to Fuka. More attention seemed to be paid to the problems of pursuit than to the break-in.' The men of Eighth Army were therefore well aware of what was intended. They were also experienced enough to realize the great advantages in their favour. Hence the inevitable discouragement when, despite those advantages, the intentions were not fulfilled.[1]

Auchinleck began his first offensive, Operation EXALTATION, on 5 July, though he had made a preliminary move on the 4th. On both days his plan was to hold Rommel in front with XXX Corps while XIII Corps attacked Rommel's flank and rear, but the aims of XIII Corps would be very different. On 4 July it was intended only to disrupt the enemy's offensive which Auchinleck did not yet know had been abandoned, whereas on the 5th it was hoped that Gott would destroy Panzerarmee Afrika 'as far east as possible'. It may be added that on neither day did Auchinleck mass his artillery and on neither day did he direct his attack against Italians. XXX Corps would engage 15th Panzer and XIII Corps would be opposed by 21st Panzer which had been moved back by Rommel on 4 July to counter the threat from the south of which he had been warned by intercepted signals.

Considering Eighth Army's limited aims on the 4th, its actions then were reasonably successful. XXX Corps pushed its armour forward from the eastern end of the Ruweisat Ridge, driving back 15th Panzer before being halted by Rommel's 88mms. XIII Corps, hampered by Stuka raids, made little progress but at least clearly established that Rommel was not attempting any further advance. This was confirmed by 'Ultra' that evening, whereupon Auchinleck quite rightly went onto the offensive.

Auchinleck's tactical plan for EXALTATION was that of 'containing the enemy's eastern front and southern flank and attacking his rear'. From this it is clear that the main blow was to be delivered by XIII Corps; it would be the 'hammer' and XXX Corps the 'anvil'. So it was unfortunate that the Eighth Army Commander left almost all his tanks with XXX Corps, presumably in order to 'husband' them. Gott commanded all three New Zealand Brigades plus 9th Indian Brigade but to support them he had only the armoured cars of 7th Motor Brigade together with just eight Stuarts from 1st Royal Tanks.

Nor did Gott receive adequate protection from the Desert Air Force. On the contrary the lack of liaison between the Services enabled the Stukas to deliver several attacks against the New Zealanders on 5 July, one of which hit the Headquarters of 4th New Zealand Brigade and as Paul Carell rather gleefully records, 'put the entire brigade staff out of action', leaving the troops 'without direction'.

For that matter XIII Corps also suffered from other problems that were not so dramatically obvious. As even the usually undemonstrative Official History confirms, it was by now:

> . . . very weak and becoming weaker by separating (or, as some would say, disintegrating) into its 'mobile artillery battle groups', the latest development of the 'Jock Columns' which, in the Commander-in-Chief's own words of the previous April, could not 'press home an attack against anything but very weak resistance'.

And it did not help Gott that his superior changed his mind at the very last moment. As we have seen, Auchinleck had originally intended that XIII Corps should assault the enemy's rear. On 5 July therefore the Corps moved to 'jumping-off places' ready for just such an attack, but hardly had it reached them when, reports the Official History, Auchinleck 'decided that he had not the superiority to justify the dispersal of his forces in making such a wide movement, and a new plan was made.' This directed roving columns only to operate to the rear of the enemy while the bulk of XIII Corps attacked Rommel's right flank by thrusting towards Deir el Shein. In consequence, all Gott's arrangements had to be altered with the minimum of notice.

What made all this so tragic was that an effective assault by XIII Corps would, Paul Carell tells us, have had a marvellous chance of 'putting an end to Rommel'. Von Mellenthin concurs, stating that on 4 July Panzerarmee Afrika 'could not have resisted a determined attack by Eighth Army' and 'on 5 July our position was little better.'

In the existing circumstances, however, XIII Corps had been given little chance of achieving success and by the evening of 7 July its main advance had petered out. That night a column from 7th Motor Brigade did get as far behind the enemy lines as Fuka, where it shelled an Axis landing-ground for thirty minutes before retiring. At the same time the newly arrived 24th Australian Brigade delivered a raid in the area of the Ruweisat Ridge. Unfortunately neither of these actions did any real damage and by 8 July Auchinleck's first offensive had failed.

It had also left the New Zealanders in particular somewhat exposed. Hitherto Rommel had been forced to rely on his three German divisions to do his fighting, but from 6 July his Italian infantrymen were at last beginning to join him, although there were only about 4,000 of them available at first. He now sent them to hold the northern and central sections of his front while the Littorio Armoured Division with a strength of fifty-four tanks joined the German divisions, increased by reinforcements to no less than 2,000 infantry and from forty-five to fifty tanks, in opposing Gott. Warned by Intelligence of this move, Auchinleck ordered that XIII Corps was to fall right back to the line of a desert track called the 'Springbok Road' running almost due north to south from El Alamein to Himeimat. This meant abandoning the 'boxes' at 'Kaponga' and Naqb abu Dweiss, as well as the vital good going near Djebel Kalakh, but it also had a highly valuable if unintentional consequence.

For as if Auchinleck did not enjoy enough advantages, he now had a wonderful stroke of luck. On learning of this withdrawal, Rommel was filled with a sudden wild hope that Auchinleck, as at Mersa Matruh, was going to order an inexplicable and unnecessary retreat. Accordingly, as Gott's men fell back, Rommel eagerly pressed after them. On 9 July, 21st Panzer and Littorio dramatically stormed 'Kaponga', only to find it had already been evacuated; after which 90th Light and Reconnaissance Units 3 and 33 moved on to the south-east next day. So Rommel's striking force had been concentrated in the south of the Alamein Line – at the very moment when Auchinleck, by sheer good fortune, had planned to launch his second offensive in the coastal area.

This was entrusted to XXX Corps under the command of Ramsden, who in turn gave the main role to Morshead's 9th Australian Division. Its objective was the low hill of Tell el Eisa near the coast, from which it was hoped that the Australians would be able to break through the Axis defences altogether and enforce the retreat, or better still the destruction of Panzerarmee Afrika. The inland flank would be covered by the South Africans who were directed against another smaller feature, Tell el Makh Kadh, to the south-east of Tell el Eisa and almost due west of El Alamein. The attackers were fresh, greatly outnumbered their enemies and, with Rommel at 'Kaponga', would for the first time be opposed mainly by Italians. As more good luck would have it, the particular Italian unit to be engaged was the Sabratha Infantry Division, which was the weakest of the Axis formations, being inexperienced, well below strength and lacking supporting artillery.

For the Australians, however, their greatest advantage was that Morshead, though as Lucas Phillips tells us, 'not without sharp words', had flatly refused to follow Auchinleck's wish to split up his division into battle groups, thereby vastly increasing its hitting power.[2] This concentration enabled him to mass the artillery not just in theory but in practice, instead of keeping it 'fluid and mobile'. In consequence, at 0330 on 10 July, an artillery bombardment fell with devastating effect on the hapless Italians who had no means of retaliating. At 0500 the infantry attacked and by 0730 had broken through the enemy's forward positions.

It seems probable that total victory could have been obtained if only the Australians had been properly assisted. Unhappily, though the Desert Air Force was out in strength, the separation of the two headquarters again prevented its effective co-operation. Even more infuriatingly, though in his official Despatch Auchinleck would complain that he had had 'no reserves available with which to reinforce the attack', he made virtually no use of his very large reserves of tanks, of which he now had over 200. Of these he allocated only thirty-two Valentines from 8th and 44th Royal Tanks to aid the Australians and just eight of the ageing Matildas to support the South Africans.

Even so, the Australians were able to complete the rout of the luckless Sabratha Division, taking over 1,500 prisoners. They then over-ran the German Wireless Interception Section which had given vital Intelligence reports to Rommel in the past. Its leader, Captain Alfred Seebohm, was captured badly wounded; he died in hospital in Alexandria soon afterwards. Paul Carell calls this 'an irreparable loss for the whole army' and laments that 'this handicap could not be overcome during the decisive battles for the El Alamein positions' – an interesting comment as showing that the Germans did not believe that these had yet been fought. By about 1000, the Australians had gained the eastern end of Tell el Eisa, while the South Africans had secured their southern flank by capturing Tell el Makh Kadh.

Further progress was prevented by von Mellenthin in temporary charge of Rommel's headquarters. He hastily formed 'a rough battle line' with his headquarters personnel together with those advanced elements of 164th Light Division which, as was related earlier, had just reached the front line. With this scratch force von Mellenthin 'succeeded in holding the Australians.' During the afternoon more reinforcements from 164th Light helped to strengthen the defences, while Rommel also arrived on the scene, having raced up from the south with part of 15th Panzer to launch a counter-attack which the Australians successfully resisted.

At 0630 on 11 July, the Australians renewed their pressure eastwards and southwards, the former move capturing the remainder of the Tell el Eisa position, the latter inflicting heavy casualties on the Trieste Division. However, by now the remainder of Rommel's striking force had returned from the south. The attackers were met with heavy artillery fire, and the lack of liaison again ensured that the Allied airmen would be unable to prevent the Luftwaffe from delivering a number of effective raids with Stukas or the faster more modern Junkers Ju 88s. Indeed, the only interception achieved by the Desert Air Force on 11 July came about as the result of an accidental encounter. The Kittyhawks of No 2 Squadron SAAF and the older Tomahawks of No 5 Squadron SAAF were escorting a raid by Boston bombers when they sighted a group of thirty Stukas, heavily escorted. Leaving their own bombers, the South Africans attacked these, shooting down two Stukas and two 109s, but losing four of their own aircraft.

By the end of 11 July, Auchinleck's second offensive had failed. During the next three days Rommel delivered a series of local counter-attacks which were unable to dislodge either the Australians or the South Africans from their captured hills but made it quite clear that they would make no further advances from them. Nonetheless, the offensive had only just failed and it might be thought that Auchinleck would have been well advised to mount a new assault as soon as possible before his enemies could regain their balance and before their attempts to prepare fixed defences, including mine-fields, could make much progress.

Unhappily, as we saw earlier, it was at this time that Auchinleck was expecting a response from his superiors in London to his suggestion that he divert forces to guard against a possible German breakout from the Caucasus. That response proved to be a flat negative but while Auchinleck was awaiting it Panzerarmee Afrika was given a chance to recover, and furthermore, as the Official History complains, while his attention was thus distracted, Auchinleck took no measures towards 'finding out about the enemy's dispositions'. The result of this omission would become apparent in the action which Eighth Army would call the First Battle of the Ruweisat Ridge, or more familiarly, 'First Ruweisat'.

This was Auchinleck's third offensive which began late on 14 July. The main role was entrusted to Gott's XIII Corps, its initial objective being the western part of the Ruweisat Ridge which had fallen into enemy hands at the beginning of the month. Its capture, Auchinleck believed, would allow Eighth Army to exploit north-westwards, 'break through the enemy's centre and destroy his forces.' As a subsidiary move, XXX Corps was ordered to attack south from the Tell el Eisa salient towards the Miteirya Ridge. Much of the effect of this diversionary effort would, however, be lost by the strange decision not to begin it until the main assault had already been defeated.

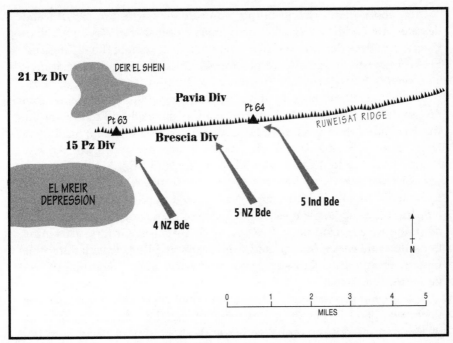

Map VIIA: 'First Ruweisat'.

Map VIIB: 'Second Ruweisat'.

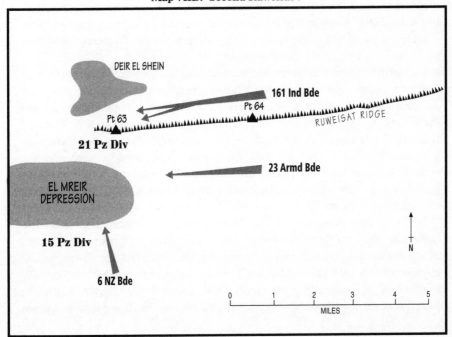

Once more there was no proper co-ordination with the air arm and despite Morshead's successful preliminary bombardment before Tell el Eisa, Auchinleck decreed that there should be none before 'First Ruweisat' in the interests of surprise. And though Morshead had achieved enviable results by fighting his division as a division, the assault at 'First Ruweisat' was to be made by three separate brigades, all advancing from the south-east. 4th New Zealand Brigade was directed on Point 63 at the western end of the Ruweisat Ridge just south of Deir el Shein; 5th Indian Brigade from 5th Indian Division attacked another prominent feature, Point 64, further to the east; and 5th New Zealand Brigade made for that part of the Ridge lying between these two features. At least this time Lumsden's 1st Armoured Division was ordered to provide support for the attack and he had ample means with which to do so since his division now contained 2nd Armoured Brigade with forty-six Grants, fifty-nine Crusaders and eleven Stuarts, and 22nd Armoured Brigade with thirty-one Grants, twenty-three Crusaders and twenty-one Stuarts – a total of 191 gun-armed tanks.

Again the attack was directed against the unhappy Italians – in this case the Brescia and Pavia Infantry Divisions – though there was also a stiffening of German infantry present together with about twenty tanks from 8th Panzer Regiment of 15th Panzer Division, their existence being quite unsuspected by the attackers as a result of the inadequate reconnaissance. The advance began at 2300 and during the fierce fighting that took place on the night of 14–15 July, 5th Indian Brigade was thrown back in some disorder, but both New Zealand brigades, despite sizable casualties, secured their objectives, capturing some 1,600 Italians. They also encountered and killed the crews of three of the German tanks.

Unfortunately, in the confusion inevitable in a night-action, a number of German posts were overlooked. With daybreak, these engaged the New Zealanders from behind, cutting them off from their anti-tank guns. At the same time the remaining German armour fell on the rear of 5th New Zealand Brigade, forcing the surrender of 350 men. One who did not surrender was Sergeant Keith Elliott, who took his platoon northward where, despite wounds in chest, back and both legs, he directed the capture of five machine-gun posts and some 200 prisoners, an achievement for which he was awarded the Victoria Cross.

It had been intended that the British armour should proceed to the Ruweisat Ridge at first light on 15 July – but this simply did not happen. 22nd Armoured Brigade had been moved well south of the Ridge on the evening of the 14th to guard against enemy tanks reported to be operating in this area. Kippenberger personally drove over to 2nd Armoured Brigade which was stationed to the south-west of Point 64 in an attempt to obtain help for his men, but he tells us that its commander, Brigadier Raymond Briggs, 'received me coolly.'

For this perhaps Briggs should not be blamed too severely. The repeated orders that the armour must be 'husbanded' had undoubtedly had a deadening effect but as Kippenberger would later accept, 'the fundamental fault was the failure to co-ordinate infantry and armour. This is impossible without a common doctrine, a sound system of inter-communication and training together.' Briggs would later succeed to the command of 1st Armoured Division and under a later regime would rightly earn high praise for, among other things, ensuring just such a co-ordination. At the time of 'First Ruweisat', as the Official History sadly notes, 'co-operation between an armoured division (as distinct from 'I' tank units)' – Matildas and Valentines – 'and one or more infantry divisions had not been really studied and had certainly not been practised.'

Shortly after Kippenberger's arrival, Lumsden also drove up. His presence induced a greater sense of urgency and 2nd Armoured moved forwards, but by that time the enemy had already retired in triumph with their prisoners. The British tanks, though troubled by minefields, then went to the assistance of 5th Indian Brigade when it renewed its attempts to take Point 64. This finally fell early that afternoon.

Meanwhile, however, the remaining tanks of 15th Panzer, most of 21st Panzer and Reconnaissance Units 3 and 33 had hurriedly been collected together by Nehring to the west of Ruweisat Ridge. At 1700, these forces attacked the unprotected 4th New Zealand Brigade at Point 63, inflicting heavy losses and capturing another 380 New Zealanders, including Captain Charles Upham who had been wounded in one arm and both legs but whose gallantry in directing the resistance to the German onslaught, coupled with that displayed by him on the previous night, won a bar to the VC he had earned in Crete – a double award unique in the Second World War.[3] The Brigade Headquarters was then over-run. Brigadier Burrows managed to escape but the total New Zealand losses rose to 1,405 dead, wounded or captured.

Not until 1815, when 22nd Armoured Brigade made a belated appearance, was Nehring's progress checked, and next day, 16 July, he delivered attacks on 5th Indian Brigade which were repulsed but which ended any hopes that this brigade would be able to make further advances. At least 5th Indian did manage to lift the gloom slightly by spreading spectacular stories of the casualties it had inflicted on its attackers. These no doubt had a good effect on morale but, sad to say, it is now known that they bore no resemblance to reality.

Also on the 16th, the Australians began their move southwards from Tell el Eisa. They completed the ruin of the wretched Sabratha Division but were then thrown back by the 382nd Infantry Regiment from 164th Light which was now in strength in the north of the Axis positions. Next day, the Australians resumed their advance under cover of heavy but not very well co-ordinated air-raids. The Valentines of 44th Royal Tanks provided useful assistance, Corporal Raistrick earning a DCM for rescuing two crew-members from his blazing tank – though sadly both died later – despite his own injuries which were so serious that he subsequently lost a leg. Again the Italians bore the brunt of the attack. Trieste and Trento Divisions suffered heavily but resisted bravely, while the 32nd Battalion, African Combat Engineers fought with such determination that only two officers and four-teen men survived unwounded out of a strength of one hundred. Once more powerful counter-attacks, well supported by the Luftwaffe, drove the Australians back. They did not escape without losses either, for 24th Australian Brigade alone incurred some 300 casualties.

Auchinleck's third offensive had failed – and failed disgracefully. 'There is nothing in the whole record of the Afrika Korps' states Ronald Lewin bluntly, 'to compare with the abandonment of the New Zealanders naked before an armoured attack in the opening stages of this first Ruweisat battle.' Like many another he laments the tragic waste of the 'ardent young lives simply thrown away'.

There would be even greater waste in Auchinleck's fourth offensive, the Second Battle of the Ruweisat Ridge, which began in the evening of 21 July. Its objective was declared by Dorman-Smith to be 'cutting Rommel's battle front in two parts' and the orders issued by Auchinleck and his subordinate commanders laid great stress on the need 'to continue the pursuit as far as the frontier without pause' and to 'pursue the enemy relentlessly and inflict the maximum destruction.'

Of course before Eighth Army had the luxury of pursuing Panzerarmee Afrika, it first had to defeat it. Its ability to do so was not assisted by the fact that Auchinleck, in the words of the Official History, had once more 'allowed insufficient time for the study of a multitude of details.' There was no proper reconnaissance, though it is interesting to learn that a certain Sergeant Rycroft was later awarded a DCM for some effective 'recce' work carried out on his own initiative. The preliminary bombardment was restored but Auchinleck still persisted in using independent brigade groups rather than divisions for making his assault.

On the other hand Auchinleck did not persist with his intention of attacking the Italians. John Connell is quite lyrical about Auchinleck's decision to 'attack wherever Afrika Korps was not. He would go on attacking the Italians and compelling Afrika Korps to come to their rescue until he had eliminated the Italians and exhausted Rommel and the Afrika Korps. Call this an expedient, call it a master-plan (but without all the flummery associated with that overworked noun): its justification was that it worked.' The men who took part in 'First Ruweisat' would not have agreed and in 'Second Ruweisat' the 'master-plan' was abandoned altogether, possibly without flummery but certainly without any apparent regret.

For in 'Second Ruweisat', Auchinleck, says Ronald Lewin, 'went straight for the Afrika Korps.' He deliberately 'chose to attack German strength rather than Italian weakness' agrees General Jackson, 'hoping thereby to destroy the backbone of Rommel's Panzer Army.' Nor was that hope unreasonable, as to oppose this offensive Rommel could find just forty-two German tanks, plus fifty Italian ones. Of the forty-two German ones moreover, only thirty-six were gun-armed and of these only eight were the new 'Specials'.

The main assault was again to be carried out by Gott's XIII Corps. 6th New Zealand Brigade would attack from the south against the El Mreir Depression lying to the south-west of the Ruweisat Ridge, while 161st Indian Motor Brigade from 5th Indian Division – a new reinforcement for Eighth Army which had originally come from Iraq but had more recently been stationed in the Nile Delta – attacked from the east, its objectives being the Deir el Shein Depression and Point 63 on the Ridge. The infantry would be assisted by 1st Armoured Division, its 2nd and 22nd Armoured Brigades between them mustering sixty-one Grants, eighty-one Crusaders and thirty-one Stuarts, to say nothing of almost another hundred tanks in reserve. The armoured brigades were not, however, intended to advance before first light on 22 July. Much criticism has been levelled against their commanders for being unwilling to move at night when the Germans had no compunction about doing so, but there was the important difference that the British tanks would have to make their way through enemy minefields while their opponents would not.

In addition to their other tasks, 6th New Zealand and 161st Indian Motor Brigades were to clear a gap in those minefields. Through this were to pass the 40th and 46th Battalions, Royal Tank Regiment, both from 23rd Armoured Brigade, recently arrived in the Middle East, and between them containing ninety-eight Valentines. The Axis forces would thus indeed be cut in two and the ground won would be secured by 9th Indian Brigade which would follow the Valentines through the gap. As diversionary moves 69th (British) Brigade would attack in the south, the South Africans would thrust to the north of Deir el Shein and the Australians would strike southwards towards the Miteirya Ridge, supported by 23rd Armoured's third unit, 50th Royal Tanks, which was equipped with six Matildas and some forty-five Valentines.

Such was the plan – but not the realization. During the night of 21–22 July, 161st Brigade seized Deir el Shein, only to be driven out by counter-attacks; it failed to capture Point 63. 6th New Zealand Brigade, after ferocious fighting which cost it 200 casualties, secured the eastern part of El Mreir, but the tanks did not move up to support it in time. In consequence at 0515 on the 22nd, Nehring fell on the New Zealanders with both 15th and 21st Panzer and shattered them. Brigadier George Clifton was taken prisoner but concealed his badges of rank and was later able to make good his escape.[4] Some 700 men were killed, wounded or captured, and twenty-three guns, thirteen being the new 6-pounders, were lost.

There was some excuse for the ineffectiveness of the British armour. On 18 July another successful Luftwaffe attack had wounded both Lumsden and Briggs. Command of 1st Armoured Division was therefore given to Gatehouse, now a major general, but he only arrived at the front from the Nile Delta on the evening of the 20th and he also was wounded at about 0900 on the 22nd, his place being taken by Brigadier Fisher. Yet it is hardly surprising that, in the bitter words of Kippenberger: 'At this time there was throughout Eighth Army, not only in the New Zealand Division, a most intense distrust, almost hatred, of our armour. Everywhere one heard tales of the other arms being let down; it was regarded as axiomatic that tanks would not be where they were wanted on time.'

As a result of all these misfortunes, no gaps were cleared through the minefields for the Valentines of 40th and 46th Royal Tanks. Nonetheless Gott ordered that they should still advance, though a mile south of their intended route. Communications failures prevented this change of plan reaching the Valentines, but since the new line of approach was also mined it probably made little difference. The tanks set off at about 0800. They suffered heavy losses first from mines, then from anti-tank guns against which they charged valiantly but in vain. Private Günther Halm, a nineteen-year-old gun-layer from Westphalia, was responsible for the destruction of nine of them, for which feat he received a Knight's Cross, as well as promotion to corporal. Finally the surviving Valentines were counter-attacked by 21st Panzer.

By mid-day it was all over. Forty Valentines had been destroyed, forty-seven more crippled. Thirty officers and 173 other ranks had been killed or wounded. Just eleven tanks returned to their start-line. Nothing was left to 23rd Armoured Brigade except its spirit. 'We'd like to have another crack at them, sir', Trooper Gordon Redford told Alan Moorehead.

At 1700, 2nd Armoured Brigade, after experiencing problems with the enemy's minefields, at last approached El Mreir from the south, but meeting heavy fire, it retired with a loss of twenty-one tanks. At 0200 on 23 July, 9th Indian Brigade began another series of attempts to capture Deir el Shein and Point 63. These also failed with heavy casualties.

The main diversionary attack in the north, which began at 0600 on 22 July, went equally badly. The Australians displayed limitless valour, symbolized by the posthumous VC awarded to Private Gurney who had attacked several machine-gun posts single-handed, but again the lack of co-operation between armour and infantry was all too apparent. That evening, 50th Royal Tanks at last broke through to the Miteirya Ridge but since the infantry necessary to hold the ground that had been won never joined them, the Valentines fell back after about an hour, leaving behind twenty-three of their number.

Even allowing for the fact that some of its crippled tanks were later salvaged, Eighth Army had lost a total of 118 in this offensive. The Germans had lost just three. If General Auchinleck had intended 'to husband the armour', it can only be said that he had not succeeded.

So ended 'Second Ruweisat', which Auchinleck had code-named Operation SPLENDOUR. The Eighth Army Commander had no doubt who was responsible for its failure. In a report to Brooke on 25 July, he would complain that: 'The 23rd Armoured Brigade, though gallant enough, lost control and missed direction. The infantry too, seem to have made some avoidable mistakes. Perhaps I asked too much of them.'

Others took a different view. 'My opinion' declares Kippenberger, 'was that we would never get anywhere until the armour was placed under command of infantry brigadiers and advanced on the same axis as the infantry. In some operations I conceded that the armour commander should control and the infantry employed should be under him and still both arms should operate on the same axis. We fought one more unsuccessful battle on the old lines and then the principle for which I argued, and which must have had very much more influential protagonists, was adopted.'

Since Gott's XIII Corps had endured the heaviest losses in the two Ruweisat actions, Auchinleck's fifth offensive, the Battle of the Miteirya Ridge – Kippenberger's 'one more unsuccessful battle on the old lines' – was made the task of Ramsden's XXX Corps, reinforced by the bulk of the armour. It began at midnight on 26–27 July, and unbelievably it repeated all the errors made in the two previous disasters.

Indeed the action was bedevilled by those same disasters before it even commenced. It had been intended that it should start forty-eight hours earlier but neither Morshead nor Pienaar would agree to participate unless the attacking force was strengthened. The 'indiscipline at the top' displayed by the leaders of the Dominion divisions, and which they justified by their responsibilities to their own governments, was such that Major General Douglas Wimberley, commander of 51st Highland Division, who reached the Desert at this time in advance of his men, is quoted by Lucas Phillips as remarking: 'Really! If this is the form, I shall have to consider referring any orders I don't like to the Secretary of State for Scotland!' On the other hand it must be admitted that Morshead and Pienaar had been given every excuse for scepticism, especially since both had in the past achieved success by disregarding Auchinleck's wishes, the former at Tell el Eisa, the latter at 'First Alamein'.

In the event, Auchinleck met their demands and did provide a reinforcement in the form of 69th (British) Brigade from 50th Division which had previously been stationed in the south. Needless to say the attack would be made by independent brigade groups, though 24th Australian Brigade, on Morshead's insistence, was backed by the whole of 9th Australian Division's artillery. Its task was to seize the eastern end of Miteirya Ridge. This would protect the flank of South African units which were to break into the enemy minefields south-east of the Ridge. Here they would make gaps through which would pass the infantry of 69th Brigade. Although this formation was new to the area, however, General Richardson reports that all reconnaissance 'by company and platoon commanders was prohibited "to secure surprise".' The result, he adds, was that some units 'got lost' – but the responsibility for this would be laid not on the prohibition but on certain luckless officers in 69th Brigade.

Having passed through the minefields, 69th Brigade was to strike southwestwards to capture the Deir el Dhib, a small depression north of Deir el Shein, clearing a path through any further minefields discovered on the way. With the Deir el Dhib in British hands, 2nd Armoured Brigade and 4th Light Armoured Brigade would advance to it, then swing to the north-west and burst clean through the enemy's defences.

The first moves were successful. The South Africans had carried out their tasks by 0130 on the 27th. By 0300 the Australians were on the Miteirya Ridge. By 0800 69th Brigade, despite the confusion mentioned earlier, had reached Deir el Dhib. But of course co-operation with the armour broke down. 2nd Armoured Brigade, wrongly advised as to the extent of the South Africans' mine-clearing activities, held back until the gaps could be widened. It was a decision for which Brigadier Fisher has been much abused but his attitude is surely understandable when the misfortunes of 23rd Armoured are recalled. 50th Royal Tanks did try to aid the Australians but was repulsed by heavy anti-tank fire with the loss of thirteen Valentines. For the third time running, the infantry were left 'naked before an armoured attack'. By mid-morning, the Afrika Korps, backed by 200th Infantry Regiment from 90th Light, was already counter-attacking. The isolated 69th Brigade was driven back through the minefields, having suffered 600 casualties which necessitated its removal from the front line. 24th Australian Brigade was pushed off Miteirya Ridge with a casualty list of 400. This brought the total of Australians dead, wounded and missing in a period of just over three weeks to 146 officers and 3,070 other ranks, and the Eighth Army's total casualties for July to over 13,000.

Panzerarmee Afrika had not escaped unscathed either, having lost in July over 7,000 men as prisoners of war. Over 6,000 of these were Italians and if the Italians had suffered severely they had certainly not been eliminated, while the Germans were far less exhausted at the end of July than they had been at the beginning. And there would be no sixth offensive. On the 31st, Auchinleck signalled to London that it would not be 'feasible' to resume 'offensive operations before mid-September'.

The Axis forces had in fact survived their time of greatest peril astonishingly well, and as the realization spread, so there was a great uplift in their morale. This was entirely justified for they had every reason to believe that if Eighth Army could not defeat them with the advantages it had enjoyed in July 1942, then it was scarcely likely to be able to stand up to them once they had received their own promised reinforcements of men and improved equipment. No wonder von Mellenthin concludes his account of this series of actions on a note of triumph: 'The Panzerarmee had failed to reach the Nile, but on 15, 22 and 27 July we had won important defensive victories and the balance of losses was highly favourable to us.'

No wonder either that it was the British and Commonwealth soldiers who were disheartened. For all their efforts, for all their sacrifices, they had not driven their enemy out of Egypt, let alone destroyed him 'as far east as possible'. At the end of their five offensives they were left only with defeat, humiliation, an increase in 'indiscipline at the top', a worsening relationship with their air-arm, and bitter mutual recriminations among the different branches of their own army. John Connell complains that July, 1942, was 'the month that was ignored by the historians and the writers of memoirs'. Perhaps they were all too ashamed of it.

Notes

1   On 9 November, 1942, i.e. after El Alamein, Leopold Amery, Secretary of State for India, assured Auchinleck who was a personal friend, that 'there would have been no champagne' – celebrations – for Eighth Army at that time if Auchinleck 'hadn't put the cork in the bottle in July.' A more relevant comment, though less welcome to the recipient, might have been that Eighth Army felt it could have had its 'champagne' much earlier if Auchinleck 'hadn't smashed the bottle' in the latter part of July.

2   Morshead's distaste for battle groups was such that he expressly warned the commanders of later British divisions to arrive in the Middle East that they should be on their guard against this pernicious practice, telling them that: 'The staff here are mad on breaking up divisions.'

3   It shows no disrespect for an astonishing, though astonishingly modest, man whose complete indifference to danger was legendary, to point out that he was not captured while preventing the enemy breaking through to the Nile in 'The First Battle of El Alamein' as most accounts of his exploits have related. He was captured because he and his men were cut off after the failure of an offensive which had been neither adequately planned nor adequately executed.

4   Brigadier Clifton was again taken prisoner during the Battle of Alam Halfa. He escaped once more but this time was recaptured before being able to regain the Allied lines.

11

TALK OF RETREAT

There is universal respect for General Auchinleck as a big man, and a strong personality. No one openly criticises him. Nevertheless, he has not created a coherent Army, and most of the criticisms and explanations which people give are directed to matters which are his immediate concern.

Colonel Jacob's Diary.

6 August, 1942.

Silence now fell on a battlefield littered with the shattered, burned remains of vehicles and the graves into which the shattered, burned bodies of the dead had hurriedly been consigned. But in London and throughout the Eighth Army the sounds of discontent grew louder. It was the 'nonsenses of July', as they were called by the troops, which convinced Churchill and Brooke that they should visit the Middle East in an attempt to discover what had gone wrong. When they arrived they would not be gratified by the picture that was presented to them.

The basic problem in Eighth Army was a loss of confidence. Few doubted their own abilities or those of their immediate commanders. 'The most general and the most dangerous tendency' reports Field Marshal Carver in his book *El Alamein*, 'was that of different arms or formations to lay the blame on others.' If the infantry had 'a most intense distrust, almost hatred' of the armour, the tank commanders, says Lucas Phillips, accused the infantry of 'always screaming for tank support on every possible occasion.' Neither the infantry nor the armour had any real knowledge of the difficulties facing the other or of the ways in which co-operation between them might be achieved.

Not even the recollection of Eighth Army's undoubted success in checking Rommel's advance in the first three days of July served to raise morale. After all, Rommel had been stopped before; at Tobruk and near Sollum during his first offensive, at the Gazala Line after his counter-attack in early 1942. He had even been thrown back by Operation CRUSADER. Yet in each case the successes had proved only temporary; had been followed by further failures. Now in July, 1942, this depressing pattern had been repeated once again. Moreover there was a growing realization that the main factor in halting Rommel had been the enemy's exhaustion. This did not encourage hopes of Eighth Army's ability to meet the new attack which Rommel was known to be planning for late August.

Urgent action was needed to rectify this state of affairs, but none was forthcoming. Auchinleck's main desire, according to de Guingand, was that of 'returning to Cairo to re-assume his appointment as Commander-in-Chief.' He seems to have abandoned making any constructive suggestions or indeed giving any positive directions to Eighth Army at all. His attitude was made worse because it was obvious to his staff, to his field commanders and even to knowledgeable onlookers.

Thus General Richardson notes sadly that Auchinleck, rather than 'visiting his forward commanders' remained in his Headquarters, 'day after day sitting in the sand spending long hours staring through binoculars at the distant void horizon.' 'For a long time', confirms Kippenberger, 'we had heard little from Army except querulous grumbles that the men should not go about without their shirts on, that staff officers must always wear the appropriate arm-bands, or things of that sort.' 'In itself' declares Alan Moorehead, the Eighth Army 'was ready for anything. But the things it lacked badly were a clearly defined purpose and a leader.'

Inevitably, in these circumstances, increasingly few in Eighth Army believed that their present commander, for all his fine qualities and for all his good intentions, had the ability to lead them out of the quagmire into which they had fallen. General Richardson, for instance, expresses his admiration for Auchinleck's 'striking personality, which dominated almost without speech, his courage and his manifest integrity' but then adds bluntly: 'I was unconvinced that General Auchinleck could turn the tide no matter what new resources might come our way.'

This was the general opinion. In particular, as Field Marshal Carver relates, mistrust was growing 'between the Dominion divisions and the Higher Command. That there was such mistrust by this time cannot be denied.' Not that it was only the Dominion divisions who were mistrustful. As Carver continues:

> The degree of demoralization must not be exaggerated, as it often
> has been since, but there is no doubt that even those who had

been spared the Battle of Gazala, such as the New Zealanders and the recently arrived 23rd Armoured Brigade, were severely affected by their experiences in the July battles round Ruweisat Ridge.'

23rd Armoured Brigade of course was a purely British formation. Mistrust of the Higher Command was in fact widespread.

For that matter, the Higher Command was also mistrustful. If Auchinleck in his reports to Brooke blamed his troops for the defeats – as he did – he clearly cannot have had too much confidence in their abilities. He might urge on his men with stirring exhortations such as his Order of the Day on 25 July: 'We must not slacken. If we can stick it we will break him. Stick to it!' Yet at the same time he was turning his attention to matters that would be irrelevant unless Eighth Army not only could not break its enemy but could not hold its present positions either. No wonder that Lieutenant Colonel Harry Llewellyn in his autobiography *Passports to Life: Journeys into Many Worlds*[1] should comment cynically: 'We had all become used to lies, more lies and election promises.'

The matters with which Auchinleck was concerned can be summed up in one word: 'Retreat'. Rumours of planned retreats would persist throughout Eighth Army in early August, doing immense harm to morale. In 1958, Auchinleck, in a letter to the *Sunday Times*, would expressly deny the truth of those rumours, declaring:

> It is absurd and incorrect to say that, at that time, I was contemplating a withdrawal from the Alamein position. Such a plan had ceased to be seriously considered since early in July, 1942, when Rommel had been forced on the defensive and the Eighth Army had regained the power to attack.

On the other hand, the express statements of individual officers, supported by a whole mass of written records,[2] indicate that not only were plans for withdrawal being considered very seriously indeed at this time but that the two main concerns of General Headquarters, Middle East and to a lesser extent of the various subordinate formations as well, were what defensive positions should be held and what other measures should be taken if Eighth Army did have to withdraw from the Alamein position.

The proposed retreats took three forms. The most extreme dealt with the abandonment of Egypt altogether. Thus Field Marshal Lord Harding, who was then a major general and the Deputy Chief of the General Staff at Middle East Headquarters, would reveal to the biographer of Field Marshal Alexander[3] that Auchinleck had ordered the preparation of plans 'to extricate the bulk of his forces south of Cairo, and then over the Suez Canal into

Palestine.' Harding could speak with some authority on this point; it was he who was entrusted with drawing up the plans. General Richardson confirms that he personally was also ordered to prepare plans, in his case 'for the possible withdrawal of Eighth Army to Khartoum'. De Guingand agrees that Eighth Army or at least its leaders were 'still looking over their shoulder' and that already 'a new site for the Headquarters had been selected on the Nile, sixty miles south of Cairo.'

Finally, Major General Sir Miles Graham, who was the Eighth Army's Deputy Chief Administrative Officer, recorded in a BBC radio broadcast of 24 September, 1958, that he too was made responsible for 'arrangements to evacuate Eighth Army' should this prove necessary; they included 'having different coloured flags put into the sand to take the various units out.' Indeed at the moment he first met Auchinleck's successor as Commander of Eighth Army, Graham was marking up a large map to indicate the logistical situation that would apply if the Army was forced to leave Egypt in a hurry. It says much for his ability that his career survived this unfortunate encounter.

As well as these extreme moves, there was at this time much serious and detailed consideration of retreats from Alamein to alternative defences protecting Cairo and Alexandria. On 25 July after Operation SPLENDOUR – 'Second Ruweisat' – had ended far from splendidly, Auchinleck, in a report to Brooke, specifically accepted that 'we may have to face a withdrawal from our present forward positions.' If this should become necessary, he had 'a strong defensive position, organized in depth for thirty miles or more' within which his forces could be 'fully mobile' and if this also failed there was a 'similar but smaller system' in reserve. 'Whatever happens' Auchinleck assured the Chief of the Imperial General Staff, 'I intend to keep the Eighth Army or the greater part of it as a mobile field force.'

Auchinleck's reserve system, as he informed Brooke, was 'based on the Wadi Natrun obstacle, which fits in with the western defences of Alexandria, the defences along the water line of the Delta and . . . covering Cairo'. The main positions in this system were at Amiriya, south-west of Alexandria, at Khatatba, on the north-western approaches to Cairo, and particularly, as Auchinleck indicated, at Wadi Natrun, situated between Alexandria and Cairo and blocking a rough desert road called the 'Barrel Track', which ran towards the Egyptian capital from the southern part of the Alamein position.

Clearly then, Auchinleck already had serious doubts as to the ability of Eighth Army to drive back the enemy; which would mean that he would have to face a new assault by Rommel in the comparatively near future. That his thoughts should promptly turn to reserve positions indicates that he also doubted whether his army could hold their present defences when this assault was delivered.

As we know, Auchinleck mounted one further offensive of his own, but this also failed on 27 July. Thereupon a signal was dispatched from Eighth Army Headquarters enquiring urgently as to 'the progress of the Wadi Natrun defences'. On the same day also, Dorman-Smith presented an 'Appreciation of the Situation in the Western Desert' which was approved by Auchinleck, but which must rank as the most depressing document to be found in the entire story of the war in North Africa.

It begins with a ringing declaration: 'Object: The defence of Egypt by the defeat of the enemy forces in the Western Desert'. But not just yet! Hastily Dorman-Smith concludes that for the time being an assault on the enemy's northern or central sectors is pointless since 'the enemy's positions are now too strongly held to be attacked with success with the resources available'; that even in the southern sector an attack 'hardly seems advisable at present'; that in general Eighth Army is 'hardly fit at present to do any more attacks'; that 'the enemy now holds in sufficient strength for his purpose a front from which he cannot be dislodged by manoeuvre or any attack Eighth Army can at present deliver'; that 'unless the enemy's position deteriorates', Eighth Army will not be 'strong enough to attack' until 'mid-September at the earliest'; and that even then it may not have 'a superiority sufficient to justify a direct attack on what may be by then a strongly organized front' and it might perhaps be better to consider a flanking move 'to the enemy's rear via Siwa' – an oasis south-west of the Qattara Depression – which would have necessitated a march of some 400 miles over difficult country.

In any event, Dorman-Smith realizes that Rommel 'will certainly try to attack before the end of August.' The prospect appears to fill him with dread: 'The enemy is attempting to build up his strength'; Rommel may be 're-inforced in the second part of August'; 'the Axis may make great efforts to strengthen Panzer Armee in the shortest time'; 'during August the enemy may build up to between 150 and 200 German Tanks'; 'there may be a critical period late in August' before Eighth Army's 'new divisions' are ready. In short Dorman-Smith doubts whether in these circumstances Eighth Army could hold its present position, and naturally therefore he spends much time assessing what would happen should it fail to do so.

'To us', announces Dorman-Smith, 'the two vulnerable points are Cairo and Alexandria' and he refers with obvious relief to the forces that are being built up to guard them. He declares that the task of Eighth Army should be to hold not only 'the El Alamein defended area and to prevent it being by-passed' but to hold the 'Natrun area' as well. Yet elsewhere in his Appreciation Dorman-Smith specifically states that 'there is little danger of the enemy getting any value out of by-passing the Eighth Army on its present ground.' Presumably therefore the reason why he regards it as so important to hold the 'Natrun area' is his fear that Eighth Army might in fact be not just by-passed on but driven out of 'the El Alamein defended area'.

No doubt it is also for this reason that Dorman-Smith records so thankfully that 'the critical period for the preparation and manning of the Delta and Cairo defences is now over' and that 'the defences of Alexandria-Cairo-the Delta proper east of the Nubariya canal and the Wadi Natrun area will be well forward by August 14 and should be complete, in so far as defences are ever complete, by the end of August.' He further remarks that 'bottle-necks exposed to air action are the Nile crossings at Cairo and northwards.' These again would only be of real importance should Eighth Army be defeated, but Dorman-Smith notes with satisfaction that they are 'being supplemented by two floating bridges south of Cairo and by improving the routes from these bridges eastwards.' He is further consoled by the knowledge that 'all arrangements for demolitions in the Delta are being made.' He laments, however, that in contrast 'the enemy has few really vulnerable points' though 'morally his Italians are always vulnerable.'

Finally Dorman-Smith rejoices that: 'The soft sand areas of the country east of El Alamein, notably the "Barrel Track" axis, the Wadi Natrun, the sand area to its north, are all added difficulties for the enemy's movement, particularly as they cannot be widely known to him.' This is the most disheartening comment of all, for the only reason why the enemy would be moving into these areas would be because he had broken through the existing defences at Alamein.

The pessimism contained in these passages – General Jackson goes so far as to call it 'defeatism' – is reflected and confirmed by a mass of instructions which pour out from General Headquarters Middle East dealing with the actions to be taken in the event of an Eighth Army defeat at Alamein. On 2 August, for instance, orders are given to cut down 'fig and palm trees' which might otherwise block lines of fire from the reserve defences. On 14 August, in response to previous directions from Auchinleck, a War Game is organized to test the best ways in which to protect Alexandria. On the same day, plans are issued for the removal of civilians living between Alamein and the Nile, 'should the Battle of the Delta have to be fought'.

If Eighth Army was defeated it would of course become necessary to deny vital supplies or equipment to the enemy, and this consideration is certainly not absent from the orders issued during early August. On the 1st, the railway bridge over the Nubariya canal is scheduled for destruction. On the 4th, so are water sources in the area of Wadi Natrun. Two days later, 'wells and water supplies' in the Sinai Desert, and incidentally also those in the desert parts of southern Palestine, are added to the list. So too are 'loco-motives' and 'rolling stock' on the 11th. Earlier on the 7th, attention had been given to the possible destruction of oil supplies, not only in Palestine but in Syria, Trans-Jordan, the Sudan, Iraq, Persia, Saudi Arabia, Bahrein and Aden – which does appear to anticipate a fairly total collapse.

Of course it can rightly be argued that the retreats to Cairo and Alexandria, let alone to Palestine and the Sudan, would be carried out only if this became inevitable; that just because the plans existed it did not mean that they would be put into operation. The trouble was that there was far too much interest shown in the plans and in the reserve positions that were required by them. In Field Marshal Alexander's official Despatch there appears the definite declaration that 'it was fairly well known' that Eighth Army 'would retreat again in accordance with the theory that it must be kept in being.' Alexander does add that this would be 'in the last resort' but this was not a qualification likely to be made by the troops in the heated atmosphere of August, 1942.

As a result, 'the whole attitude of Eighth Army', in Kippenberger's words, 'was that of having one foot in the stirrup.' 'I don't say that it is not prudent to be prepared for the worst' declares de Guingand, 'but on the other hand, if there is too much of this sort of thing it is most unlikely that the troops will fight their best in their existing positions.'

And how important it was that they should fight their best in their existing positions becomes clear when it is realized that, for all the concern over reserve defences, it was felt by many that there was no real hope of holding them. Certainly this was the opinion of Auchinleck's successors and of some of his own chief subordinates. Field Marshal Harding for instance, in the interview already quoted, states that if Rommel had broken through at Alamein:

> . . . the time-factor, the topography and the effect on the general political and social situation in the Delta would have been such that nothing could have stopped him from entering Cairo. . . . If you were realistic, you had to admit to yourself that if the Alamein position became untenable through penetration and subsequent exploitation by Rommel, there was no other place in which you could fight an effective battle.

Moreover Harding believed that Auchinleck was aware of this and only 'intended to impose delay on Rommel in the Delta.'

How then was Eighth Army to defeat Rommel's renewed advance? The tactical answers given in Dorman-Smith's Appreciation make sorry reading.[4] There are no anxieties over the effectiveness of Rommel's anti-tank guns. There are no suggestions as to how to improve co-operation between the various branches of Eighth Army or between Army and Air Force, though Dorman-Smith does remark glibly that air superiority is 'a very considerable, if somewhat indefinable asset'. On the other hand he refers with obvious approval to the use of battle groups and he proclaims that 'it is necessary to husband our armour carefully' – a comment which must have aroused grim reflections in the minds of any infantry commanders who read it. Worst of all, although Eighth Army had won 'First Alamein' by a largely static defence in fixed positions, Dorman-Smith had very different ideas for the coming action. As Auchinleck expressly confirms in his official Despatch, the whole 'essence of the defensive plan' was 'fluidity and mobility'.

The Appreciation ignores not only the lessons of the past but the problems of the present. The northern part of the Alamein Line was now held firmly by the divisions of XXX Corps: 9th Australian, 1st South African and 5th Indian, reading from north to south. In the XIII Corps area, however, the situation was far more dangerous. The position of 2nd New Zealand Division was potentially perilous and south of the New Zealanders there was a yawning gap which provided an invitation that Rommel was unlikely to refuse.

In his Appreciation, Dorman-Smith does rightly anticipate that 'Eighth Army may have to meet an enemy's sortie developing into manoeuvre by the southern flank'. Yet his only reaction is to remark with cheerful lack of concern: 'We have no defences in depth opposite this sector, which is lightly covered by mobile troops.' It does not seem to occur to him that it might be a good idea to strengthen the defences in that sector.

Had Auchinleck and Dorman-Smith only held different views, they might have found ways of rectifying the situation. They might for instance have remembered from 'Second Ruweisat' how effectively minefields could ruin an armoured thrust. Instead minefields are simply ignored in Dorman-Smith's Appreciation and neither he nor Auchinleck appear to have had the slightest interest in them – after all, nothing is less fluid and mobile than a mine. Some mined areas were prepared but it seems that the general feeling, in Field Marshal Carver's words, was that 'to lay too many mines would only limit the ability of Eighth Army's own armoured forces to make a counter-thrust when their turn came.'

Then again it might have been possible to find armoured forces to guard the southern part of the front. 1st Armoured Division had suffered such casualties in July that it was soon to be pulled out of the combat zone, but it had already been decided that 22nd Armoured Brigade, now commanded by Roberts, should be transferred to 7th Armoured Division. In his Appreciation, Dorman-Smith proposes to 'organize and train a strong mobile wing based on 7th Armoured Division' but he clearly envisages it as being more mobile than strong for he specifically states it shall comprise 'divisional artillery, 7th Motor Brigade, 4th Light Armoured Brigade and possibly extra Crusader units' but not 22nd Armoured which provided 7th

Armoured Division's main tank strength. Its omission becomes under-standable when it is realized that Dorman-Smith intended his 'strong mobile wing' to impose delaying tactics only on the enemy. It must, he declares, 'be well trained in harassing defensive technique.'

If Rommel broke through in the south as thus seemed inevitable and was thus implicitly accepted, what would happen to the infantry divisions further north, particularly 2nd New Zealand Division, which would automatically be outflanked? There was a line of high ground, running from the ridge at Alam Nayil through the Bare Ridge to the ridge at Alam Halfa, which would provide an admirable reserve line of defence, but how was this to be secured? 2nd New Zealand Division was very much under strength. Its 4th Brigade had had to be withdrawn from the battle area altogether after the losses incurred in July, while both its remaining brigades had suffered heavily. It simply did not have enough men to hold both its front line and its left flank which rested on the Alam Nayil Ridge, let alone the Bare Ridge and the Alam Halfa Ridge as well.

Again though, if only Auchinleck and Dorman-Smith had held different views, they could have found an answer to this problem in the shape of an entire new division. 44th (British) Division, commanded by Major General Ivor Hughes, had recently arrived in the Middle East and might so easily have been added to the defenders of the Alamein position. Sadly the C-in-C Middle East and his adviser favoured a 'fluid and mobile' battle and believed, probably correctly, that 44th Division was not sufficiently well trained to fight such an action. Moreover they wished to use it to guard the cities of Egypt in case Eighth Army failed to hold the Alamein Line, for which task it was divided into brigade groups. On 7 August, one of these, on the instructions of General Headquarters, Middle East, was held back 'as a general reserve located east of the Nile', while three days later the duty of the others was announced as being 'to prevent a rush break-through' to Cairo 'by armoured or mechanized forces either eluding Eighth Army or arriving on the heels of a withdrawing Eighth Army.'

Deprived of 44th Division, there was no possibility of Eighth Army adequately protecting the New Zealand position or adequately defending the Bare Ridge or Alam Halfa Ridge – neither of which, it may be added, is mentioned anywhere in Dorman-Smith's Appreciation. The Bare Ridge was left completely unguarded. So was Point 102, the high ground just to the west of Alam Halfa. On 3 August, 21st Indian Brigade was instructed to maintain 'a garrison of infantry and guns in the Alam Halfa position' but this brigade was very much under strength and had made scarcely any progress in the construction of defences by mid-August.

This no doubt mattered little to Auchinleck and Dorman-Smith since they had determined on a different form of defence – another retreat, this

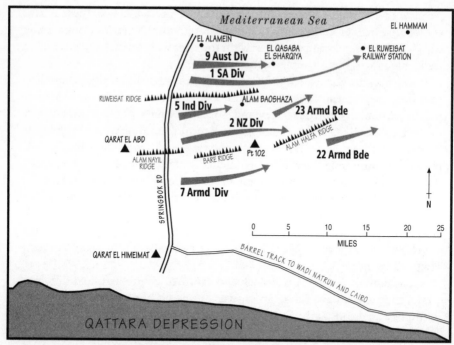

Map VIIIA: Alam Halfa – Auchinleck's Plan.

Map VIIIB: Alam Halfa – Montgomery's Plan.

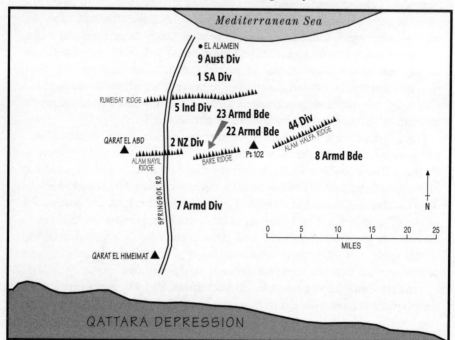

time as a tactical manoeuvre. Not only does Dorman-Smith's Appreciation envisage a retirement in the south using a 'harassing defensive technique', but in the north, he proclaims that: 'We have to be prepared to fight a modern defensive battle in the area El Alamein-Hammam.' El Hammam (in other accounts confusingly called El Hamman or El Hamma) lay some forty miles by road eastward of El Alamein.

The tactics for Dorman-Smith's 'modern defensive battle' were based on the fact that the Alamein defences, as he notes in his Appreciation, were of two types: 'FDLs' (Forward Defended Localities) which formed the existing front line and 'reserve positions'. These latter were strong-points or 'boxes', ten in number, which were known also as Defended Observation Posts (or OPs) and were established on prominent features some way to the rear. In the north they lay around Qasaba – or to give it its formal name El Qasaba el Sharqiya – on the railway line some ten miles east of El Alamein, in the centre around Alam Baoshaza east of the Ruweisat Ridge, and in the south on the ridge of Alam Halfa. 'Should it be desired to avoid the full effect of an enemy attack in great strength' announces the Appreciation, 'the above FDLs can become the outpost line and the main front can be withdrawn accordingly.'

Such was the scheme which Dorman-Smith '"sold" to the C-in-C' as he personally boasted to General Richardson. Shortly thereafter, as the War Diaries report, a series of orders was issued which set out the detailed moves necessary to put the scheme into practice. Thus on 29 July in its Operation Order 144, XIII Corps states that the Alamein defences consist of 'a forward position (the present FDLs) and the main position'. The elevation of the rear defences to the status of 'main position' is surely significant. The Order then announces that the current policy is 'to hold the forward position in strength and prepare the main defensive position' but, it continues, 'it may be necessary to occupy the main defensive position' and the remainder of the Order in fact deals almost entirely with the action required in that case.

XXX Corps adopts a similar attitude. In its Operation Order 70 of 31 July, it declares that it will 'hold present FDLs' but it then goes on to discuss the necessity to construct reserve defended localities which can be 'occupied at short notice by any formation' and to which 'personnel not required for the immediate defence of the El Alamein-El Ruweisat area will be sent forthwith.' Presumably it was as a result of these considerations that the forward dispositions of XXX Corps remained, in the words of General Jackson, 'too shallow and over-influenced by the possible need for quick withdrawal'.

By 10 August when XXX Corps issues its Operation Order 71, any remaining doubts about retiring from the forward defences had disappeared. So at least reports Field Marshal Carver and since he was the staff officer who wrote this Operation Order he can speak with exceptional authority. Its first paragraph does pay lip-service to the choice of fighting in the existing positions 'depending on the scale of the attack', but the remaining twenty-six paragraphs are concerned only with the need to 'occupy and defend the main zone of the Alamein position' and 'to thin out the forward zone' accordingly.

Operation Orders 144 and 71 both go on to describe the specific actions that will be adopted when Rommel's offensive takes place. The infantry formations 'will withdraw to the main zone' their retirement being protected by 'light covering forces on the forward position' according to XIII Corps, 'outposts in the forward area' according to XXX Corps. These covering forces will 'keep in contact with the enemy and prevent any infiltration towards our main defences.' 9th Australian Division will proceed to the northern group of 'boxes' and 2nd New Zealand Division to the southern group at Alam Halfa. 5th Indian Division will retreat to the 'Army Reserve area' near El Ruweisat railway station according to XIII Corps – confirming a suggestion in Dorman-Smith's Appreciation – but the later XXX Corps Order states that this division will make for the central group of 'boxes' while it is 1st South African Division which will 'pass through 9th Aust and 5th Ind Divs into Army Reserve.'

On reaching the Defended Observation Posts, the divisions will split up. Part only of the infantry and artillery will be allocated to them – Operation Order 71 says that each OP should contain 'two infantry battalions, one field battery and one anti-tank battery'. The remaining infantry and the bulk of the artillery will be formed into battle groups. Operation Order 71 states that 'between defended localities, battle groups will counter-attack any enemy who may attempt to attack or outflank our positions.' 'The defences of the Alam Halfa position' agrees Operation Order 144, 'will include the operation of mobile battle groups.' It is pointed out that if necessary the battle groups can always fall back into the OPs.

'The theory was' remarks de Guingand sardonically:

> . . . that in the event of enemy attack and penetration, these strong points would be occupied in accordance with the situation, and from them would be directed powerful artillery fire. I never quite understood how it was to be done, but the artillery was to be concentrated in support of the threatened sector or sectors, and then be linked up and controlled from these OPs. It was all too uncertain and fluid a plan for a sound defence. There was a great danger of the guns being driven hither and thither, and confusion setting in.

It was also a plan which would have delighted Rommel. Eighth Army would be giving up its secure defences, and incidentally the few gains it had made at such cost in July, in order to engage in mobile manoeuvres against an enemy who had repeatedly proved his superiority in this type of conflict. It was Rommel's own determination that when he delivered his offensive, events must 'move fast'; the engagement was 'on no account to become static' – and although he did not know it, his opponents were thus playing straight into his hands.

This was doubly the case because Eighth Army's armoured formations were also to be 'fluid and mobile'. Operation Order 71 directs the Valentines of 23rd Armoured Brigade, which had been detailed to support XXX Corps, to take station well to the east of the 'boxes' around Qasaba but to be 'prepared to counter-attack in the event of an enemy break-through between 9 Aust and 5 Ind Divs.' Operation Order 144 tells 7th Armoured Division that its tasks will be to 'protect the southern flank during and subsequent to the occupation of the main position; take over the forward position or part of it in conjunction with other armoured forces; maintain an armoured reserve.'

This last task was entrusted to 22nd Armoured Brigade; Roberts tells us it was 'to be in reserve in an area just south of Alam Halfa.' On 1 August, however, its duties were elaborated upon and complicated. It was told to 'impose maximum delay on enemy advance' or alternatively to restore the 'local situation' if the New Zealand position should be penetrated or alternatively again to cover a 'withdrawal of 5th Ind Div and 2nd NZ Div to the rear position' – being ready, like 23rd Armoured Brigade, to counter-attack when necessary, presumably, as so often before, straight at the muzzles of Rommel's 88mms.

Indeed 22nd Armoured was presented with a wide variety of potential duties and potential plans. 'On code word "so-and-so",' says Roberts, 'we would move to a specific area with a certain task; on another code word we would move somewhere else, etc. etc.' Since the chances were high that the wrong plan might be followed in the confusion of combat or as a result of communications problems. Roberts felt strongly that this situation 'did not inspire the greatest confidence.'

He was not alone in this belief. Field Marshal Carver declares that: 'A good many people, including notably Freyberg' (who had resumed command of 2nd New Zealand Division) thought the tactics proposed would fail. 'It would be difficult', complains General Richardson, 'to conceive a tactical plan more unsuited to the units of the Eighth Army at that time.' The 'suicidal notions' embodied in Dorman-Smith's Appreciation, approved by Auchinleck and set out in subsequent commands to formations, 'might almost', grumbles Lucas Phillips, 'have been written for Rommel's express benefit.'

Fortunately Rommel would never gain any benefit from them. On

16 August, XXX Corps issues Operation Order 72. Its opening paragraphs ring out like trumpet-blasts:

> All orders and instructions which refer to withdrawal from or thinning out of our present positions are hereby cancelled.
>
> XXX Corps will defend the present FDLs at all costs. There will be no withdrawal.
>
> The above intention is to be explained to and impressed on all ranks immediately.

Montgomery had arrived.

Notes.

1 At that time a young captain in Eighth Army, Llewellyn is best known in the equestrian world. In 1936 he had ridden 'Ego' into second place in the Grand National. After the war he would achieve fame in show-jumping, his 'Foxhunter' being the only horse to win the King George V Gold Cup on three occasions. Another of his best horses, by the way, was 'Monty' but we are told he was not named after anyone in particular.

2 Notably the War Diaries of General Headquarters, Middle East, Eighth Army HQ, XIII Corps HQ and XXX Corps HQ, all of which may be found in the Public Record Office, Kew. Any subsequent quotations from the War Diaries come from this source.

3 Nigel Nicolson: *Alex: The Life of Field Marshal Earl Alexander of Tunis.*

4 The Appreciation is equally depressing in matters of strategy. It displays, for example, great concern for the Caucasus, remarking that 'the operations of Eighth Army are linked to the fate of Russia.' On the other hand it shows no appreciation whatever of the importance of Malta, which is not so much as mentioned.

12

ARRIVALS AND DEPARTURES

The Prime Minister's visit will have been worthwhile, if only for the stimulus which he has given to the Army, and for the new blood which he has introduced.

Colonel Jacob's Diary.
6 August, 1942.

The first of the new arrivals from Britain was in fact the Chief of the Imperial General Staff. Brooke reached Cairo in time for breakfast on 3 August, deeply concerned about the situation in the Middle East, fully aware of the problems he would have to face and only too conscious of the probably calamitous consequences of any errors of judgement. Churchill, with an impressive entourage, which included the indispensable Colonel Jacob, Sir Alexander Cadogan, Permanent Secretary to the Foreign Office and the Prime Minister's doctor Sir Charles Wilson (later Lord Moran), joined him soon afterwards. So did Field Marshal Smuts whom Churchill had summoned from South Africa, while on the following day General Wavell flew in from India to complete a formidable council of war.

The series of interviews, discussions and decisions which followed have often been described and may be dealt with briefly.[1] When Brooke arrived in Cairo, Auchinleck had not yet returned from his headquarters at the Ruweisat Ridge. Brooke had a long talk with Corbett instead, and on the morning of 4 August, Churchill met Corbett also. Both were informed that Auchinleck was eager to resume his post as C-in-C, Middle East and wished to appoint Corbett to command Eighth Army in his stead. 'In fact', Corbett told the Prime Minister, 'I have been living with my kit packed for the last week.'

Since neither Churchill nor Brooke relished the thought of Auchinleck directing Eighth Army from Cairo through another loyal staff officer and held no high opinion of Corbett either, this suggestion did not meet with approval. After lunch on the 4th therefore, Brooke met with Auchinleck and expressed his strong dissatisfaction. Auchinleck then hastily agreed that Corbett should not command Eighth Army and should moreover cease to be Auchinleck's own Chief of Staff. Poor Corbett was duly dismissed, retiring from the Army in 1943.

On 5 August Churchill and Brooke had their 'day in the desert'. By its end Brooke was ready, says General Fraser in *Alanbrooke*, 'to agree to any solution which took Auchinleck from Cairo.' Churchill heartily agreed. Much stress has been laid on the Prime Minister's impatience with Auchinleck's proposed delay before resuming the offensive in September, but while this undoubtedly did not help Auchinleck's case, the real reason for Churchill's opinion was Auchinleck's inept explanation of how he intended to deal with the enemy's offensive at the end of August.

Thus Brigadier Sir Edgar Williams states emphatically that:

> Hugh Mainwaring and I virtually heard Winston Churchill sack the Auk because we stood outside the caravan waiting to be summoned if wanted on the Ops side or the Intelligence side – and Winston gave this astonishing description of what Rommel was doing and said to the Auk: "Well, what are you going to do about that? What's your plan?" I mean he was incredibly well-briefed, of course he'd got his "Ultra", he'd sort of thought it out: Rommel's doing this, what are we going to do? . . . The Auk, he wasn't very articulate.

As Williams walked away after this exchange, he remarked: 'Well, we'll get a new Army Commander now. Who the hell will it be?'

Next day Churchill and Brooke reached their decision. Auchinleck would cease to be Commander-in-Chief, Middle East. To replace him, Brooke, supported by Smuts, proposed General Sir Harold Alexander, who had previously been selected to command the British First Army in the TORCH landings. He would reach Cairo early on 9 August. Alexander seemed fated to be presented with one hazardous assignment after another. He had been placed in command of the rearguard during the evacuation from Dunkirk. Later he had been sent to Burma just before the fall of Rangoon, only to find that its defenders, who were desperately short of artillery and were un-supported from the air, had no possible chance of checking the Japanese advance. As a result, he had been forced to conduct another withdrawal, this time all the way to the frontier of India.

It was perhaps hardly a good omen that the new Commander-in-Chief,

Middle East had made his name carrying out retreats, but the calm courage he had displayed in desperate situations had not only mitigated the extent of the disasters but had rightly won widespread admiration. Moreover, Brooke felt that this steadfast imperturbability would serve Alexander equally well in Cairo; that he would cope with the political problems of the Middle East with tact and charm, support his subordinates loyally but only intervene if matters were going badly, and be able to win the affection and trust of all.

Alexander's appointment led to an abrupt change of fortune for an officer who had been disregarded and dismissed by his predecessor. The new C-in-C, Middle East would need a new senior staff officer. 'I at once thought of Dick McCreery' Brooke tells us. Auchinleck's ignored tank-expert would go on to lead X Corps in Italy, before taking command of Eighth Army in November 1944. He would hold this post until his Army was disbanded in July, 1945, when, as General Sir Richard McCreery, he became Commander-in-Chief of the British Forces in occupied Austria and later the British Army Representative on the Military Staff Committee of the United Nations.

McCreery was not the only officer who had fallen into disfavour with Auchinleck but would achieve success elsewhere. Ritchie had returned to Britain in mid-July, writing a last touching letter to Auchinleck regretting that he could no longer help shoulder his chief's burdens and reiterating his confidence that Eighth Army would win in the end. It was perhaps as well that he could not foresee the future.

For when John Connell produced the authorized biography of Auchinleck, he attempted to place all responsibility for Eighth Army's defeats onto Ritchie, omitting vital documents in whole or in part, misdating signals and indulging in every kind of innuendo.[2] Ritchie had been informed that Connell's version 'had been approved by Auchinleck' but he 'simply could not believe' this. He therefore sought out his former superior to discuss the subject.

He was quickly undeceived. To his 'utter amazement', Auchinleck:

> . . . made it quite clear that he would do nothing to support or help me. He would not do anything to alter the inaccuracies contained in the book about me which, if you have read it, was written very much biased against me. This he could easily have done at the time. From that day, my feelings for him completely changed. He did to me what I consider a dishonourable and disloyal thing.

Ritchie contemplated taking legal action but eventually refrained. It is possible to regret his decision since it allowed a number of legends which might otherwise have been strangled at birth to flourish and endure, but in reality Ritchie had already answered his critics in anticipation. It was appreciated by everyone who mattered that as Eighth Army Commander he had been placed by Auchinleck in an impossible position. On his return from the Middle East therefore, he was given command first of 52nd Lowland Division, then of XII Corps which he led with distinction throughout the victorious campaign in North-Western Europe. After the war, as General Sir Neil Ritchie, he became Commander-in-Chief, Far East Land Forces and later head of the British Army Staff in the Joint Services Mission to the United States. 'A very fine man who did a wonderful "come-back" after suffering a serious blow' is how Brooke describes him.

Brooke also had no doubts about the ability of Whiteley. He was soon to find employment as Deputy Chief of Staff (Operations) to General Eisenhower in North Africa, served on Eisenhower's staff throughout the North-Western Europe campaign and rose to become General Sir John Whiteley, Deputy Chief of the Imperial General Staff.

The subsequent career of Lieutenant General Sir Willoughby Norrie was more disappointing. Though at one time he held high rank in 21st Army Group under General Paget, he was not on good terms with the new leaders who took over in early 1944, so he did not participate in the North-Western Europe campaign. Instead he was sent overseas to become Governor of South Australia. Later he was appointed Governor General of New Zealand, but despite these honours and his elevation to the rank of 1st Baron Norrie of Wellington, New Zealand and of Upton, Gloucestershire, it must be a matter of regret that the officer who above all others had ensured that Eighth Army stood firm in early July 1942, should not have received another active command. It was undoubtedly regretted by Norrie who was a man of outstanding personal courage.

The man who had been Norrie's somewhat reluctant supporter in the art of ignoring unsuitable orders, Major General Dan Pienaar, suffered a still sadder, indeed a tragic fate. He would lead 1st South African Division through the triumphs of Alam Halfa and Alamein, but after the latter the South Africans – and the Australians as well for that matter – returned to their own countries. Pienaar was killed in an aircraft accident on the way home.

He was not the only great Eighth Army figure to die in an aircraft. When Auchinleck was dismissed from his post of C-in-C, Middle East, he also ceased to be Commander, Eighth Army. There was some dispute as to who should succeed him. Brooke favoured Lieutenant General Bernard Law Montgomery who had performed splendidly under his command during the retreat to Dunkirk and whom, according to General Fraser, he considered 'without question, the best tactical commander in the Army' and just the man to 'instill a new spirit of self-confidence in the Eighth Army.'

Churchill by contrast preferred Gott, by whom he had been most impressed during his 'day in the desert'. Brooke argued that Gott was 'no longer as fresh as he might be' – as indeed Gott had, with complete honesty, made clear to both Brooke and his political master. Yet by the evening of 6 August, Churchill had had his way, though Brooke personally still considered that 'Montgomery was far better qualified for the job.' 'I may have been weak' Brooke would admit later. He may also have been mentally exhausted after his labours on the preceding days. 'It is not easy' he explains feelingly, 'to be absolutely certain between the relative qualifications of two very able commanders.'

Tragedy now intervened. On the afternoon of 7 August, a Bristol Bombay of 216 (Air Transport) Squadron RAF, flown by Sergeant Pilot Hugh James, arrived at Burg el Arab to take a number of wounded soldiers back to Heliopolis Airport, Cairo. Gott, who had been ordered to return to the Egyptian capital, also boarded this aircraft, which took off at 1645. The route was normally considered safe, so much so that it had been used by Churchill and his party when they visited Eighth Army two days earlier. For this reason, no fighter escort had been provided. Unfortunately, because of an over-heated engine, James was forced to climb to 500 feet instead of proceeding at ground level as was usual.

Meanwhile at 1618, six Messerschmitt Bf 109Fs from II Gruppe of Jagdgeschwader (Fighter Wing) 27 had taken off on an intruder mission. They encountered the Bombay, apparently by sheer chance, and two of them promptly attacked it. Unteroffizier Schneider riddled the helpless transport with cannon shell, setting both engines alight, but James with great skill landed his machine in the desert. Gott who was unhurt gave James a thumbs-up sign. Then, however, the 109s, perhaps guessing that the Bombay might be carrying important passengers, strafed it repeatedly on the ground. Only the four crew members, a medical orderly and one wounded soldier escaped from the blazing wreck. Gott was buried in the military cemetery in Cairo. 'He was the last of the old desert rats to go' relates Alan Moorehead. 'He was a great man for England.'

Brooke was not to be denied a second time. 'CIGS decisively recommends Montgomery for Eighth Army' Churchill signalled to London. 'Pray send him by special plane at earliest moment.' Montgomery was duly sent. Bursting with self-confidence, full of ideas, eager to take up a command in the field again, delighted to be serving under Alexander whom he liked very much, he arrived in Cairo on the morning of 12 August – to be confronted with an absurdly anomalous situation.

Four days earlier, an embarrassed Colonel Jacob had carried a letter to Auchinleck informing him of his dismissal but offering him a new Persia-Iraq Command[3] which was to be detached from the control of the Middle

East. In view of Auchinleck's previous concerns over the defence of the area, this might seem rather an appropriate post, but though urged by Jacob and later by de Guingand to accept, Auchinleck flatly declined it. The Command went instead to Wilson, for whom it proved a path which led to his becoming Commander-in-Chief, Middle East, Supreme Allied Commander, Mediterranean, head of the British Joint Staff Mission in Washington, a field marshal and a peer.

Auchinleck officially refused the Persia-Iraq Command on the ground that his removal from the Middle East implied a lack of confidence in him – as was certainly the case – and that a commander who was replaced in such circumstances should not accept another post. Since only a year later Auchinleck did accept another post, it seems far more probable that he regarded the Persia-Iraq Command as insufficiently important and was outraged by what he regarded as his demotion.

At first Auchinleck's innate dignity allowed him to mask his feelings. He received Jacob with calm control, earning the admiring tribute: 'A great man and a fighter'. On 9 August a meeting between Auchinleck and Churchill was, says the latter, 'at once bleak and impeccable'. But an interview with Brooke, who as Auchinleck knew was ultimately responsible for his dismissal, was very different. 'I tried to soften the blow as much as I possibly could' Brooke would recall. 'In the end I had no alternative but to turn on him and put him in his place; he left me no alternative. I had to bite him back as he was apt to snarl; that kept him quiet.'

Perhaps therefore it was wounded vanity that persuaded Auchinleck to take a step for which no explanation was ever offered either at the time or later. Churchill's party left for Teheran on the first stage of their flight to Moscow in the early hours of 11 August. They had hardly done so when, despite the Prime Minister's wish that 'the transfer of responsibility' should take place on the 12th, Auchinleck declared that he did not propose to give up his leadership either of the Middle East or of Eighth Army until the 15th, and took advantage of Alexander's good nature to get him to agree.

This then was the situation which Montgomery found when he reached Cairo. His unease was increased by an interview with Auchinleck soon after his arrival. This must have been particularly difficult for Auchinleck because he had disliked Montgomery ever since the summer of 1940 when Auchinleck had been commanding Southern Command in a Britain expecting invasion at any moment while Montgomery had been one of his subordinates, having taken over Auchinleck's previous command, V Corps guarding the coasts of Dorset and Hampshire.

Oddly enough, the two men, though poles apart in temperament, did share one important belief. At the end of the Norwegian campaign, Auchinleck had called for 'our methods of man-mastership and training for war' to be made 'more realistic and less effeminate'. Montgomery's training exercises earned many epithets but 'effeminate' was certainly not among them. Here surely could have been a basis for mutual respect. Unhappily Montgomery had strongly criticized the tactics Auchinleck had laid down for V Corps, as well as the lack of training and of operational efficiency in general which he had found in the Corps on Auchinleck's departure. Auchinleck, never happy with criticisms of any sort, retaliated either by dismissing Montgomery's ideas on training as 'mostly rubbish', or by damning them with faint sneer: 'All very inspiring and made me feel a bit inadequate. But I doubt if runs before breakfast really produce battle winners of necessity.'

Understandably therefore, Auchinleck kept his meeting with Montgomery as short as possible and it seems that, as on an earlier occasion, he 'wasn't very articulate.' It is clear that he mentioned both his planned major retreats and his planned tactical withdrawals from the Forward Defended Localities to the Defended Observation Posts. It is equally clear that his listener, who considered that all these plans undermined the morale and determination of the troops, did not realize that while Auchinleck had intended to execute the limited retirements in any case as part of his battle-plan, he would carry out the major evacuations only if they became absolutely essential. As a result, Montgomery would later indicate that Auchinleck proposed to retire from the Alamein position automatically when Rommel attacked. This was of course quite incorrect and Montgomery has been subjected to much abuse in consequence.

Forgotten, however, among all the indignation is another statement made by Auchinleck at this meeting about which there is no doubt whatever. Because he insisted that any transfer of Eighth Army should be delayed so as to coincide with the change in the Middle East Command, Auchinleck, as Field Marshal Carver cynically recalls, told Montgomery he was 'to go down to the desert and look round but not to take over command until the 15th.'

Yet ever since the end of the previous month, Eighth Army Intelligence had predicted that during August, Rommel would deliver an attack vastly more powerful and dangerous than at the time of 'First Alamein'. Moreover by now it was believed that this assault was planned for the 26th, which would give Montgomery as little as fourteen days in which to prepare for it. In these circumstances, Auchinleck's instruction that the new Eighth Army Commander should in effect simply waste one-seventh of the precious time available to him, is utterly astounding.

Montgomery next sought out Alexander whom he found, he tells us in his *Memoirs*, 'calm, confident and charming – as always' – but who did not feel that the changes they both favoured could be put in hand until after the official transfer of command. Montgomery was already beginning to be irritated by the postponement and his irritation increased after he had discussed his new ideas with Harding, the only senior officer of the General Staff who would not be leaving. From Harding he received a forthright account of the present state of Eighth Army, which included a warning that 'at brigade and divisional level they were very good and efficient and morale was very good. But as a total, no, they were disorganized and they were rattled. They had lost their confidence.'

Next morning Montgomery drove out to the Ruweisat Ridge, accompanied by de Guingand, from whom he heard another lengthy review of the current situation. It could not have been a very encouraging one for de Guingand had spent most of the previous day drawing up a list of 'matters which I thought required urgent attention.' These, interestingly enough, were the 'unsound fashion' of fighting in 'battle groups', the 'unsatisfactory headquarters set-up', the separation of 'the Army and Air Headquarters' and first and foremost 'the dangerous "looking over the shoulder" defensive policy'.

Following the equally direct comments of Harding, this information must have convinced Montgomery that steps to rectify the position must be taken without delay. The sight of Eighth Army's dismal, fly-encrusted headquarters did nothing to dispel his belief. On his arrival, Montgomery cross-examined Ramsden, to whom Auchinleck had entrusted temporary command of Eighth Army. 'By the time he had finished' reports Field Marshal Carver, 'Montgomery had decided that he could not tolerate two days hanging about under these conditions. He therefore told Ramsden to return to his corps, having decided, in spite of Auchinleck's orders, to assume command immediately' – at 1400 to be precise.

Montgomery did not have an easy task ahead of him. How great was the disillusionment throughout Eighth Army would be demonstrated by the way that its consequences lasted well into the future. At Alam Halfa the benefits that might have been gained from a planned counter-move would be lost because the best part of a day would be wasted by 'indiscipline at the top'. At Alamein Montgomery would discover that his armoured commanders knew 'very little about the co-operation of all arms on the battlefield' – naturally not, because they had never received any training in this respect. And during the pursuit from Alamein and even as late as the Battle of the Mareth Line in March, 1943, opportunities would be missed because infantry formations, especially the New Zealanders, would be concerned about being left 'naked before an armoured attack'.

Fortunately almost the first action that Montgomery took would serve to impress his men with his ability, silence the grumblers and unite his entire army behind him in relieved approval. He countermanded all existing plans for retreat either to the Defended Observation Posts or to the Nile Delta. To his assembled staff he announced curtly: 'I do not like the general atmosphere I find here. It is an atmosphere of doubt, of looking back to select the next place to which to withdraw, of loss of confidence in our ability to defeat Rommel, of desperate defence measures by reserves in preparing positions in Cairo and the Delta.' It may be remarked that no one who was present on this occasion would ever query the accuracy of this assessment.

Calling for a 'new atmosphere', Montgomery proclaimed: 'The defence of Egypt lies here at Alamein and on the Ruweisat Ridge. What is the use of digging trenches in the Delta? It is quite useless; if we lose this position we lose Egypt; all the fighting troops now in the Delta must come here at once, and will. *Here* we will stand and fight; there will be no further withdrawal. I have ordered that all plans and instructions dealing with further withdrawal are to be burnt, and at once. We will stand and fight *here*. If we can't stay here alive, then let us stay here dead.'

In those few sentences, Montgomery ended for ever the doubts that had so crippled Eighth Army, the uncertainties, the glances 'over the shoulder'. The news spread like wildfire. 'Thank God!' exclaimed Morshead, the Australians' commander. Montgomery followed up his announcement with a number of ostentatious acts designed to emphasize his determination. Kippenberger recounts for instance that:

> Our troop-carrying transport was sent a long way back so that we could not run away if we wanted to! There was no more talk of the alternative positions in the rear. We were delighted and the morale of the whole Army went up incredibly.

Montgomery then relieved more anxieties by embarking on an almost total alteration of the battle-plan prepared by Auchinleck and Dorman-Smith. Even the 'essence' of that plan, 'fluidity and mobility', was abandoned. There would be no 'fluid and mobile' retirement to the Defended Observation Posts. As was mentioned earlier, on 16 August the divisions in XXX Corps were directed by Operation Order 72 to 'defend the present FDLs at all costs.' Two days earlier the New Zealanders had been instructed by XIII Corps Operation Order 145 to hold their front-line defences 'to last man and last round'. Labour units, hitherto employed on tasks in the Delta, were summoned to strengthen and give as much depth as possible to the forward positions of all the infantry divisions, while food, water and ammunition were hurriedly brought up to enable them to conduct a lengthy resistance if needed.

In addition Montgomery declared that the infantry divisions would never in future be split up into battle groups. De Guingand tells us that he gave orders that 'the expression ceased to exist. Divisions would fight as divisions and be allowed to develop their great strength.' This insistence meant that the divisions' artillery would henceforth not be scattered but would be able to deliver concentrated fire, a task made easier in the Battle of Alam Halfa by Montgomery's determination that the fighting should remain static.

Since Montgomery was interested only in standing fast at Alamein and not in any reserve positions guarding Alexandria or Cairo, and since he thought that even comparatively inexperienced units should be able to hold prepared defences, he could reinforce his front-line still further. On the evening of 13 August, he personally rang Harding to demand that 44th Division be sent to the combat-zone. Harding went to see Auchinleck who weakly suggested that he consult Alexander. At 2200, 44th Division was ordered to join Eighth Army. 50th Division, which Montgomery claimed for his army reserve, also moved up from Amiriya during the coming action. Unfortunately, it contained only one brigade, the 151st, after the maulings received by 150th Brigade in the Cauldron and 69th Brigade in July.

Only Wimberley's 51st Highland Division remained to hold the defences of Cairo. By some extraordinary thought-process this has been taken as evidence that Montgomery accepted the value of Auchinleck's dispositions. In fact this decision was made by Alexander. It did not please Montgomery who would see that the division was sent to the front as soon as Rommel's offensive had been quelled – though since Wimberley's men were not at this time considered fit for action, even in a purely defensive role, Alexander had really had little choice in the matter. Montgomery's own opinion of Auchinleck's ideas about defending the cities of Egypt would be made crystal clear on 14 August. When Auchinleck, then of course still Commander-in-Chief, Middle East, was so unwise as to enquire about the progress of the Wadi Natrun defences, Lieutenant Colonel Mainwaring, on Montgomery's behalf, retorted that: 'In view of Eighth Army Commander's new order for "no looking over your shoulder" and "fighting on present position" there is no need for a Wadi Natrun defensive position, therefore there is no action required.'

Not that the location of 51st Highland Division was of much relevance in any event. The crucial move was that of 44th Division. On 16 August its 131st and 133rd Brigades relieved 21st Indian Brigade to provide an adequate defence for the Alam Halfa Ridge. At the same time, its 132nd Brigade came under command of 2nd New Zealand Division, thereby giving Freyberg sufficient troops with which to guard both his front line and his flank on Alam Nayil.

South of the New Zealand position the defences were reinforced by other means. On 14 August, during a conference at XIII Corps Headquarters, Montgomery proposed an 'enlarging and strengthening of the minefields' in this area. By the end of the month these were formidable indeed – two wide belts, containing, says Major General Strawson, 'a judicious mixture of anti-tank and anti-personnel mines'. Moreover the minefields, 'hindering and canalizing movement as they did, were ideally complimented by the RAF.'

Montgomery regarded 'his' 'magnificent air striking force' as he rather arrogantly considered it, as one of the main keys to success. By 16 August, his headquarters was again side by side with that of the Desert Air Force, the two staffs co-operating fully in planning future moves. Their task also was aided by the decision that the coming battle would no longer be 'fluid and mobile', for this inevitably reduced the possibilities of errors arising from mistaken identity.

Eighth Army's armoured units would cease to be 'fluid and mobile' as well. 23rd Armoured Brigade was ordered to transfer a squadron of tanks each to the Australians, the New Zealanders and 5th Indian Division. Its remaining Valentines were brought up from Qasaba to a position behind the Ruweisat Ridge from which Brigadier Richards, who now commanded them, could provide close support to the front-line infantry. Once he considered there was no further danger of a break-through in the Ruweisat area, however, Richards was to move south to occupy the Bare Ridge.

Further south still, 7th Armoured Division was to fight from behind the protection of the minefields. It was to contain, for this purpose, only 4th Light Armoured Brigade and 7th Motor Brigade, since 22nd Armoured Brigade was sent to Point 102. Here, reinforced by a number of anti-tank guns, it was, as Roberts delightedly told his men on 19 August, 'for once' to await an enemy attack 'in good positions of our own choosing'. The mass of alternative plans were 'gladly destroyed' and, Roberts reports, 'we all felt better.'

Finally, towards the end of August, 10th Armoured Division, under the command of Gatehouse, arrived to replace 1st Armoured Division. Richards and Roberts were transferred to Gatehouse's control but apart from them he had only Brigadier Custance's 8th Armoured Brigade, of which two-thirds of the armoured regiments were totally inexperienced, having seen no action previously in the war, or indeed since they had ceased to ride horses. Nonetheless, it was again felt that 8th Armoured would do well enough if it stood on the defensive. It was also strengthened with anti-tank guns and stationed ten miles east of Roberts to the south-east of Alam Halfa.

Thus, in a miraculously short time, Montgomery had brought about not only a complete change of atmosphere by restoring Eighth Army's flagging morale, but also a complete change of tactics which would achieve victory in the battle so soon to be fought. And if any would query this statement it can only be said that this was the opinion of almost every officer who was present at the time, regardless of differences in rank, in nationality and in the branches of the army from which they came: Belchem, Carver, de

Guingand, Freyberg, Graham, Harding, Jacob, Kippenberger, Lewin, Llewellyn, Lucas Phillips, Morshead, McCreery, Oswald, Richardson, Roberts, Stirling, Williams, Wimberley . . . the list is endless. To these names add Nehring and von Vaerst who provided most of the information for this period to Paul Carell, who in turn calls Montgomery simply 'the man who was to defeat Rommel' adding 'and how dangerous he was'. Add also Major General von Mellenthin who gives a more detailed but equally clear verdict:

> There can be no question that the fighting efficiency of the British improved vastly under the new leadership, and for the first time Eighth Army had a commander who really made his will felt throughout the whole force. . . . Montgomery is undoubtedly a great tactician – circumspect and thorough in making his plans, utterly ruthless in carrying them out. He brought a new spirit to Eighth Army, and illustrated once again the vital importance of personal leadership in war.

It may be suspected that General Auchinleck did not share this opinion, but then it would hardly have been fair to have asked him to do so. Since he stayed on in Cairo for a few days after his transfer of command to Alexander on 15 August, however, he will have seen how his successor immediately gave his unqualified support to Montgomery's actions, in particular to his 'no withdrawal' orders and his refusal to allow the break-up of divisions. Auchinleck then retired to India where in June 1943 he was re-appointed Commander-in-Chief, receiving promotion to field marshal three years later. It is only right to say that this was entirely deserved for he once again proved a conspicuous success in a post which he must often have wished that he had never left.

Yet in the end he must have wished even more fervently that he had never resumed it, for an unkind fate decreed that his final acts should be to preside, with great dignity, over the destruction of that magnificent Indian Army to which he had devoted his life, and afterwards to watch helplessly as the various races of the sub-continent, for all of whom he had a sincere and genuine regard, embarked on an orgy of mutual slaughter which he was powerless to prevent. It must have broken his heart.

Auchinleck's 'evil genius' fell with his master – to the great relief of the whole of Eighth Army. On returning to Britain, Dorman-Smith reverted to the rank of colonel and, as his desert reputation did not recommend him to potential superiors, he remained inactive until he was given command of an infantry brigade in the Anzio bridgehead in March 1944. It proved a mistake.

Since astonishingly enough Dorman-Smith still has admirers eager to find excuses for him, it seems best to relate what followed in the words of General

Sir Charles Richardson. In an article for *The Royal Engineers Journal* in April 1991, he describes how Dorman-Smith's three battalion commanders:

> . . . became appalled at the prospect of an offensive operation under 'Chink's' command. Eventually, when this became officially known, he was relieved; he retired, an embittered man, to Eire, but not before he had made a prolonged, emotional appeal against the adverse report which had followed the Anzio incident.

Thereafter Dorman-O'Gowan, as he became known in 1949, divided his time between explaining how the 'Military Establishment' had decreed his ruin and attempting to magnify his war-time achievements. His views found some acceptance far from the battlefield but not among many of those who had served with him. Accordingly in an outburst of spite he decided to offer his services elsewhere. At the time of his death he was giving advice on future objectives to, and conducting tactical studies in his cellar for, the benefit of the Irish Republican Army.

For the officers and men of Eighth Army, the change of command was not only their salvation but their justification. All they needed was an experienced Commander and a C-in-C Middle East who gave him steadfast support but did not attempt to control the battle from afar, and there would be no holding them. The same soldiers who had been accused by their previous leader in late July of losing 'control' and making 'avoidable mistakes' would be congratulated by their new leader in early September for their 'devotion to duty and good fighting qualities'.

Most of them would moreover gain further distinction during the rest of the war and after it. None more so than de Guingand who served as Montgomery's Chief of Staff throughout that officer's tenure as Eighth Army Commander in North Africa, Sicily and Italy, and remained his Chief of Staff when Montgomery was entrusted with command of Twenty-First Army Group during the North-Western Europe campaign. After the war they quarrelled, which is another, sadder story. Nonetheless in his *Memoirs* Montgomery openly acknowledges the debt he owed to his 'trusted Chief of Staff' without whom he 'could not possibly have handled' his military duties.

To name just a few of Eighth Army's other staff officers: Williams would soon be appointed head of that army's Intelligence staff and later of the Intelligence staff of Twenty-First Army Group. He served under Montgomery throughout the rest of the war and was afterwards a distinguished Fellow of Balliol College, Oxford and Editor of the 'Dictionary of National Biography'. Robertson left Montgomery before the end of the North African campaign but later became Chief Administrative Officer to

General Alexander in Italy, Deputy Military Governor, then Governor and Commander-in-Chief of the British zone of occupied Germany and finally High Commissioner, before retiring as General Lord Robertson of Oakridge. Richardson also left Montgomery after the campaign in Sicily to take up the post of Deputy Chief of Staff (British) in General Mark Clark's Fifth United States Army, which included British units. He rejoined his old leader in Twenty-First Army Group in March 1944 as head of Plans, and later rose to be Quartermaster General, Master General of the Ordnance and finally Chief Royal Engineer.

Of the other officers who have been mentioned earlier, Kippenberger served with Eighth Army during the remainder of the North African campaign and subsequently in Italy. He would command the New Zealand Division and survive the loss of both feet on a mine, to be appointed Editor-in-Chief of the New Zealand War History. Roberts stayed with Eighth Army until the fall of Tripoli, after which he was transferred to command a brigade in the British First Army during the campaign in Tunisia. Promoted to major general, he again saw service under Montgomery throughout the North-Western Europe campaign in command of 11th Armoured Division, later becoming Director of the Royal Armoured Corps. Harding left the staff in Cairo after Alam Halfa, leading 7th Armoured Division until he was badly wounded during the final advance on Tripoli. On his recovery he was appointed Chief of Staff to Alexander in Italy, and after the war C-in-C, Far East Land Forces, C-in-C, British Army of the Rhine and Chief of the Imperial General Staff, becoming a field-marshal and the 1st Baron Harding of Petherton.

When Harding was wounded he probably owed his life to his rapid evacuation to hospital organized by his senior staff officer. This was none other than Carver, then a lieutenant colonel, who was shortly to command 1st Royal Tanks and later 4th Armoured Brigade at the early age of 28, being yet another who saw combat with Montgomery's Twenty-First Army Group. He later followed in Harding's footsteps as C-in-C, Far East Land Forces, Chief of the General Staff and then Chief of Defence Staff, earning a peerage and a field marshal's baton in the process.

All that would be in the future. At the end of August, 1942, the officers and men of Eighth Army were concerned only with Rommel's coming offensive, which they awaited with a mixture of determination and anxiety. Rommel's numbers had increased far more than Eighth Army's. Reinforcements had restored his three original German divisions to full strength, the remaining units of 164th Light had reached the front-line and he had been joined by Colonel Bernhard Ramcke's 288th (German) Parachute Brigade and the finest of all Italian formations the Folgore Parachute Division, both of which were used in an infantry role.

Eighth Army was still superior in tanks. Of the 772 it officially contained, 693 were serviceable:- 197 Crusaders, 169 Stuarts, 163 Valentines, 164 Grants. Nonetheless the Axis armour had made a remarkable recovery. The Afrika Korps, which had mustered sixty tanks at Mersa Matruh, as few as twenty-six on 3 July, and only forty-two when it had won 'Second Ruweisat', now possessed 232 tanks, of which 203 were gun-armed. The Italian Ariete and Littorio Armoured Divisions could find another 243 medium and thirty-eight light tanks - albeit of limited value.

In the case of the German armour moreover, Rommel had gained in quality as well as quantity. His Mark III Specials which could out-gun all British tanks except Grants, but of which he had never had more than twenty-seven in June or sixteen in July, numbered seventy-three when his attack began on 30 August. He had also at last received suitable armour-piercing ammunition for his twenty-seven Mark IV Specials which, as the British armoured commanders were well aware, were far superior to the Grants and indeed to the Shermans. In addition, Rommel had doubled the number of his formidable anti-tank guns.

The Axis air forces had also gained in strength and, in sharp contrast to the situation in early July, were well forward in close support. Major General Max Seidemann, who had taken up the post of *Fliegerführer Afrika* in August, commanded 720 machines divided almost equally between the Luftwaffe and the Regia Aeronautica. The Italian aircraft were mainly fighters, ranging from biplane Fiat CR 42s through Fiat G 50s and Macchi MC 200s to the excellent Macchi MC 202s of which about forty-five were serviceable. Apart from reconnaissance machines, the German warplanes consisted of three Gruppen of Junkers Ju 87 Stuka dive-bombers, the equivalent of three Gruppen of Junkers Ju 88 bombers, a Gruppe of Messerschmitt Bf 110 twin-engined fighter-bombers – which arrived in late August – and four Gruppen of Messerschmitt Bf 109s, which oddly enough contained 109 machines of which about sixty-five were serviceable. In addition there were 230 German aircraft, mainly Ju 88s and Bf 110s, in Crete which could be used for long-range attacks on Allied bases or aerodromes.

By contrast, Coningham's Desert Air Force contained 565 machines, though the percentage of aircraft serviceable was higher in the Allied than in the Axis units. Apart from reconnaissance aircraft, among which was an entire Hurricane squadron, No 208, the RAF contributed two squadrons of Baltimore light bombers, three squadrons of Spitfires, No 92 having become fully operational on 13 August, three of Kittyhawks, and a further eight squadrons of Hurricanes, including No 6 Squadron with its anti-tank Hurricane IIDs. There were also two squadrons of Royal Australian Air Force Kittyhawks, seven squadrons from the South African Air Force – two with Boston light bombers, two with Kittyhawks, one with Tomahawks, two with Hurricanes – and two squadrons from the United States Army Air Force, the 81st flying Mitchell bombers and the 64th with Warhawks, both of which had joined the Desert Air Force during August. Coningham, like Seidemann, also had the support of some 230 aircraft not under his direct control; six squadrons of Wellingtons, the equivalent of a squadron of Halifaxes, two squadrons of Beaufighters and two of Fleet Air Arm Albacores.

In short, as Liddell Hart records, 'the strength of the two sides was nearer to an even balance than it was either before or later.' No wonder then that just before the Battle of Alam Halfa began on the night of 30–31 August, Rommel told his wife that, despite some supply problems, it would be 'a long time before we get such favourable conditions of moonlight, relative strengths etc again.' He did not consider that his assault this time would be a 'try-on'. He called it a 'decisive battle' which he believed would result in 'the final destruction of the enemy' and would carry Panzerarmee Afrika to the Nile.

The officers and men of the Eighth Army, ably supported by the officers and men of the Desert Air Force, smashed the assault. They would never lose another battle.

Notes.

1   Detailed accounts will be found in Field Marshal Carver's *El Alamein* and General Sir David Fraser's *Alanbrooke*. The statements of Williams and Harding, however, come from Nigel Hamilton's biography *Monty: The Making of a General 1887–1942*.

2   For instance, Connell accuses Ritchie of deliberately concealing information from Auchinleck during the Battle of Gazala, declaring: 'It is to be noted that the Auchinleck papers contain no communications of any kind from Ritchie to the Commander-in-Chief between June 4 and June 11.' Even if one ignores the fact that Ritchie's own information was scanty for some time, it is also to be noted that Connell does not mention that Corbett had gone to Ritchie's HQ early on the morning of 7 June, had stayed two days and had met Ritchie's Corps Commanders. He could thus give Auchinleck a sufficiently detailed report to make any communication from Ritchie redundant. A detailed examination of Connell's misrepresentations is set out in Field Marshal Carver's *Dilemmas of the Desert War*, from which the account of Ritchie's reactions is also taken.

3   Churchill did not like the modern name Iran which he felt caused confusion with Iraq.

BIBLIOGRAPHY

ALEXANDER Field Marshal the Earl: *The African Campaign from El Alamein to Tunis*. (London Gazette Supplement 1948.)

ARNOLD-FORSTER Mark: *The World at War*. (Collins 1973.)

AUCHINLECK Field Marshal Sir Claude: *Operations in Middle East 1/11/41 to 15/8/42*. (London Gazette Supplement 1948.)

BEHRENDT Hans-Otto: *Rommel's Intelligence in the Desert Campaign*. (Kimbers 1985.)

BRYANT Sir Arthur: *The Turn of the Tide 1939–1943*. (Collins 1959.)

CARELL Paul: *The Foxes of the Desert: The Story of the Afrika Korps*. (Macdonalds 1960.)

CARVER Field Marshal Lord: *Dilemmas of the Desert War: A New Look at the Libyan Campaign 1940–1942*. (Batsford 1986.)

CARVER Field Marshal Lord: *El Alamein*. (Batsford 1962.)

CARVER Field Marshal Lord: *Harding of Petherton*. (Weidenfeld & Nicolson 1978.)

CARVER Field Marshal Lord: *Out of Step* (Memoirs). (Hutchinson 1989.)

CARVER Field Marshal Lord: *Tobruk*. (Batsford 1964.)

CHURCHILL Sir Winston: *The Second World War. Volume III: The Grand Alliance*. (Cassell 1950.)

CHURCHILL Sir Winston: *The Second World War. Volume IV: The Hinge of Fate*. (Cassell 1951.)

CONNELL John: *Auchinleck*. (Cassell 1959.)

COWLES Virginia: *The Phantom Major: The Story of David Stirling and the SAS Regiment*. (Collins 1958.)

DE GUINGAND Major General Sir Francis: *Generals at War*. (Hodder & Stoughton 1964.)

DE GUINGAND Major General Sir Francis: *Operation Victory*. (Hodder & Stoughton 1947.)

FRASER General Sir David: *Alanbrooke*. (Collins 1982.)

FRASER General Sir David: *And We Shall Shock Them: The British Army in the Second World War*. (Hodder & Stoughton 1983.)

FULLER Major General J.F.C.: *The Decisive Battles of the Western World. Volume III.* (Eyre & Spottiswoode 1957.)

FULLER Major General J.F.C.: *The Second World War 1939–1945.* (Eyre & Spottiswoode 1948.) (Revised Edition 1954).

HAMILTON Nigel: *Monty: The Making of a General 1887–1942.* (Hamish Hamilton 1981.)

HINSLEY F.H. with THOMAS E.E., RANSOM C.F.G. and KNIGHT R.C.: *British Intelligence in the Second World War: Its Influence on Strategy and Operations. Volume II.* (HMSO 1981).

JACKSON General Sir William: *The North African Campaign 1940–43.* (Batsford 1975.)

KESSELRING Field Marshal Albert: *Memoirs.* (Kimbers 1963.)

KIPPENBERGER Major General Sir Howard: *Infantry Brigadier.* (Oxford University Press 1949.)

LEWIN Ronald: *The Life and Death of the Afrika Korps.* (Batsford 1977.)

LEWIN Ronald: *Montgomery as Military Commander.* (Batsford 1971.)

LEWIN Ronald: *Rommel as Military Commander.* (Batsford 1968.)

LEWIN Ronald: *Ultra Goes to War: The Secret Story.* (Hutchinson 1978.)

LIDDELL HART Captain B.H.: *History of the Second World War.* (Cassell 1970.)

LIDDELL HART Captain B.H.: *The Tanks: The History of the Royal Tank Regiment and its Predecessors.* (Cassell 1959.)

LLEWELLYN Harry: *Passports to Life: Journeys into Many Worlds.* (Hutchinson 1980.)

LUCAS PHILLIPS Brigadier C.E.: *Alamein.* (Heinemann 1962.)

MACINTYRE Captain Donald: *The Battle for the Mediterranean.* (Batsford 1964.)

MACKSEY Kenneth: *Kesselring: The Making of the Luftwaffe.* (Batsford 1978.)

MASTERS David: *With Pennants Flying: The Immortal Deeds of the Royal Armoured Corps.* (Eyre & Spottiswoode 1943.)

MELLENTHIN Major General F.W.von: *Panzer Battles.* (Cassell 1955.)

MONTGOMERY Field Marshal the Viscount: *Memoirs.* (Collins 1958.)

MOOREHEAD Alan: *The Desert War: The North African Campaign 1940–1943.* (Hamish Hamilton 1965.)

NICOLSON Nigel: *Alex: The Life of Field Marshal Earl Alexander of Tunis.* (Weidenfeld & Nicolson 1973.)

OWEN Roderic: *The Desert Air Force.* (Hutchinson 1948.)

PLAYFAIR Major General I.S.O. with FLYNN Captain F.C., MOLONY Brigadier C.J.C. and GLEAVE Group-Captain T.P.: *The Mediterranean and Middle East. Volume III: British Fortunes Reach their Lowest Ebb.* (HMSO 1960.)

RICHARDS Denis: *Royal Air Force 1939–1945. Volume I: The Fight at Odds.* (HMSO 1953.)

RICHARDS Denis and SAUNDERS Hilary St G.: *Royal Air Force 1939–1945. Volume II: The Fight Avails.* (HMSO 1954.)

RICHARDSON General Sir Charles: *Flashback: A Soldier's Story.* (Kimbers 1985.)

RICHARDSON General Sir Charles: *From Churchill's Secret Circle to the BBC: The Biography of Lieutenant General Sir Ian Jacob.* (Brasseys UK 1991.)

RICHARDSON General Sir Charles: *Send for Freddie: The Story of Montgomery's Chief of Staff Major General Sir Francis de Guingand.* (Kimbers 1987.)

ROBERTS Major General G.P.B.: *From the Desert to the Baltic.* (Kimbers 1987.)

ROMMEL Field Marshal Erwin (Edited by LIDDELL HART Captain B.H.): *The Rommel Papers.* (Collins 1953.)

ROSKILL Captain S.W.: *The War at Sea 1939–1945. Volume II: The Period of Balance.* (HMSO 1956.)

SHORES Christopher and RING Hans: *Fighters over the Desert: The Air Battles in the Western Desert June 1940–December 1942.* (Neville Spearman 1969.)

SMITH Peter C.: *Pedestal: The Malta Convoy of August 1942.* (Kimbers 1970.)

STEWART Adrian: *Eighth Army's Greatest Victories: Alam Halfa to Tunis 1942–1943.* (Leo Cooper – Pen & Sword Books 1999.)

STEWART Adrian: *Hurricane: The War Exploits of the Fighter Aircraft.* (Kimbers 1982.)

STRAWSON Major General John: *The Battle for North Africa.* (Batsford 1969.)

War Diaries of GHQ Middle East, Eighth Army, X Corps, XIII Corps, XXX Corps and individual divisions and brigades in Eighth Army. (Public Record Office, Kew.)

INDEX OF EIGHTH ARMY

FORMATIONS AND UNITS

171

GENERAL INDEX

Note: All service personnel are given the rank they held at the time of the incidents described.

Messervy, Major General F., 11, 36, 44, 47–8, 60, 66, 68–70, 76–7, 79, 88
Mickl, Lieutenant Colonel J., 35
Minquar Qaim, 97
Miteirya Ridge, 103, 126, 131, 133–4
Miteirya Ridge, Battle of, 133–4
Montgomery, Lieutenant General B.L.:
  takes command of Eighth Army, 150, 154–8, 163–4
  raises morale, 158–9, 161–2
  plans for Alam Halfa, 158–62
Morshead, Major General L., 112, 124–5, 128, 133–5, 159, 162
Mreir El (Depression), 131–2
Msus, 43–4, 47–8
Munassib, Deir el (Depression), 103
Mussolini, Benito, 5, 46, 52, 93–5

Naqb abu Dweiss, 103, 124
Navarini, Lieutenant General E., 12
Nehring, Lieutenant General, later General W., 61, 91, 106, 129, 132, 162
Neumann-Silkow, Major General W., 12, 25, 34–5, 37
Newman, Corporal W., 82
Newton-King, Lieutenant Colonel D., 68
Nile Delta, 13, 98, 105, 118, 131–2, 140, 142–3, 159
Nile River, 58, 103, 111, 136, 140, 142, 145, 166
Norrie, Lieutenant General C.W.:
  commands XXX Corps, 11
  during CRUSADER, 11, 16–17, 27, 30, 35–6, 38, 40
  during Gazala, 68–9, 74–5, 77, 79, 88
  during 'First Alamein', 103–8, 118
  mentioned, 47, 60, 65–6, 77, 109, 154
Norton, Sergeant G., 92
Norway, 14, 52–3, 156

O'Connor, Lieutenant General Sir R., 10–11
Operational Code Names:
  ABERDEEN, 76–8
  ACROBAT, 43, 45–6
  CRUSADER, 9, 12–37, 40–1, 43–4, 49, 56, 60–1, 79, 88, 90, 105, 115, 138
  EXALTATION, 121–3
  FREEBORN, 83
  HERCULES, 94
  LIMERICK, 73–4, 76–7
  SINBAD, 69
  SPLENDOUR, 133, 140
  TORCH, 3, 152
Oswald, Major M. St J., 117, 162

Palestine, 94, 140, 142–3
'Pedestal' (Convoy), 4
Percy, Lieutenant Colonel J., 85
Persia, See under Iran
Pienaar, Brigadier, later Major General D., 6, 20, 25, 34, 60, 74, 83–5, 104, 106–7, 118, 133–4, 154
Pinney, Major B., 23
Point 63, 128–9, 131–2
Point 64, 128–9
Point 102, 145, 161
Point 171, 60, 63, 69
Point 175, 20, 32, 35
Point 178, 20, 23
Point 186, 78
Point 187, 82, 89
Point 204, 38
Powell, Captain R., 78
Pownall, Lieutenant General Sir H., 55
Pyman, Lieutenant Colonel H., 130

Qasaba El, 147, 149, 161
Qattara, Bab el (Pass), 103, 124
Qattara Depression, 103, 121, 141

Raistrick, Corporal S., 130
Ramcke Colonel B., 164
Ramsden, Major General, later Lieutenant General W., 60, 74, 83–4, 97, 108, 124, 133, 158
Ravenstein, Major General J. von, 12, 25, 34
Redford, Trooper G., 132
Reid, Brigadier D., 88
Renton, Brigadier J.M.L., 68–9
Retma, 60, 63, 69
Richards, Brigadier G., 60, 69–70, 79, 87–8, 161
Richardson, Lieutenant Colonel C., 114, 117, 119, 134, 138, 140, 147, 149, 162–4